THE INTERVAL

THE
INTERVAL

The Brief Window That Shapes
Your Eternal Soul

Jarred Fenlason, D.Min.

Copyright © 2026 by Jarred Fenlason

Published by
Encounter Press
Charlotte, North Carolina
www.encounterpress.com

All rights reserved. No part of this publication may be reproduced, distributed, or transmitted in any form or by any means, including photocopying, recording, or other electronic or mechanical methods, without the prior written permission of the publisher, except in the case of brief quotations embodied in critical reviews and certain other noncommercial uses permitted by copyright law.

Scripture Quotations. Unless otherwise indicated, all Scripture quotations are from The ESV® Bible (The Holy Bible, English Standard Version®), copyright © 2001 by Crossway, a publishing ministry of Good News Publishers. Used by permission. All rights reserved.

Free Companion Resource. To help you study this book with others, a complimentary Discussion Guide is available for download. Designed for an 8-week small group or church study, it includes discussion questions for each chapter and practical exercises for applying the principles together. It can be downloaded at: **www.intervalbook.com**

Printed in the United States of America
First Edition: 2026

ISBN: 979-8-9941752-0-0 (Paperback)
ISBN: 979-8-9941752-1-7 (Hardcover)
ISBN: 979-8-9941752-2-4 (Ebook)

ALSO BY JARRED FENLASON

Encounter Discipleship: An Interactive Biblical Discipleship Program

*To my father, who showed me what it looks like to walk with Jesus—
and who now stands on the far side of the interval.
You have finished your race well.
I am still running mine. I will see you when the work is done.*

The only thing that you and I will get out of our lives one day when we die and stand before God, when everything is stripped away and who we really are is made known, is the person we will have become.

— Dallas Willard

CONTENTS

Introduction — 1

PART ONE
THE AWAKENING

1. The Waiting Room Fallacy — 11
2. The Mathematics of Forever — 21
3. The Two Pillars — 31

PART TWO
THE THEOLOGY OF BECOMING

4. The Continuity Principle — 43
5. The Kiln of Death — 55
6. The Patristic Witness — 67
7. The Mystical Vision — 79
8. The Modern Recovery — 87
9. Objections Answered — 97

PART THREE
THE THEOLOGY OF DOING

10. The Differentiated Kingdom — 111
11. The Stewardship Test — 123
12. The Fire That Tests — 135
13. The Treasure Transfer — 145

PART FOUR
HEAVEN'S ECONOMY

14. The Great Inversion — 157
15. The Currency of Souls — 169
16. The Hidden Ledger — 177
17. The Compound Effect — 191

PART FIVE
THE HIDDEN CURRENCIES

18. The Crucible of Character	199
19. The Unrepeatable Resource	211
INTERLUDE	221

PART SIX
THE PRACTICE

20. The Eternal Audit	229
21. Your Eternal Vocation	233
INTERLUDE	237

PART SEVEN
THE VISION

22. The Bema Seat	241
23. The Great Reunion	247
24. The New Creation Unveiled	257
Key Phrases	271
Voices from the Cloud of Witnesses	273
Appendix	275
About the Author	285

INTRODUCTION
THE LIFE THAT SHAPES FOREVER

You are becoming someone.

Not in the vague, inspirational sense that adorns graduation cards and motivational posters. In the most literal, consequential sense possible. With every choice, every habit, every act of faithfulness or neglect, you are forming the person who will exist forever. The soul you are shaping in this brief span of years is the soul you will carry into eternity.

This is not a truth the contemporary church has taught well. We have emphasized salvation—and rightly so, for it is the foundation of everything. We have emphasized morality—and necessarily so, for how we live matters. But we have largely neglected what lies between conversion and glorification: the formation of the eternal self. We have treated the Christian life as a waiting room rather than a training ground, as if the goal were merely to arrive in heaven rather than to arrive as a particular kind of person, prepared for a particular kind of glory.

The result is a church full of believers who are saved but asleep. Justified but unformed. Bound for heaven but unprepared for what they will do when they get there.

This book is an alarm clock.

The Thesis

The argument of this book can be stated simply, though its implications are vast:

Eternal life has already begun. What we do in this life—empowered by the Spirit, patterned after Christ—deposits treasure in heaven. It qualifies us for responsibility in the coming kingdom. Who we become through those same grace-enabled acts shapes the soul that will live forever. These two realities—doing and becoming—are inseparable movements of a single life: hidden with Christ in God, now being revealed, one day fully unveiled.

The window in which this formation occurs I call *the interval of grace*—that unrepeatable span between conversion and death when the clay is still soft, when the wheel is still turning, when who we are becoming remains responsive to the pressure of faithful choices and the hands of a patient Potter. This interval will close. Death will fire the kiln. And what emerges will be the person we carry into eternity.

The stakes are eternal. The grace is sufficient. The time to begin is now.

The Problem

Most Christians operate with an impoverished eschatology. We imagine heaven as a great equalizer—everyone receives the same mansion, the same harp, the same cloud. Whatever differences existed on earth dissolve into a uniform bliss. The faithful missionary and the nominal believer, the saint who suffered and the Christian who coasted—all arrive at the same destination, indistinguishable in glory.

This is not the biblical picture.

Scripture speaks of differentiated reward. Crowns given for specific faithfulness. Cities governed in proportion to proven stewardship. Glory varying as star differs from star. A judgment seat where every believer's works are tested, some surviving the fire as gold and silver, others burning up as wood and hay—the person saved either way, but one with reward, the other suffering loss.

Scripture also speaks of continuous identity. The person who dies is the person who is raised—not replaced, not reset, but transformed. The seed becomes the tree, carrying forward everything the seed contained. The resurrection body is not a different body but this body glorified. And the character formed in earthly life persists into eternal existence.

If these things are true—and I will argue that Scripture, the early church fathers, and the most serious modern theologians all affirm them—then what we do in this brief window of earthly existence matters infinitely. Not just for reward, as if heaven were a cosmic compensation scheme. But for capacity. For assignment. For the kind of person we will be forever.

The clay is being shaped now. The kiln will fire at death. What emerges will be permanent.

The Two Pillars

This book is built on two inseparable realities.

The first is what we do. This is the stewardship dimension—action, faithfulness, fruit. We are entrusted with resources, relationships, time, and talent. What we do with these deposits treasure in heaven or squanders it. The parables of Jesus present earthly life as a proving ground: the master entrusts, departs, and returns for an accounting. Those who proved faithful receive more. Those who did not lose even what they had.

The second is who we become. This is the formation dimension—character, capacity, identity. Every choice shapes the soul. Every discipline carves a groove. Every act of love expands our capacity for love. Every refusal to love diminishes it. We are not merely doing things in this life; we are becoming someone. And that someone persists.

These two pillars are distinct but inseparable. Doing shapes becoming: every act of faithfulness forms faithful character. Becoming determines capacity for doing: the formed character enables greater stewardship. They spiral together, upward toward glory or downward toward diminishment. The stewardship shapes the steward.

Most Christian teaching emphasizes one pillar at the expense of the other. The prosperity-adjacent stream focuses on doing—works, achievements, outputs that earn reward. The quietist stream focuses on being—contemplation, inner transformation, the soul's journey toward God. Both capture something true. Neither captures enough. This book holds both together because Scripture holds both together. Everything translates—both the treasure we store and the soul we form.

What This Book Is Not

Let me be clear about what I am not arguing.

I am not arguing for works-righteousness. Salvation is by grace through faith, and nothing in this book undermines that foundation. The distinction between salvation and reward is explicit in Scripture. Paul writes of a man whose works are burned up entirely, yet who is "saved, but only as through fire." Salvation is gift. Reward is earned—but earned by works that are themselves grace-enabled, flowing from a salvation already secured. This is what I call the threefold framework: salvation by grace through faith, formation by Spirit-enabled cooperation, reward by grace-enabled faithfulness. Each is distinct. All are real.

I am not arguing for anxiety. The goal of this book is not to burden you with a new set of religious obligations or to induce terror about whether you've done enough. The grace of God is the ground beneath everything. The Spirit empowers what we could never accomplish alone. The clay is shaped by the hands of a loving Potter, not by our frantic self-effort.

I am not arguing for a heaven of competition and envy. The differentiation Scripture describes is not the zero-sum hierarchy of earthly systems. Augustine taught that the blessed in heaven rejoice in others' greater glory without any diminishment of their own joy.

Thérèse of Lisieux offered the image of a thimble and a tumbler—both filled to capacity, both overflowing with the same water, both completely full, though not holding the same volume. Heavenly psychology operates differently from earthly comparison.

I am not arguing for speculation beyond Scripture. Where the Bible is clear, I will be clear. Where it is silent or suggestive, I will acknowledge the limits of what we can know. The early church fathers and later theologians offer wisdom, but they are not Scripture. The inferences I draw are grounded in biblical text, tested against historical orthodoxy, and offered with appropriate humility about matters that remain mysterious.

What I am arguing is this: what you do and who you become in this brief life matters eternally. Not merely that you will exist forever—that is settled by grace. But what kind of existence. What capacity for joy. What assignment in the kingdom. What weight of glory.

The church has been largely silent about this. The silence has cost us.

The Path Ahead

The book unfolds in seven parts, with interludes at the center.

Part I: The Awakening disrupts the waiting-room mentality that characterizes so much of Western Christianity. We examine why this brief span matters against the backdrop of infinity. The answer: because eternal life has already begun, because the interval of grace is formative, and because small differences in starting capacity yield exponentially divergent outcomes over infinite time. The two pillars —doing and becoming—are introduced as the architecture for everything that follows.

Part II: The Theology of Becoming builds the biblical, patristic, and modern case for continuous identity and eternal formation. We examine the continuity principle—that you persist through death, the same person transformed. We confront the kiln of death—the sobering reality that formation has a deadline. We listen to the early church fathers, the mystics, and modern voices who understood what we have largely forgotten. And we answer the serious objections that arise.

Part III: The Theology of Doing builds the case for differentiated reward based on faithful action. Heaven is not a great equalizer; Scripture teaches a differentiated kingdom where faithfulness is measured and rewarded. We examine the stewardship test that earthly life represents, the fire that will try every work, and the treasure transfer that generosity enables.

Part IV: Heaven's Economy explores how eternal value is calculated differently than we expect. The great inversion reveals that what looks insignificant here often proves most valuable there. The currency of souls shows that people—not possessions—are the only treasure that transfers fully. The hidden ledger records what no human eye sees. And the compound effect demonstrates how small faithfulness, multiplied by time, produces exponential return.

Part V: The Hidden Currencies examines the investments that yield eternal weight—particularly suffering and time. We discover that the crucible of character produces what comfort cannot, and that time is the unrepeatable resource in which all formation occurs.

The First Interlude invites you to pause. *The theology must become personal. The truth must settle into the soul before it can reshape the life.*

Part VI: The Practice moves from theology to implementation. The eternal audit helps you see clearly where you stand. And we learn to live with awareness of the coming evaluation—the moment when we will stand before Christ to give account—not as threat but as clarifying hope.

The Second Interlude is an offering—*a response to all that has been considered, before the final vision is unveiled.*

Part VII: The Vision lifts eyes toward what we are being prepared for. We trace the great reunion—what death stole, resurrection returns. And we follow the city descending from heaven to earth, where embodied vocation on the renewed creation awaits those who have been formed to receive it. The everlasting morning is coming. The question is who we will be when it dawns.

A Word on Sources

This book draws on four streams of witness.

Scripture is primary. Everything rises or falls on whether it aligns with biblical revelation. I have labored to exposit texts rather than merely cite them, to let Scripture carry its own weight rather than using it as decoration for my ideas.

The early church fathers understood formation in ways the modern church has largely forgotten. Irenaeus saw human life as maturation toward capacity for God. Augustine taught differentiated glory and the persistence of personal history into resurrection. Gregory of Nyssa envisioned *epektasis*—eternal progress into the infinite God, where perfection consists not in arrival but in endless advance. Their witness confirms and deepens the biblical teaching.

The Christian mystics explored territories of the soul that our activistic age has neglected. Maximus the Confessor on Christ being formed in us through the virtues. John of the Cross on the dark night as formation's most potent crucible. Jakob Böhme on the will shaping itself into what it will remain forever. They mapped the interior landscape of becoming.

Modern theologians have recovered aspects of this vision against the grain of their contemporaries. Jonathan Edwards on degrees of eternal blessedness and vessels of different sizes, all filled to the brim. C.S. Lewis on choice-by-choice becoming and the weight of glory that awaits. Dallas Willard on discipleship as apprenticeship for eternal living. N.T. Wright on "life after life after death"—the persistence of present faithfulness into God's renewed creation. Their voices bridge ancient wisdom and present urgency.

I have tried to let these witnesses speak, not as decoration but as testimony. They are not Scripture, but they are the communion of saints reflecting on Scripture across two millennia. Their agreement strengthens confidence that we are not innovating but recovering.

An Invitation

I do not know who you are as you read these words. Perhaps you are a new believer, just awakening to the implications of eternal life. Perhaps you are a seasoned saint, sensing that something has been missing from your discipleship. Perhaps you are a pastor or teacher, looking for resources to help your people grasp what is at stake. Perhaps you are skeptical, picking up this book to see if it has substance or is merely another piece of Christian self-help dressed in theological clothing.

Whoever you are, I invite you to read with openness and seriousness. What you encounter here may disturb you. It has disturbed me. The realization that every day is forming my eternal self, that the character I'm developing is the character I'll carry forever, that the kiln will fire and what emerges will be fixed—this is not comfortable. But it is clarifying.

And it is hopeful.

The clay is still soft. The wheel is still turning. The hands of grace are still at work. Whatever you have done or failed to do, whatever years you feel you have wasted, whatever distance lies between who you are and who you could become—the Spirit is present, Christ is the pattern and the power, and today is the day of salvation in every sense of that word.

The interval of grace remains open. The becoming is happening now. You cannot stop it. The only question is whether it will be intentional or accidental, directed toward glory or drifting toward diminishment.

My prayer is that this book will help you choose wisely. The stakes could not be higher. The grace could not be greater. And the time could not be shorter.

Let us begin.

PART ONE
THE AWAKENING
CHAPTERS 1–3

CHAPTER 1
THE WAITING ROOM FALLACY

What you do in this life matters eternally. Who you become matters equally, perhaps more. These two realities are inseparable, and together they constitute the weight of *the interval of grace*—the brief span between your conversion and your death when eternal formation is still possible.

The years you spend on this earth are not a waiting room. They are a forming room, limited and closing. Every choice, every investment, every act of faithfulness or neglect is shaping the person who will exist for endless ages.

C.S. Lewis saw this with uncommon clarity in *Mere Christianity*: "Every time you make a choice you are turning the central part of you, the part of you that chooses, into something a little different from what it was before. And taking your life as a whole, with all your innumerable choices, all your life long you are slowly turning this central thing either into a heavenly creature or into a hellish creature."

The central thing. The part that chooses. The self being formed beneath the surface of daily routine—formed through every decision to serve or withhold, to give or grasp, to invest in the kingdom or bury the talent in the ground. This is what persists. This is what we carry through death into resurrection. This is what stands before Christ when the interval ends and the accounting begins.

Dallas Willard, reflecting on decades of studying spiritual formation, arrived at the same conclusion: when we die and stand before God, when everything is stripped away and who we really are is made known, the only thing we will have is the person we have become.

The works we do are tested by fire. But so is the worker. The fruit is evaluated. But so is the tree. And what we carry into eternity is the person shaped by the doing—the soul formed through a thousand faithful choices or a thousand faithless ones.

This is why the interval of grace matters. Not merely because there are rewards to be earned, though there are. Not merely because there is treasure to be stored, though there is. But because the very person storing the treasure and earning the reward is being formed in the process. The stewardship shapes the steward. The investment shapes the investor. The faithfulness shapes the faithful one.

And yet many Christians—even sincere, devoted Christians—live without grasping this reality.

The Sincere but Unaware

The moment of conversion is rightly celebrated. A soul passes from death to life, from darkness to light, from condemnation to justification. Angels rejoice. Heaven records a name. The transaction is complete, the outcome secure. Nothing can separate this new believer from the love of God in Christ Jesus.

And then the journey begins.

For many sincere believers, this journey is pursued with genuine devotion. They love God. They serve in their churches. They give generously. They study Scripture, pursue holiness, and seek to grow in Christlikeness. They are not nominal Christians going through the motions—they are committed disciples who want to please the Father.

And yet something may be missing. Not sincerity—they have that. Not effort—they bring that daily. What may be missing is the larger frame. The eternal horizon. The awareness that everything they are doing and becoming carries permanent weight into the ages to come.

This is the waiting room fallacy in its subtler form. It does not afflict only the spiritually indifferent. It can afflict the spiritually earnest who have simply never been awakened to the fuller picture. They know that faithfulness matters. They know that sanctification is the Spirit's work. They know that heaven awaits. What they may not know is how these connect—that the person being formed through every act of faithfulness is the very person who will exist forever. That the soul being shaped now is not preparation for a different existence but the beginning of an existence that never ends.

The church has not always taught this well. We have emphasized salvation, and rightly so. We have emphasized moral growth, and necessarily so. But we have often framed these within a horizon that extends only to the edge of this life. We speak of becoming better people, better spouses, better parents. We speak of spiritual growth as though its primary fruit is a more peaceful life, more meaningful relationships, greater resilience in hardship.

All of this is true. But it is not the whole truth.

The whole truth is that we are becoming eternal creatures. The character being formed in us—the patience, the love, the humility, the capacity for joy—is not merely improving our earthly experience. It is shaping the soul that will inhabit the new creation. The virtues that become second nature are not shed at death like old clothing. They are carried forward. They become part of who we are forever.

The faithful believer already pursuing holiness needs to know: your pursuit is not merely improving your character for temporal benefit. It is forming your eternal self. The generous believer already giving sacrificially needs to know: your generosity is forming a generous soul, expanding your capacity for the self-giving love that characterizes God himself. The serving believer already pouring out time and energy for others needs to know: your service is shaping your will toward the posture of Christ. That servant heart is not temporary equipment for earthly ministry. It is eternal equipment for kingdom vocation.

The implications are staggering. Every choice toward love is forming eternal capacity for love. Every discipline of patience is building eternal patience. Every habit of attention to God is deepening eternal capacity for his presence. Nothing is wasted. Nothing is merely temporal. Everything translates.

The Starting Gun, Not the Finish Line

Scripture nowhere presents salvation as the conclusion of spiritual life. It presents salvation as the beginning.

Consider Paul's language. He writes to the Philippians not as a man who has arrived but as one pressing forward: "Not that I have already obtained this or am already perfect, but I press on to make it my own, because Christ Jesus has made me his own" (Philippians 3:12). The grammar is instructive. Christ has already laid hold of Paul—that transaction is complete. But Paul has not yet laid hold of that for which Christ laid hold of him. Something remains to be pursued, obtained, made one's own.

This is not Paul in his early years, still unsure of his standing. This is Paul the aged apostle, writing from prison, decades into his ministry. If anyone had grounds to consider himself arrived, it was Paul. Yet he describes himself as one still pressing, still reaching, still running.

To the Corinthians he writes: "Do you not know that in a race all the runners run, but only one receives the prize? So run that you may obtain it" (1 Corinthians 9:24). The imagery is not of passengers waiting for departure but of athletes in competition. Training. Discipline. Exertion toward a goal. The crown is not handed out at registration; it is awarded at the finish.

To Timothy he writes: "Share in suffering as a good soldier of Christ Jesus... An athlete is not crowned unless he competes according to the rules. It is the hard-working farmer who ought to have the first share of the crops" (2 Timothy 2:3-6). Three metaphors in rapid succession—soldier, athlete, farmer—and all three assume active engagement, not passive waiting. The soldier is enlisted, but the soldier's life is not the enlistment ceremony. It is the campaign that follows. The athlete is registered, but registration is not victory. The farmer has planted, but planting is not harvest.

The consistent witness is that conversion initiates rather than concludes. We are saved—and now we train. We are justified—and now we run. We are enlisted—and now we fight. The starting gun has fired. The race is underway.

The Servant and the Master

Jesus told a parable that illuminates the interval of grace with unforgettable clarity.

"It will be like a man going on a journey, who called his servants and entrusted to them his property. To one he gave five talents, to another two, to another one, to each according to his ability. Then he went away" (Matthew 25:14-15).

The structure is significant. The master entrusts resources. The master departs. A period of absence follows—a span of time when the servants are left with what they have been given, unsupervised, unobserved. What they do in this interval is entirely up to them.

The amounts are staggering. A talent was not a coin but a measure of weight—roughly seventy-five pounds of precious metal. A single talent represented approximately twenty years of wages for a common laborer. Even the servant with one talent held a fortune.

"Now after a long time the master of those servants came and settled accounts with them" (Matthew 25:19). The phrase "a long time" matters. This was not a brief absence. The servants had years to work with what they had been given—long enough for character to crystallize around choices.

The two faithful servants doubled their investments. The master's response to each was identical: "Well done, good and faithful servant. You have been faithful over a little; I will set you over much. Enter into the joy of your master" (Matthew 25:21, 23). Five talents—a century's wages—is called "a little." What awaits the faithful servant is "much." The reward is not retirement but promotion. Not rest but increased responsibility.

But the third servant buried his talent in the ground. His excuse was fear. The master's response was severe: "You wicked and slothful servant!" The talent was taken and given to the one who had ten. And the principle was stated: "For to everyone who has will more be given, and he will have an abundance. But from the one who has not, even what he has will be taken away" (Matthew 25:29).

Whatever else this parable teaches, it teaches that the interval of grace matters. The period between the master's departure and return is not empty time. It is testing time. Stewardship time. The servants are not waiting for the master; they are working in his absence. And their work—or their failure to work—shapes both their outcome and their capacity. The faithful servants have become faithful people. The unfaithful servant has become an unfaithful person. The interval has formed them.

The Judgment Seat

The judgment Jesus describes is not limited to the final judgment between saved and lost. Scripture also speaks of a judgment for believers—what Paul calls the "judgment seat of Christ" (2 Corinthians 5:10), what theologians call the Bema Seat.

"For we must all appear before the judgment seat of Christ, so that each one may receive what is due for what he has done in the body, whether good or evil."

The Bema was familiar to Paul's readers—the raised platform where magistrates rendered judgment and athletes received crowns. This is not the great white throne of condemnation. This is evaluation of those already saved, already secure, already belonging to Christ.

But evaluation it remains. Every believer will appear. The outcomes will vary.

Paul develops this in his first letter to the Corinthians: "Each one's work will become manifest, for the Day will disclose it, because it will be revealed by fire, and the fire will test what sort of work each one has done. If the work that anyone has built on the foundation survives, he will receive a reward. If anyone's work is burned up, he will suffer loss, though he himself will be saved, but only as through fire" (1 Corinthians 3:13-15).

The builder himself is saved. This is not loss of salvation but loss of reward. Loss of what could have been built. Loss of the "well done" that was available but not obtained.

And there is more than works at stake. If the person we become is what we carry into eternity, then the Bema Seat is not merely evaluation of what we did but revelation of who we have become. The fire tests the works. But it also reveals the worker. The soul formed through decades of choices stands before Christ, and what has been forming in secret is made manifest.

The Weight of the Interval

Jonathan Edwards understood this gravity perhaps better than any theologian in the American tradition. Among his resolutions, written when he was only nineteen, appears this:

"Resolved, that I will live so, as I shall wish I had done when I come to die."

Edwards understood that the deathbed reveals what daily life conceals. From that vantage point, the investments that seemed prudent often appear foolish, and the sacrifices that seemed excessive appear insufficient. He resolved to live by the deathbed evaluation rather than the comfortable assumptions of mid-life.

He also wrote: "Resolved, to endeavor to obtain for myself as much happiness, in the other world, as I possibly can, with all the power, might, vigor, and vehemence, yea violence, I am capable of."

Note the language: power, might, vigor, vehemence, violence. This is not the vocabulary of passive waiting. Edwards understood that eternal happiness was not merely assured but variable—that more or less could be obtained—and he resolved to pursue the maximum with every faculty he possessed.

This was not works-righteousness. Edwards trusted entirely in grace for salvation. But he understood what many have forgotten: grace does not preclude reward. Salvation does not eliminate differentiation. What we do and who we become in the interval carries eternal consequence.

Two Dimensions, One Life

This book will argue that two dimensions of the interval require our attention—what we do and who we become. These are not the same, though they are inseparable.

What we do involves stewardship—the investment of time, treasure, talent, and opportunity. The parables of Jesus speak directly to this dimension. Talents are entrusted and expected to multiply. Faithfulness in small things qualifies for stewardship of large things. This is the doing dimension, and it matters eternally.

Who we become involves formation—the shaping of character, the cultivation of virtue, the deepening of capacity for God and others. The writings of Paul speak directly to this dimension. We are being transformed from glory to glory. We are being conformed to the image of Christ. This is the becoming dimension, and it matters eternally—perhaps even more fundamentally, since the doing flows from the being, the fruit flows from the tree.

The sincere believer may be faithfully engaged in the doing dimension—serving, giving, working for the kingdom—while insufficiently aware of the becoming dimension. They may not realize that every act of service is also forming a servant heart. Every act of generosity is also expanding a generous soul. The doing is forming the being. And the being is what persists.

This book aims to hold both dimensions together and to trace their implications into eternity. The interval of grace matters—both for what we do and for who we become. Both translate into the new creation. Both carry permanent weight.

The Invitation

This book is for the sincere believer who wants to understand the fuller picture.

Not a rebuke for insufficient effort—you are already pursuing faithfulness. Not a burden of additional obligation—grace remains the ground beneath your feet. But a reframe. A wider lens. An invitation to see that the life you are already living carries weight you may not have fully grasped.

The service you render is forming a servant. The generosity you practice is expanding a generous soul. The patience you cultivate is building an eternally patient self. Nothing is wasted. Nothing is merely temporal. Everything translates.

The starting gun has fired. The race is underway. You are already running. The question is not whether you will run but whether you will run with full awareness of what is at stake—not merely the prize at the end, but the person you are becoming in the running.

You are not waiting. You are becoming.

The only question is: becoming what?

CHAPTER 2
THE MATHEMATICS OF FOREVER

Eighty years against eternity. A single lifetime measured against ages without end. The mathematics seem to argue for insignificance. What could possibly matter about so brief a span when set against infinite duration?

Consider the disproportion. If eternity were a line stretching from one end of the universe to the other, your earthly life would not be a millimeter of that line. It would not be a fraction of a millimeter. Mathematically, any finite number divided by infinity approaches zero. Your eighty years—or sixty, or forty, or a hundred—register as negligible against the backdrop of forever.

This is not a new observation. The psalmist felt it: "You have made my days a few handbreadths, and my lifetime is as nothing before you. Surely all mankind stands as a mere breath" (Psalm 39:5). James pressed the point with unsparing directness: "What is your life? For you are a mist that appears for a little time and then vanishes" (James 4:14). Moses prayed from the weight of this awareness: "So teach us to number our days that we may get a heart of wisdom" (Psalm 90:12). The brevity is acknowledged. The disproportion is real.

And yet Scripture insists, with equal force, that what happens in this brief span carries eternal weight. The same Bible that calls life a vapor also says we will give account for every idle word (Matthew 12:36). The same apostle who speaks of life as a mist also warns that faith without works is dead (James 2:26). The same tradition that acknowledges our days as few handbreadths also insists that what we do in the body determines what we receive in eternity (2 Corinthians 5:10).

How can both be true? How can something so brief matter so much?

The answer lies in understanding what kind of moment this is—and what kind of weight it carries into what follows.

Eternal Life Has Already Begun

The first reframe is this: the interval of grace is not preparation for eternal life. It is eternal life in its opening movement.

We tend to think of eternal life as something that begins after death. We live our earthly years, we die, and then eternal life commences—as if heaven were a separate program that launches only after the current one terminates. Chapter 1 introduced the image of the starting gun—salvation as beginning, not conclusion. But the reframe goes further still. This is not merely the start of a race that will one day reach eternal life. This *is* eternal life, already underway.

"This is eternal life," Jesus said, "that they know you, the only true God, and Jesus Christ whom you have sent" (John 17:3). The verb is present tense. Eternal life is defined not as endless duration in a future location but as knowing God—a relationship that begins now and continues forever. The believer who knows God today has already entered eternal life. The age to come has broken into the present age. The symphony has begun.

Paul understood this. He wrote of believers as those who have already been "raised with Christ" (Colossians 3:1), who are already "seated with him in the heavenly places" (Ephesians 2:6). The language is past tense and present tense, not merely future. Something has already happened. Something is already underway. The eternal has invaded the temporal.

This reframes the disproportion entirely. The eighty years are not a waiting room before the concert begins. They are the opening movement of an endless symphony, already playing, already counting. What happens in this movement shapes what follows. The themes introduced here will be developed forever. The motifs established now will echo through endless ages.

The interval of grace is not prelude. It is commencement.

Brevity Means Intensity, Not Insignificance

The second reframe concerns the nature of brevity itself. We assume that brief means unimportant. But in the logic of formation, the opposite is true. Brief means intense. Brief means unrepeatable. Brief means this window and no other.

Consider what happens in the interval of grace that cannot happen after it closes. Formation happens here. The soul is shaped, the character is forged, the will is bent toward God or away from him. This shaping occurs through resistance, through choice, through the friction of a fallen world and the pressure of daily faithfulness. After death, the friction ceases. The choices that shape are complete. The clay has entered the kiln.

This is why brevity amplifies rather than diminishes significance. A brief window for formation that will never reopen is not less important than an endless opportunity. It is infinitely more important. The scarcity creates the weight.

If you had endless time to shape your soul, the pressure of any given moment would be negligible. But you do not have endless time. You have this life—this interval of grace, limited and closing. What you become in this window is what you will be forever. The brevity is not a problem to be overcome. It is the very condition that makes formation possible and urgent.

The exam is not less important because it lasts only three hours. The exam is more important because those three hours determine everything that follows. So it is with life.

Differentiated Glory

The third reframe concerns what Scripture actually teaches about eternal outcomes—and it teaches differentiation.

We sometimes imagine heaven as a great equalizer, where all believers arrive at the same destination with the same reward, all differences dissolved in uniform bliss. But this is not the biblical picture. Scripture consistently presents eternal outcomes as varied, proportioned to earthly faithfulness and formation.

Jesus made this explicit in the parable of the minas. The servant whose mina earned ten more was told, "Well done, good servant! Because you have been faithful in a very little, you shall have authority over ten cities." The servant whose mina earned five more received authority over five cities (Luke 19:17-19). The reward was proportioned to the faithfulness. Ten cities and five cities are not the same.

Paul taught the same principle. Writing about the resurrection, he said: "There is one glory of the sun, and another glory of the moon, and another glory of the stars; for star differs from star in glory. So is it with the resurrection of the dead" (1 Corinthians 15:41-42). The differentiation is real. Not all stars shine equally. Not all resurrection bodies carry the same glory. The variation is established at death and becomes the starting point for eternal life.

Elsewhere Paul warned that believers' works would be tested: "Each one's work will become manifest, for the Day will disclose it, because it will be revealed by fire, and the fire will test what sort of work each one has done. If the work that anyone has built on the foundation survives, he will receive a reward. If anyone's work is burned up, he will suffer loss, though he himself will be saved, but only as through fire" (1 Corinthians 3:13-15). Some arrive with reward. Others arrive saved but stripped—their works burned, their loss real.

Jonathan Edwards, the eighteenth-century theologian, reflected deeply on these passages and articulated the principle with characteristic precision: "There are different degrees of happiness and glory in heaven. As there are degrees among the angels, viz. thrones, dominions, principalities, and powers; so there are degrees among the saints. In heaven are many mansions, and of different degrees of dignity. The glory of the saints above will be in some proportion to their eminency in holiness and good works here. Christ will reward all according to their works."

The biblical testimony is consistent: eternal outcomes vary. What we do and who we become in the interval of grace determines not merely whether we enter the kingdom but how we enter—with what glory, what reward, what capacity for the life to come.

Vessels of Different Sizes

But how can differentiated glory coexist with perfect happiness? If some have more and others less, will heaven not be poisoned by envy, regret, or dissatisfaction?

Edwards addressed this with a metaphor that has endured: "Every vessel that is cast into this ocean of happiness is full, though there are some vessels far larger than others." The small vessel cast into the ocean of happiness is as completely full as the large one. Both hold all they can contain. Neither lacks anything. Yet they do not hold the same volume.

So it is with the saints in glory. All are perfectly satisfied—filled to capacity with the joy and love and presence of God. But capacities differ. The vessel that enters eternity is the vessel shaped in the interval —sized by faithfulness, expanded by love, formed by the daily pressure of grace-enabled choices. Whatever eternal progress may hold, this much is clear: what we carry through death is the vessel we have become.

Edwards continued: "But yet there will be different degrees of both holiness and happiness according to the measure of each one's capacity, and therefore those that are lowest in glory will have the greatest love to those that are highest in happiness, because they will see most of the image of God in them."

There is no envy because there is no lack. Each vessel is full. But there is differentiation because capacities vary—and the capacities were formed in the interval of grace.

Eternal Progress

But there is a further principle that suggests the differentiation extends beyond the moment of judgment into eternal increase.

Jesus said, "To everyone who has will more be given, and he will have an abundance. But from the one who has not, even what he has will be taken away" (Matthew 25:29). The principle appears in the context of the parable of the talents, but its implications may reach further than the immediate story. What you have becomes the basis for receiving more. Capacity generates greater capacity. Faithfulness in little qualifies for faithfulness in much.

Edwards believed this principle operated eternally. In his *Miscellanies*, he wrote: "The knowledge of those in heaven will increase to eternity; and if their knowledge, doubtless their holiness. For as they increase in the knowledge of God and of the works of God, the more they will see of his excellency; and the more they see of his excellency... the more will they love him; and the more they love God, the more delight and happiness... will they have in him."

The saints do not reach a plateau and remain static. They grow—in knowledge, in holiness, in love, in happiness. And this growth continues forever because God himself is inexhaustible. There is always more of him to know, more of his glory to behold, more of his love to receive. The eternal life that began in the interval of grace continues to deepen across endless ages.

Gregory of Nyssa, the fourth-century church father, developed this insight into a comprehensive vision he called *epektasis*—a Greek term drawn from Paul's language in Philippians 3:13 of "straining forward" toward what lies ahead. Gregory wrote in his *Life of Moses*: "The perfection of human nature consists perhaps in its very growth in goodness."

This was a striking claim. Greek philosophy had taught that perfection meant stasis—reaching a final state and remaining there unchanged. Gregory reversed this: perfection is not arrival but perpetual advance. Because God is infinite, the soul can never exhaust him. There is always further to go, always more to receive, always deeper to grow.

Gregory elaborated: "Thus, no limit would interrupt growth in the ascent to God, since no limit to the good can be found nor is the increasing of desire for the good brought to an end because it is satisfied." And again: "Activity directed toward virtue causes its capacity to grow through exertion." Moses, he observed, "always found a step higher than the one he had attained."

If Edwards and Gregory are right—if the principle of "more given to those who have" operates eternally, and if heavenly progress continues without end—then the formation established in the interval of grace is not merely a starting point. It is a trajectory. What may seem like small differences in earthly formation become significant differences across eternal ages.

In 1999, NASA's Mars Climate Orbiter disintegrated in the Martian atmosphere. The cause: one engineering team had used metric units, another imperial. The discrepancy was small—a matter of conversion factors. But compounded over 286 million miles, it meant total loss. The mathematics of small differences over vast distances suggest something similar about formation: small differences in starting capacity, extended across eternal duration, may yield differences we cannot fully calculate.

This is not mathematical certainty. Scripture does not give us the formulas of eternity. But it gives us the principles: rewards differ, glory varies, capacity determines experience, and more is given to those who have. The weight of these principles, extended into endless ages, suggests that what happens in the interval of grace carries consequence beyond our present ability to measure and comprehend.

The Eternal Weight of Glory

Paul captured this dynamic in a remarkable passage.

"For this light momentary affliction is preparing for us an eternal weight of glory beyond all comparison, as we look not to the things that are seen but to the things that are unseen. For the things that are seen are transient, but the things that are unseen are eternal" (2 Corinthians 4:17-18).

Notice the language. Paul calls present suffering "light" and "momentary." He acknowledges the disproportion—this life is brief and its hardships are passing. But then comes the turn: this light momentary affliction is *preparing* eternal weight. The brief is producing the permanent. The small is generating the vast.

The word "preparing" is significant. The Greek *katergazomai* suggests working out, producing, bringing about. Present experience is not merely endured until something better arrives. It is actively generating what arrives. The affliction is producing the glory. The formation happening in the interval is creating the capacity for what follows.

And the result is described as "beyond all comparison"—literally, "from excess to excess" or "surpassingly surpassing." Paul reaches for language and finds even superlatives insufficient. The weight of glory prepared by faithful formation in the interval exceeds our ability to measure or describe.

This is why earthly formation matters so intensely. The soul formed here is the soul that receives there. The character shaped in the interval is the character that inherits the kingdom. What is built in the light momentary affliction shapes our capacity for the eternal weight of glory.

Numbering Our Days

Moses prayed, "So teach us to number our days that we may get a heart of wisdom" (Psalm 90:12). The prayer is not merely for awareness of mortality—though it includes that. It is for a particular kind of vision: seeing the interval clearly enough to live it wisely.

To number our days is to recognize their limit. But it is also to recognize their weight. Each day is a day of formation. Each day the soul is being shaped—toward greater capacity for God or lesser, toward deeper love or shallower, toward character that will shine in the kingdom or character that will enter impoverished. The numbering is not morbid. It is clarifying.

The mathematics of forever do not diminish the interval of grace. They magnify it. Because eternity stretches endlessly, what happens in this brief window carries weight that extends beyond calculation. Because glory differs as star differs from star, what we become here determines how we shine there. Because more is given to those who have, the capacity formed now shapes the capacity we carry forever.

This is the weight beneath the weight. When we speak of the interval of grace mattering, we are not speaking of religious obligation or divine arbitrariness. We are speaking of the structure of reality as Scripture reveals it. We are speaking of how God has ordered the relationship between time and eternity, between present formation and future glory.

The interval is brief. But brief, in this case, means everything.

Two Implications

Two implications follow from the mathematics of forever, and they will occupy us for the remainder of this book. These are the two dimensions we introduced in Chapter 1—now seen through the lens of eternal mathematics.

The first concerns what we do. If formation in the interval shapes capacity for eternity, then how we invest our time, our resources, our energy matters profoundly. The talents entrusted to us are not merely to be preserved but multiplied. The treasure laid up in heaven is not merely stored but generating returns. Faithful stewardship in the interval qualifies for faithful stewardship in the kingdom—authority over ten cities or five, each proportioned to what was proven in the proving ground of earthly life.

The second concerns who we become. If the soul shaped here is the soul that continues forever, then character formation is not merely self-improvement for temporal benefit. It is the construction of an eternal self. The patience cultivated now becomes eternal patience. The love developed here becomes capacity for infinite love. The habits of attention to God formed in the interval become the permanent posture of a soul oriented toward him forever.

These two dimensions—doing and becoming—are the twin pillars of the interval's weight. They cannot be separated. What we do shapes who we become. Who we become determines what we are entrusted to do. Together, they constitute the forming work that happens in this brief, unrepeatable window.

The mathematics of forever make one thing clear: the interval of grace is among the most consequential spans of time you will ever experience. Not despite its brevity, but because of it. Not in spite of eternity's vastness, but precisely because that vastness extends whatever is formed here beyond our present ability to comprehend.

You are in the interval now. The formation is happening. The trajectory is being set.

What you do with these numbered days will echo forever.

CHAPTER 3
THE TWO PILLARS

We have established that the interval of grace matters. We have seen why brevity amplifies rather than diminishes its significance. Now we must examine more closely the two dimensions of eternal weight that operate within it.

What we do and who we become. These are the twin pillars on which the interval's significance rests. They are distinct but inseparable—two realities so interwoven that separating them distorts both. Yet distinguishing them clarifies what is at stake and how we might live in light of it.

The doing concerns stewardship. The becoming concerns formation. The doing deposits treasure in heaven. The becoming shapes the soul that will enjoy that treasure forever. The doing is tested by fire at the Bema Seat. The becoming is revealed—the worker behind the works, the tree behind the fruit, the heart behind the hands.

Scripture speaks to both. The parables of Jesus emphasize the doing—talents invested, minas multiplied, servants held accountable for what they produced. The epistles of Paul emphasize the becoming —transformation into Christ's image, the fruit of the Spirit cultivated, character refined through suffering. Neither testament ignores the other dimension, but different texts carry different emphases.

Holding them together is essential for understanding what the interval of grace is for.

This chapter explores both pillars, then traces their inseparability. What emerges is not a balance between two competing concerns but a unified vision of a life that matters eternally.

The First Pillar: What We Do

The parables of Jesus return again and again to the theme of stewardship. Resources are entrusted. Accounts are required. Faithfulness is rewarded. Unfaithfulness is judged.

We examined the parable of the talents in Chapter 1. But it is not alone. In Luke's account, Jesus tells a similar parable with different details—servants given minas rather than talents, with explicit connection to kingdom authority: "Because you have been faithful in a very little, you shall have authority over ten cities" (Luke 19:17). The parable of the shrewd manager commends a man who used resources wisely to secure his future, then applies the principle: "One who is faithful in a very little is also faithful in much, and one who is dishonest in a very little is also dishonest in much. If then you have not been faithful in the unrighteous wealth, who will entrust to you the true riches?" (Luke 16:10-11).

The logic is consistent. Earthly stewardship is a test. What we do with "unrighteous wealth"—the resources of this present age—reveals what we can be trusted with in the age to come. Faithfulness here qualifies for responsibility there. The doing matters because it determines what we are entrusted to do eternally.

Jesus made this explicit in his teaching on treasure: "Do not lay up for yourselves treasures on earth, where moth and rust destroy and where thieves break in and steal, but lay up for yourselves treasures in heaven, where neither moth nor rust destroys and where thieves do not break in and steal. For where your treasure is, there your heart will be also" (Matthew 6:19-21).

The command is not merely to avoid earthly treasure but to actively store heavenly treasure. Something is being deposited. Something is being accumulated. The treasure laid up in heaven is real

—not metaphorical, not merely spiritual sentiment, but actual wealth in the economy of the kingdom.

What constitutes this treasure? Scripture suggests several categories.

First, there is the treasure of souls. Paul wrote to the Thessalonians: "For what is our hope or joy or crown of boasting before our Lord Jesus at his coming? Is it not you? For you are our glory and joy" (1 Thessalonians 2:19-20). The people brought to faith, the disciples made, the lives transformed through faithful witness—these constitute treasure that endures. Daniel was told, "Those who are wise shall shine like the brightness of the sky above; and those who turn many to righteousness, like the stars forever and ever" (Daniel 12:3). The currency of souls is the currency of heaven.

Second, there is the treasure of generosity. Paul instructed Timothy: "They are to do good, to be rich in good works, to be generous and ready to share, thus storing up treasure for themselves as a good foundation for the future, so that they may take hold of that which is truly life" (1 Timothy 6:18-19). Generosity here becomes treasure there. The mechanism is mysterious but the teaching is clear: what is given away in this life is somehow retained—transformed and stored—for the life to come.

Third, there is the treasure of faithful service. The servants who multiplied their talents were commended and promoted. The faithful steward was set over the master's household. The cup of cold water given to a disciple does not go unnoticed or unrewarded (Matthew 10:42). Every act of service rendered in Christ's name accumulates in the heavenly ledger.

The first pillar, then, concerns what we do with what we have been given. The resources entrusted to us—time, money, gifts, relationships, opportunities—are to be invested for kingdom return. The treasure laid up in heaven is real. The account will be rendered. And what we have done determines what we receive.

The Second Pillar: Who We Become

But there is more than doing at stake. There is becoming.

Paul's letters are saturated with the language of transformation. "We all, with unveiled face, beholding the glory of the Lord, are being transformed into the same image from one degree of glory to another. For this comes from the Lord who is the Spirit" (2 Corinthians 3:18). "Put off your old self, which belongs to your former manner of life and is corrupt through deceitful desires, and... put on the new self, created after the likeness of God in true righteousness and holiness" (Ephesians 4:22-24). "Work out your own salvation with fear and trembling, for it is God who works in you, both to will and to work for his good pleasure" (Philippians 2:12-13).

The Christian life is not merely about doing right things. It is about becoming a certain kind of person. The goal is Christlikeness—the actual transformation of character into the image of Jesus. This transformation is the Spirit's work, but it requires our participation. We put off and put on. We work out what God works in. We cooperate with grace in the remaking of our souls.

The fruit of the Spirit describes what this transformed character looks like: "love, joy, peace, patience, kindness, goodness, faithfulness, gentleness, self-control" (Galatians 5:22-23). These are not merely behaviors to perform but qualities to embody. They are the character of Christ being formed in us. And as we argued in Chapter 2, this formed character is what we carry into eternity.

Peter wrote of this formation in terms of participation: "His divine power has granted to us all things that pertain to life and godliness, through the knowledge of him who called us to his own glory and excellence, by which he has granted to us his precious and very great promises, so that through them you may become partakers of the divine nature, having escaped from the corruption that is in the world because of sinful desire" (2 Peter 1:3-4).

Partakers of the divine nature. The Eastern church calls this *theosis*—divinization, the process by which humans come to share in God's own life and character. This is not becoming God, but becoming like God—participating in his nature, reflecting his character, embodying his love and holiness and goodness. The interval of grace is where this participation begins. It continues and deepens forever.

What we become, then, is not peripheral to the Christian life. It is central. The doing matters, but the doing flows from the being. The works are tested, but so is the worker. The fruit is examined, but so is the tree.

Jesus made this connection explicit: "A healthy tree cannot bear bad fruit, nor can a diseased tree bear good fruit" (Matthew 7:18). The fruit reveals the tree. The works reveal the worker. What we do flows from who we are. And who we are is being formed—for better or worse—through the choices we make in the interval of grace.

The Inseparability of Doing and Becoming

These two pillars cannot be separated. They are not two competing priorities to be balanced. They are two aspects of a single reality that must be held together.

Consider: What we do shapes who we become. This is the formative power of action. Every choice bends the will in one direction or another. Every discipline carves a groove in the soul. The servant who invests the talents is not merely producing a return; he is becoming a faithful person. The servant who buries the talent is not merely failing to produce; he is becoming an unfaithful person. The doing is forming the doer.

Scripture affirms this dynamic and grounds it in grace. James writes: "Be doers of the word, and not hearers only, deceiving yourselves" (James 1:22). And again: "Faith apart from works is dead" (James 2:26). The doing is not merely evidence of faith—it is the very means by which faith remains alive and character is formed. Paul instructs the Philippians to "work out your own salvation" (Philippians 2:12)—not to earn what has been given, but to actualize it, to make real in character what has been declared in justification.

And consider the reverse: Who we become determines what we can do. This is the enabling power of character. The servant with a faithful character can be trusted with more. The servant with an unfaithful character cannot be trusted with anything. "One who is faithful in a very little is also faithful in much" (Luke 16:10)—not merely as prediction but as principle. The character enables the stewardship.

The tree determines the fruit. The worker determines the work. The soul that has been formed into a generous soul is capable of greater generosity. The soul that has been formed into a loving soul is capable of deeper love. The becoming enables the doing at ever greater capacity.

This is why the two pillars must be held together. A focus on doing alone produces activism without formation—much labor but a shriveled soul. A focus on becoming alone produces quietism without fruit—much contemplation but no kingdom impact. The integrated vision is a soul being formed through faithful action, whose formation enables greater action, in an ascending spiral of grace.

Dallas Willard captured this dynamic in *The Great Omission*: "Grace is not opposed to effort. It is opposed to earning." The effort of doing—the discipline, the service, the generosity, the faithful stewardship—is not earning salvation. Salvation is gift. But the effort is cooperating with grace in the formation of a soul that will reflect Christ and serve his kingdom forever.

The Virtuous Spiral

When doing and becoming operate together, they create what we might call a virtuous spiral—an ascending dynamic in which faithful action forms faithful character, and faithful character enables greater faithful action, and so on without limit.

Consider generosity. A believer gives sacrificially. The act of giving stretches the soul and weakens the grip of greed. A more generous character begins to form. That more generous character enables the next gift to come more freely, with less internal resistance. The greater gift further expands the generous soul. And so the spiral ascends—each act of generosity forming greater capacity for generosity, each increase in capacity enabling greater acts.

Consider patience. A believer chooses patience in a difficult circumstance. The choice to wait, to endure, to refrain from reactive anger, forms the soul in patience. The next difficulty is met with slightly more patience, because patience has been forming. Each exercise of patience deepens the habit of patience. And the spiral ascends —character enabling action, action forming character.

Consider service. A believer pours out time and energy for others. The serving forms a servant heart. The servant heart delights in more serving. The more serving deepens the servant heart. And the spiral ascends.

This is how the two pillars work together across the interval of grace. The doing is never merely producing external results; it is always also forming internal character. The becoming is never merely internal development; it is always also enabling external fruit. The spiral ascends through both dimensions simultaneously.

And here is the weight: the character formed in the interval does not dissolve at death. It persists. The book of Revelation offers a glimpse of this permanence: "Let the righteous still do right, and the holy still be holy" (Revelation 22:11). The character is fixed. The righteous continue in righteousness. The holy continue in holiness.

If Edwards and Gregory are right—if heavenly growth continues eternally as the soul advances into the inexhaustible God—then the formation established in the interval shapes not merely the moment of judgment but the eternal trajectory that follows. Scripture does not give us the precise mechanics. But the principles it teaches—differentiated glory, continuous identity, more given to those who have— suggest that the level the soul reaches when the interval closes is the level from which eternal life continues.

We will return to these spirals in greater depth in the chapters ahead—both the ascending spiral of faithful formation and its dark counterpart, the descending spiral of unfaithfulness that atrophies capacity. For now, we note the dynamic: the two pillars are not merely parallel; they are intertwined, each feeding the other in patterns that compound across a lifetime and echo into eternity.

The Vicious Spiral

But spirals can descend as well as ascend.

Consider the one-talent servant. He did nothing with what he was given. The doing—or rather, the not-doing—formed a character of fearful inaction. The fearful character made future action even more unlikely. The inaction deepened the fear. And the spiral descended—until the master returned and found a servant who had become the kind of person who buries talents in the ground.

Consider the rich fool of Jesus's parable, who built bigger barns to store his surplus and said to his soul, "Soul, you have ample goods laid up for many years; relax, eat, drink, be merry" (Luke 12:19). The hoarding formed a hoarding heart. The hoarding heart saw no reason to stop hoarding. And the spiral descended—until God said, "Fool! This night your soul is required of you" (Luke 12:20).

Consider Pharaoh, whose heart was hardened. Each refusal to release Israel hardened the heart further. The hardened heart made the next refusal more certain. And the spiral descended—until Pharaoh became a man incapable of yielding, incapable of responding to God, incapable of anything but hardened resistance.

The vicious spiral is the dark mirror of the virtuous spiral. Every choice away from faithfulness forms a less faithful character. Every act of selfishness deepens the self-centered soul. Every refusal to love diminishes the capacity for love. The spiral descends—each failure making the next more likely, each hardening making the next easier.

This spiral, too, does not stop at death. For those who never turn to Christ, the character formed in the interval is the character that enters eternity. "Let the evildoer still do evil, and the filthy still be filthy" (Revelation 22:11). The spiral has descended to where it has descended—and that is where eternity finds it. But the principle extends, in a different register, even to believers: the Christian who drifts through the interval in spiritual negligence arrives saved but diminished. The soul is rescued; the capacity is stunted. Such a person enters glory—but as one arriving with little rather than much, the thimble rather than the ocean, filled with joy yet holding less than faithful formation might have built.

This is the sobering counterpart to the hopeful message. The interval of grace is not only an opportunity for ascending formation; it is also an arena of risk. For those outside Christ, the vicious spiral leads to final fixity. For those within Christ, it may lead not to condemnation but to diminishment—saved, but as through fire. The soul is being shaped either way. The only question is which direction.

Grace and Effort

At this point, a crucial clarification is needed. Everything said about the two pillars—the doing and the becoming, the virtuous spiral and the vicious spiral—must be understood within the framework of grace.

We do not earn our salvation by doing. Salvation is gift, received by faith, secured by Christ's work alone. The doing is not meritorious in the sense of creating a claim on God. We are justified by grace through faith, not by works, lest anyone should boast (Ephesians 2:8-9).

But grace does not preclude doing. The very next verse continues: "For we are his workmanship, created in Christ Jesus for good works, which God prepared beforehand, that we should walk in them" (Ephesians 2:10). Grace creates workers. Grace prepares works. Grace enables the walking. The doing flows from the gift, not toward it.

Similarly, we do not form ourselves by sheer effort. The becoming is the Spirit's work. "He who began a good work in you will bring it to completion at the day of Jesus Christ" (Philippians 1:6). We are being transformed—passive voice—by the Lord who is the Spirit. The formation is God's initiative, God's power, God's grace.

But grace calls for cooperation. "Work out your own salvation with fear and trembling"—here is the human responsibility—"for it is God who works in you, both to will and to work for his good pleasure" (Philippians 2:12-13). God works in; we work out. God provides the willing and the working; we provide the actual willing and working. It is synergy, not independence—cooperation, not autonomy.

The two pillars stand on the foundation of grace. Everything we do that matters is enabled by grace. Everything we become that lasts is formed by grace. The interval of grace is called what it is because grace pervades it. The doing and the becoming are not alternatives to grace but expressions of it.

Yet they are real. The choices are real. The formation is real. The spirals—ascending or descending—are real. Grace does not override human action; it empowers and evaluates it. The steward who multiplied the talents did so by grace—but he did so. The servant who buried the talent refused grace—and bore the consequence.

The Integration

What, then, is the integrated vision?

A life of doing that forms becoming. A character of becoming that enables doing. An ascending spiral of grace-empowered faithfulness in which every act of stewardship shapes the steward, and the shaped steward is entrusted with greater stewardship.

The treasure laid up in heaven is real—but so is the soul being formed to enjoy that treasure. The works that survive the fire are real—but so is the worker who stands revealed. The authority over ten cities is real—but so is the character that qualified for such authority.

In the interval of grace, the believer is not choosing between doing and becoming. The believer is living a single life in which both dimensions are always operative. Every day of faithful service is forming a faithful servant. Every act of generous giving is expanding a generous soul. Every discipline of patience is building an eternal patience.

This is the life that echoes into eternity. This is what the interval of grace is for. This is why it matters—not as two separate concerns to balance, but as one unified reality to embrace.

The two pillars hold up a single structure: a life that matters forever, forming a person who will shine forever, equipped for a vocation that will unfold forever.

The foundation is now laid. What we do and who we become are the twin realities that give the interval of grace its weight.

You are doing something right now. You are becoming something through the doing. Both matter. Both translate. Both will be revealed.

PART TWO
THE THEOLOGY OF BECOMING
CHAPTERS 4–9

CHAPTER 4
THE CONTINUITY PRINCIPLE

The question is not whether we will exist after death. The question is whether *we* will exist—the same self, the same person, continuous with who we are now.

Much of what passes for Christian hope is actually a kind of erasure. We imagine death as a reset, a do-over, a merciful deletion of everything we have been. The struggles, the failures, the slowly formed habits of soul—all wiped clean, replaced by some generic heavenly existence. We will float, we will sing, we will be happy. But we will not, in any meaningful sense, be *us*.

This is not the biblical hope. Scripture presents something far more weighty: transformation, not replacement. The person who dies is the person who rises. The seed becomes the plant—not a different organism, but the fullness of what the seed contained. The acorn becomes the oak. And the soul shaped in the interval of grace is the soul that enters eternity.

This is the continuity principle. It is what makes the interval matter so intensely. If death were a reset, the choices of this life would carry no permanent weight. But death is not a reset. It is a transition—and we carry ourselves through it.

The two pillars we examined in Chapter 3—what we do and who

we become—assume this continuity. If death erased the self, neither pillar would carry weight. The treasure laid up would belong to no one. The character formed would simply vanish. But death does not erase. It transforms. And what we carry through that transformation is precisely what the interval has been forming.

The Seed and the Plant

Paul addressed this directly when the Corinthians asked a skeptic's question: "How are the dead raised? With what kind of body do they come?" (1 Corinthians 15:35).

His answer was not philosophical abstraction. It was agricultural imagery:

"What you sow does not come to life unless it dies. And what you sow is not the body that is to be, but a bare kernel, perhaps of wheat or of some other grain. But God gives it a body as he has chosen, and to each kind of seed its own body" (1 Corinthians 15:36-38).

The metaphor is precise. The seed is sown; the seed dies; a plant rises. But the plant is not unrelated to the seed. It is the seed transformed. The wheat kernel becomes a wheat stalk, not a rose bush. The acorn becomes an oak, not a maple. There is continuity of kind, continuity of identity, even as there is radical transformation of form.

Paul continued: "So is it with the resurrection of the dead. What is sown is perishable; what is raised is imperishable. It is sown in dishonor; it is raised in glory. It is sown in weakness; it is raised in power. It is sown a natural body; it is raised a spiritual body" (1 Corinthians 15:42-44).

The contrasts are stark: perishable and imperishable, dishonor and glory, weakness and power, natural and spiritual. But through every contrast, the subject remains the same. *It* is sown; *it* is raised. The same thing—transformed, glorified, but continuous.

Randy Alcorn has documented this biblical vision extensively in his book *Heaven*, correcting the Platonic distortions that have led many Christians to imagine the afterlife as a realm of disembodied spirits floating on clouds. The resurrection is physical. The new creation is material. The hope of Scripture is not escape from the body but redemption of the body—the same body, transformed and glorified.

But there is a further implication that Alcorn's descriptive work opens up and that we must press into. If the body is continuous through resurrection, what about the soul? What about the character that has been forming? What about the person who inhabits the body?

The answer, we will argue, is the same: continuity. The self that has been shaped through the interval of grace is the self that rises. The soul that has been forming is the soul that enters eternity. The transformation is real—but so is the continuity.

This does not mean we rise with our sins intact. The resurrection completes the sanctification that grace began. The sinful residue is purged. The struggle against sin is finally over. But the *character* that was being formed through that struggle—the patience forged in difficulty, the love cultivated against resistance, the faithfulness proven through testing—this persists, now perfected. Sanctification does not erase what was formed; it purifies and completes it. The real you, finally freed from sin, is still *you*—with all the virtue that grace was building.

Recognition: The Biblical Evidence

Scripture provides evidence of this continuity through recognition. The dead are not anonymous. They are known. They remember. They are themselves.

At the Transfiguration, Jesus took Peter, James, and John up a high mountain, and "he was transfigured before them, and his face shone like the sun, and his clothes became white as light. And behold, there appeared to them Moses and Elijah, talking with him" (Matthew 17:2-3). Moses had been dead for over a thousand years. Elijah had been taken up centuries before. Yet both appeared—recognizable, identifiable, themselves. Peter knew who they were. They had not become generic spirits. They were Moses and Elijah, continuous with who they had been on earth.

In Jesus's account of the rich man and Lazarus, the continuity is even more explicit. The rich man, in torment, "lifted up his eyes and saw Abraham far off and Lazarus at his side" (Luke 16:23). He recognized Lazarus—the same beggar who had lain at his gate. He remembered his own life, his brothers, his failure to heed Moses and the prophets. Memory persisted. Identity persisted. Relationship persisted. The rich man was still himself, and that was precisely his torment.

After the resurrection, Jesus appeared to his disciples and was recognized—though sometimes only after a moment of revelation. Mary Magdalene recognized him when he spoke her name (John 20:16). The disciples on the road to Emmaus recognized him in the breaking of bread (Luke 24:31). Thomas recognized him by his wounds (John 20:27-28). The recognition was not of a stranger who resembled Jesus. It was recognition of Jesus himself—the same person they had known, now risen.

These passages are not merely evidence that individuals persist. They are evidence that the *same* individuals persist—with memory, with identity, with relational history intact. The dead are not reset. They are themselves, continuous with who they were.

Scarred Yet Glorified

The resurrection of Jesus reveals something crucial about the nature of continuity: our histories are not erased. They are carried forward.

When Jesus appeared to his disciples after the resurrection, he showed them his hands and his side (John 20:20). The wounds were still visible. When Thomas doubted, Jesus invited him to touch the scars: "Put your finger here, and see my hands; and put out your hand, and place it in my side" (John 20:27).

This is remarkable. The resurrection body of Jesus was glorified. It was no longer subject to death. It could appear in locked rooms, vanish from sight, ascend to heaven. And yet it bore the marks of the cross. The wounds that killed him were not erased in resurrection. They were transformed—no longer bleeding, no longer fatal, but still present. Still visible. Still part of who he was.

The wounds were not a defect in the resurrection. They were, in some sense, its glory. The Lamb in Revelation appears "as though it had been slain" (Revelation 5:6). The marks of sacrifice are eternal marks. The history of redemption is written on the body of Christ forever.

This has profound implications for our own continuity. If Christ's earthly history is carried into his resurrection body—if the wounds remain—then our histories are not erased either. The life we have lived, the choices we have made, the character we have formed, the sufferings we have endured—these are not deleted at death. They are carried forward into resurrection, transformed and redeemed, but still ours. Still part of who we are.

We will not arrive in the new creation as blank slates. We will arrive as the people we have become—with histories, with memories, with the marks of our earthly pilgrimage written into who we are. The question is not whether our histories will persist. The question is what kind of histories we are writing.

What of Our Sins?

But what of our sins? Scripture declares that God "will remember their sin no more" (Jeremiah 31:34), that he removes our transgressions "as far as the east is from the west" (Psalm 103:12). If God does not remember our sins, do they persist in our histories?

We must be careful here. God's "not remembering" is covenantal, not cognitive. It does not mean God suffers amnesia regarding our past. It means he will not hold our sins against us. They are forgiven. They do not condemn. They are removed as grounds for judgment. The record that stood against us has been nailed to the cross (Colossians 2:14). There is now no condemnation for those who are in Christ Jesus (Romans 8:1).

But this does not necessarily mean our memories are wiped clean of all awareness of our former lives.

The rich man remembered his earthly life—including, it seems, his failures. The martyrs remembered their deaths and cried for vindication (Revelation 6:9-10). Paul, even after conversion, remembered that he had persecuted the church and called himself "the chief of sinners" (1 Timothy 1:15). Memory persisted. But for Paul, this memory was not torment. It was grounds for worship. It magnified grace.

In eternity, our memories of sin may function the same way: not as sources of shame but as amplifiers of gratitude. We will remember what we were saved *from*, and it will deepen our praise of the One who saved us. The guilt is gone. The condemnation is removed. The sting is extracted. But the story remains—a story of grace, written in the history of a redeemed sinner.

Our histories persist, then, but redeemed. The sins are forgiven and will never condemn. The wounds are healed. But the scars may remain as testimonials—not of failure, but of grace. Just as Christ bears the wounds of the cross in his glorified body, so we may carry our histories into eternity: not as burdens, but as trophies of redemption. Every memory of sin becomes a memory of mercy. Every recollection of failure becomes occasion for praise.

What Survives Death

If continuity is real—continuity through sanctification, continuity with histories redeemed—we must ask more precisely: What survives? What crosses the threshold of death and persists into resurrection?

Identity survives. The "I" that exists now is the "I" that will exist forever. There is no replacement, no substitution, no exchange of selves. Paul expected to depart and be with Christ (Philippians 1:23)—not some other Paul, but himself. The martyrs under the altar cry out for vindication (Revelation 6:9-10)—the same martyrs who suffered on earth. The continuity is personal. You will be you.

Memory survives. The rich man remembered his life, his brothers, his choices (Luke 16:25-28). The martyrs remembered their deaths and cried for justice (Revelation 6:10). Moses and Elijah remembered enough to discuss Jesus's "departure, which he was about to accomplish at Jerusalem" (Luke 9:31). We will not enter eternity with amnesia. Our earthly lives will be remembered—by us, and by God—though the memories will be transformed by grace, stripped of guilt, and suffused with gratitude.

Relational bonds survive. Paul told the Thessalonians, "What is our hope or joy or crown of boasting before our Lord Jesus at his coming? Is it not you?" (1 Thessalonians 2:19). The relationships formed on earth persist. The people we have loved, served, and brought to faith will be our joy forever. We are not saved into isolation. We are saved into community—a community with history, with shared memory, with bonds forged in the interval of grace.

Personal history survives. The "glory of the nations" is brought into the New Jerusalem (Revelation 21:24-26). Human achievements, purified of sin, are not discarded but incorporated. Our stories—the places we have been, the work we have done, the lives we have touched—are woven into the fabric of the new creation. History is not erased. It is redeemed.

And character survives. This is the weight we have been building toward. The soul that has been formed in the interval of grace—the virtues cultivated, the capacities developed, the habits solidified—this is what we carry into eternity. The character is not stripped away at death. It is what persists most fundamentally, now purified of sin and perfected by grace.

This is why the interval matters so intensely. We are not merely passing time until we receive a new self. We are forming the self that will exist forever. The virtuous spiral that has been ascending continues at the level it has reached—now freed from the drag of sin, now accelerating into eternal growth. The patience being formed now is the patience we will have eternally, perfected and expanded. The love being cultivated now is the capacity for love we will carry into the new creation, finally freed to love without hindrance.

What survives death is not some abstract essence of personhood. What survives is *you*—sanctified, glorified, but recognizably and continuously *you*—with all that grace has been forming in you.

Conformed to His Image

But we must be more specific still. We are not merely persisting as generic selves. We are being conformed to a particular image.

Paul wrote: "For those whom he foreknew he also predestined to be conformed to the image of his Son, in order that he might be the firstborn among many brothers" (Romans 8:29). The goal of the Christian life is not self-improvement in the abstract. It is Christlikeness. We are being shaped into the image of Jesus—his love, his humility, his obedience, his character.

This conformity is happening now. Paul's vision of transformation "from one degree of glory to another" (2 Corinthians 3:18) is not instantaneous replacement but progressive formation—and that progression continues through death into resurrection. The transformation is degree by degree. Glory to glory. In the interval of grace, we are becoming like Christ—or failing to become like him.

And what we have become is what we carry through death, to be perfected in resurrection.

The resurrection body will be "like his glorious body" (Philippians 3:21). The saints will be "like him" when they see him as he is (1 John 3:2). But this likeness is not imposed from the outside at the moment of resurrection as if nothing had come before. It is the completion of a process that began in the interval of grace. The conformity that has been forming in us reaches its fullness. The Christlikeness being cultivated is brought to perfection.

This means the interval is not merely about self-formation in the abstract. It is about Christ-formation specifically. Every movement toward humility is movement toward his image. Every growth in love is growth into his character. Every discipline of obedience is shaping us into what we are destined to become—and what we will be forever.

The question is not whether we will be conformed to Christ's image eventually. All the redeemed will see him and be like him. The question is how much conformity has already occurred when the interval ends. How much of Christ's image has been formed in us? How deep does the likeness go?

The continuity principle means that this formation is not lost. What has been formed persists, now sanctified and completed. The degree of Christlikeness reached in the interval is the foundation on which eternal growth continues—not restarting from zero, but building on what grace has already accomplished.

The Glory of the Nations

The book of Revelation provides a stunning image of continuity extending beyond individual persons to collective human achievement.

"The nations will walk by its light, and the kings of the earth will bring their glory into it, and its gates will never be shut by day—and there will be no night there. They will bring into it the glory and the honor of the nations" (Revelation 21:24-26).

The kings of the earth bring their glory into the New Jerusalem. The glory and honor of the nations are brought into the eternal city. Human achievement is not discarded. It is purified and incorporated.

What does this mean? At minimum, it means that human culture is not erased. The work of civilization—art, music, literature, architecture, discovery, invention—is not swept away as worthless. What has been good and true and beautiful in human achievement is somehow preserved, redeemed, and brought into the new creation.

Alcorn and others have explored what this might look like—the continuation of human creativity, the redemption of cultural achievement, the bringing of tributes to the King of kings. These are magnificent possibilities to contemplate.

But there is a personal application we must not miss. If the glory of the nations is brought into the New Jerusalem, what glory will *you* bring? What has been formed in your life that will enter the city?

The kings bring their glory. The nations bring their honor. And we—we bring ourselves. We bring the persons we have become. We bring the character that has been formed, the capacities that have been developed, the Christlikeness that has been cultivated—all sanctified, all perfected, all redeemed.

The gates are open. The invitation stands. But what we bring through those gates has been shaped by what we became in the interval of grace. The glory we carry into the New Jerusalem is the glory of Christ's image formed in a redeemed human soul—a soul with a history, a story, a journey of grace that began in the interval and continues forever.

The Weight of Continuity

The continuity principle ties directly to the two pillars we examined in Chapter 3: what we do and who we become.

What we do matters because the doing forms the doer—and the doer persists, sanctified. The treasure we lay up in heaven is real treasure, and the soul that has been laying it up carries that formed generosity into eternity, now perfected. The service we render is real service, and the servant heart being formed carries that capacity into the kingdom, now freed to serve without the drag of selfishness.

Who we become matters because the becoming is not temporary. The patience cultivated now is eternal patience, completed. The love developed now is capacity for infinite love, finally unhindered. The attention to God practiced now becomes the permanent posture of a soul oriented toward him forever, no longer distracted by sin.

The continuity principle means that the interval of grace is not a waiting room. It is a forming room. And what is being formed is what will exist forever—purified, yes; perfected, yes; but continuous with what grace was building in the interval.

This is both comfort and warning.

It is comfort because our lives matter. Our struggles matter. Our growth matters. Nothing is wasted. The slow, difficult work of sanctification—the two steps forward and one step back, the gradual transformation from glory to glory—this is not busywork to fill the time before heaven. It is the construction of an eternal self. It is the forming of the person who will walk through the gates of the New Jerusalem. Every victory over sin, every discipline of love, every choice toward faithfulness is building something permanent.

It is warning because formation is happening either way. The character being shaped through neglect, through refusal to cooperate with grace, through persistent resistance to the Spirit's work—this too has consequences. The believer who arrives having built with wood, hay, and stubble will be saved, but "only as through fire" (1 Corinthians 3:15). Saved, yes. But impoverished of what might have been. The capacity that might have been developed remains undeveloped. The Christlikeness that might have been formed remains unformed.

Revelation 22:11 offers a glimpse of finality: "Let the righteous still do right, and the holy still be holy." The character reaches a point of fixity. What we have become is what we continue to be. The righteous persist in righteousness. The holy persist in holiness. The trajectory established in the interval continues into eternity.

The clay is still soft now. The form is not yet fixed. The interval of grace is still open—limited and closing, but not yet closed. What we are becoming can still be shaped. The cooperation with grace can deepen. The conformity to Christ can accelerate.

But the continuity principle means that this window is not infinite. What we become in the interval—by grace, through faith, in cooperation with the Spirit—is what we carry through death into resurrection. The self being formed now is the self that will exist forever.

The Person You Will Be Forever

You are not waiting to become someone else in heaven.

You are becoming *now* the person you will be *forever*.

The resurrection will transform you—completing the work that grace has begun, removing every remnant of sin, glorifying what has been formed. But it will transform *you*. The same self. The same person. Continuous with who you are becoming in this very moment.

This is the weight of the interval of grace. This is why the daily choices matter. This is why the slow work of sanctification carries eternal consequence. This is why cooperation with grace is not optional but essential.

The seed is being sown. The form is being shaped. The character is being built—not yet finally, not yet in perfection, but really. Every choice toward love is forming a loving soul that will love forever. Every discipline of patience is building an eternally patient self. Every act of faith is deepening a capacity that will expand without limit in the presence of God.

The continuity principle makes the interval infinitely weighty.

You will persist—sanctified, glorified, but *you*. The question is: what kind of person is being formed?

You are becoming the answer to that question right now.

But if continuity is real, we must face what follows: there is a deadline. The soul being formed will one day be fixed. The clay will enter the kiln. To that sobering reality we now turn.

CHAPTER 5
THE KILN OF DEATH

There is a deadline to your becoming.

We prefer the comfort of open-ended growth, the reassurance of endless second chances, the quiet assumption that there will always be time to become who we ought to be. Tomorrow we will pray with more focus. Next year we will love more freely. Eventually we will grow into the people we know we should be. The interval stretches ahead of us, indefinite and forgiving.

Scripture offers no such comfort. "It is appointed for man to die once, and after that comes judgment" (Hebrews 9:27). The sequence is fixed: life, then death, then evaluation. The exam follows the semester. The harvest follows the planting. The kiln fires after the shaping.

While you live, you are clay on the wheel—pliable, shapeable, still responding to pressure. Every choice presses into the material. Every discipline carves a groove. Every refusal to love leaves its mark, and every act of faithfulness leaves another. The wheel spins, the hands of grace work, and something is taking form.

But clay does not stay soft forever.

Death is the kiln. What has been forming in secret enters the fire —the thousand small choices, the habits of attention and neglect, the shape the will has taken through decades of bending toward God or away from him. What emerges is fixed. Not frozen in time, not static, but foundationally established in its essential structure. The trajectory is set. The starting point for eternity is determined by what has been formed in time.

In Chapter 4, we established the continuity principle: the self that has been shaped in the interval is the self that rises. Now we must face the corollary that makes continuity weighty: there is a deadline. The forming does not continue indefinitely. The clay enters the kiln, and what has been shaping becomes permanent.

Frozen in the Moment

In the autumn of 79 AD, Mount Vesuvius erupted, burying the Roman city of Pompeii under a torrent of ash and volcanic debris. The city's residents who had not fled in time died where they stood—in their homes, in the streets, in the act of running toward gates that would never open for them. The superheated pyroclastic flow hit at several hundred degrees, killing instantly and encasing the bodies in layers of volcanic ash.

For nearly two thousand years, those bodies remained where they had fallen. The flesh decomposed, but the compacted ash held its shape, leaving hollow voids in the precise contours of the dead. In 1863, the archaeologist Giuseppe Fiorelli recognized what these voids represented and developed a method to reveal them. He poured liquid plaster into the cavities. When the plaster hardened and the surrounding ash was chipped away, the victims appeared again—not as skeletons, but as three-dimensional casts preserving the exact postures of their final moments.

The results are haunting. A man with his arm raised defensively, mouth open in a cry. A mother curled around her child, still trying to shield the small body from what could not be shielded. A chained dog twisted in desperate contortion. A group of thirteen fugitives near the Nocera Gate, caught mid-flight in the "Garden of the Fugitives"—men, women, and children frozen in the very act of running, their positions preserved for millennia.

Whatever posture they held when the fire struck is the posture they hold forever.

The physical preservation of Pompeii offers a sobering parable of spiritual reality. Death comes, and what has been forming is fixed. The position of the soul at the moment of the kiln's firing is the position in which it is set. There is no reshaping after the plaster hardens. There is no second chance to flee after the gate is buried. The form you are becoming now is the form you will be becoming eternally.

The Sequence of Hebrews

The writer of Hebrews assumes this reality. "It is appointed for man to die once, and after that comes judgment" (Hebrews 9:27). Note the sequence: death, then judgment. Not death, then further formation, then judgment. Not death, then remediation, then assessment. Death concludes the evaluation period. Judgment reviews what has been completed.

This is why Paul urges: "We must all appear before the judgment seat of Christ, so that each one may receive what is due for what he has done in the body, whether good or evil" (2 Corinthians 5:10). The phrase is precise: *what he has done in the body*. Embodied earthly life is the arena of evaluation. The works tested at the Bema Seat are the works performed in the interval of grace, not works performed after it closes.

Scripture provides no intermediate formation stage. No waiting room where souls continue to develop before final assessment. The rich man in Jesus's parable does not request additional time to become more generous; he asks for relief from consequence and warning for his brothers (Luke 16:24-28). The five foolish virgins do not ask for more time to acquire oil; they find the door shut and hear the terrible words: "I do not know you" (Matthew 25:12). The one-talent servant does not plead for another chance to invest; he faces judgment on what he failed to do with what he was given (Matthew 25:26-30).

The exam follows the semester. When the semester ends, the exam begins.

The Fixity of the Will

Thomas Aquinas, the medieval theologian whose work shaped centuries of Christian thought, developed a philosophical argument for this biblical reality. After death, Aquinas argued, the human soul can no longer change its basic orientation—either toward God or away from him.

His reasoning was striking. During embodied life, the soul operates through the body and is subject to time, change, and development. We think discursively, moving from premise to conclusion. We deliberate between options. We experience conversion, growth, and decline. The embodied soul is mutable.

But the separated soul—the soul after death, before resurrection—operates differently. It no longer thinks discursively but apprehends truth directly, more like an angel than like an embodied human. And just as an angel's will is fixed immediately upon its creation (explaining why the fallen angels cannot repent), so the human soul's will becomes fixed at the moment of separation from the body.

The will's fundamental orientation is established. The soul that has been turning toward God continues in that turning, now permanently. The soul that has been turned away remains turned away, the choice now irreversible.

Aquinas argued this was knowable not only from divine revelation but from philosophical reasoning about the nature of the separated soul. Whether or not one follows every step of his argument, the conclusion aligns with the consistent witness of Scripture: death ends the opportunity for change of orientation. The direction you are facing when the kiln fires is the direction you face forever.

What "Fixed" Means—and Doesn't Mean

But we must be careful here. To say that death fixes the soul's essential form is not to say that eternity is static. We established in Chapter 2 that the great theologians of the church—Edwards, Gregory of Nyssa, and others—taught that the redeemed soul continues to grow into God forever. Gregory's *epektasis*, the eternal advance into the inexhaustible divine nature, means that heaven is not a frozen tableau but an endless journey further up and further in.

What, then, is fixed?

Orientation is fixed. The fundamental direction of the will—toward God or away from him—is settled at death. For the believer, this orientation was secured by grace through faith in the interval; death does not change it but confirms it. The will that was learning to bend toward God is now permanently inclined in that direction.

Formed character is fixed. The specific capacities developed in the interval—how much humility was cultivated, how deep the love grew, how expansive the generosity became—these persist as the foundation for eternal life. The virtues formed are the virtues you carry. The Christlikeness developed is the Christlikeness you possess.

Starting point is fixed. The level reached when the interval closes is the level from which eternal growth begins. All believers grow forever. But they grow from where they are, not from some equalized starting line.

What is fixed is not growth itself—the saints advance into God forever, as we will see in Chapter 6. What is fixed is the foundation from which that endless advance begins. The kiln establishes the starting point; it does not impose a ceiling.

Consider two souls entering eternity. Both are redeemed. Both are oriented toward God. Both will grow in knowledge and love and joy forever. But one has spent decades cultivating patience, developing generosity, deepening in prayer; the other has been saved, as it were, through fire—genuine faith but little formation. Both are in Christ. Both are safe. But one enters with vast capacity already developed; the other enters with capacity barely begun.

Edwards offered the illustration we encountered in Chapter 2: every vessel cast into the ocean of heaven's happiness is full, though some vessels are far larger than others. Both are filled to the brim. Both are perfectly satisfied. Neither envies the other, for perfect love reigns and each rejoices in the other's happiness. Yet the vessel with greater capacity contains more. And the capacity you bring is the capacity you formed in the interval.

Gregory of Nyssa described perfection as perpetual progress into the infinite God. Edwards taught that the saints' knowledge and holiness increase to eternity. Both were right. But the progress begins from a fixed point—the point reached when the kiln fires.

The Deadline Heightens Everything

This is what makes the interval infinitely weighty. If post-mortem formation could eventually equalize everyone, the interval would matter less. If eternal progress could erase the effects of earthly neglect, the urgency would diminish. But the fixed starting point means that formation in the interval has permanent consequence.

Scripture does not give us formulas for eternity. It does not tell us the precise mechanics of how differentiated capacities relate to one another across infinite time. But it tells us this: what is formed matters. The servant given ten minas who earned ten more received authority over ten cities. The one who earned five received five cities (Luke 19:17-19). The differentiation persists. One star differs from another star in glory (1 Corinthians 15:41).

This is why Samuel Johnson, the great lexicographer and man of letters, spent his life haunted by the deadline. Boswell records Johnson's conversation on the subject. When asked if the fear of death might be overcome, Johnson replied with characteristic directness: "It is so natural to man, that the whole of life is but keeping away the thoughts of it." Yet Johnson did not merely fear death; he feared facing God with unfinished business. At twenty-eight, he wrote in his diary: "Mayest thou, O God, enable me, for Jesus Christ's sake, to spend this in such a manner, that I may receive comfort from it at the hour of death, and in the day of judgement!"

Johnson understood that he was forming a soul that would be evaluated. His fear was not irrational; it was the appropriate response of a man who took eternity seriously while knowing his own moral frailty. Near the end, he prayed: "Grant O Lord that my whole hope and confidence may be in his merits and in thy mercy: forgive and accept my late conversion, enforce and accept my imperfect repentance." *Late conversion. Imperfect repentance.* Johnson, a Christian all his adult life, still felt he was only now—at the very end—truly surrendering. The kiln was about to fire, and he knew what shape the clay had taken.

The Logic of Judgment

If we step back, we can see why the deadline must exist. The reward system of Scripture loses coherence without it.

The parable of the talents and the parable of the minas both assume completed formation. The master returns and evaluates what each servant has done with what was given. The evaluation is final. Imagine if, after the evaluation, the servants could continue developing and eventually all reach the same outcome. The master's "well done" and his rebuke would mean nothing. The differentiated rewards—five cities versus ten—would be temporary and finally irrelevant.

But the evaluation stands because the formation period is complete. The one who was faithful over little is now entrusted with much—not as a temporary accommodation but as permanent assignment. The one who buried his talent finds that the opportunity is not extended but closed. "Take the talent from him and give it to him who has the ten talents" (Matthew 25:28). The door shuts.

This is not arbitrary divine decree. It is how souls work. Character formation requires conditions: embodiment, time, resistance, choice. The interval provides these conditions. Death removes them. The soul that has been forming no longer has the conditions for further formation of the same kind. What continues is not formation in the sense of the interval—the struggle against sin, the learning through failure, the slow reshaping through suffering. What continues is growth of a different sort: expansion of what has been formed, deepening of capacities already developed, eternal advance into what the soul has become qualified to receive.

Galatians 6:7-8 states the principle with agricultural directness: "Do not be deceived: God is not mocked, for whatever one sows, that will he also reap. For the one who sows to his own flesh will from the flesh reap corruption, but the one who sows to the Spirit will from the Spirit reap eternal life." Sowing happens in the interval. Reaping happens at the harvest. And the harvest follows the sowing with absolute fidelity.

Sanctification Completed

For the believer, death does something glorious: it completes sanctification. The sin that has been dying throughout the interval dies finally. The struggle that has marked the Christian life comes to an end. The remnants of the old nature are purged. What emerges from the kiln is not merely fixed but perfected.

This is the continuity principle from Chapter 4 pressed to its completion: we persist, but perfected. We do not enter eternity with our sins intact. We enter with our sins removed and our character completed. The patience that was being formed—always imperfect, always battling impatience—becomes perfect patience at last. The love that was growing—always tainted by selfishness, always incomplete—becomes pure love, freed from every hindrance. The kiln does not merely fix the clay; for the believer, it purifies the clay.

But here is the weight: the clay that is purified is the clay that was being formed. Sanctification completes what grace was building. It perfects the character that was developing. It does not create from nothing; it brings to completion. If little was being built, there is little to complete. If much was being formed, much is brought to perfection.

We return to Revelation 22:11: "Let the righteous still do right, and the holy still be holy." The character persists. The righteous continue in righteousness—now perfected, now unhindered, but continuous with what they were becoming. The holy continue in holiness—now complete, now freed from every contrary impulse, but recognizably the same souls who were learning holiness in the interval.

This is why the interval matters so desperately. Not because salvation depends on our performance—it does not; salvation is by grace through faith. But because the capacity to enjoy salvation is being formed. The vessel that will be filled with glory is being shaped. And the shape it has when the kiln fires is the shape it will have forever.

THE INTERVAL

The Runners at the Starting Line

Picture two runners at the starting line of an eternal race. The gun has just fired. Both will run forever. Both will grow stronger forever. Heaven is not static, and the race is endless.

But one runner trained for eighty years. Muscles developed, endurance vast, form perfected through decades of discipline. The other runner barely trained. He believed in the race—he is genuinely present at the starting line—but he spent his training period on other things. He is saved, genuinely saved, but unprepared.

The gun fires. Both run. Both grow. But they do not begin from the same place.

Scripture does not tell us the precise relationship between their journeys over infinite time. It tells us that different servants received different cities. It tells us that one star differs from another star in glory. It tells us that what was formed in the body is what is evaluated at the judgment seat. The mechanics of eternity remain mysterious; the reality of differentiation does not.

This is not cause for despair. The untrained runner still runs. He still grows. He still experiences the joy of the race—genuine joy, eternal joy. He is not second-class. He is in the race. Both runners, Edwards would say, are filled to the brim of their capacity, and neither envies the other.

But one might have brought more capacity. One might have started with more. And the training he did not do when he could have done it—that remains undone.

The interval is the training period. Death is the gun. What you have become is where you start. From there, the race continues forever.

The Grace of Now

"Behold, now is the favorable time; behold, now is the day of salvation" (2 Corinthians 6:2).

This is not meant to terrify. It is meant to clarify.

The grace is that we have *now*. The clay is still soft. The kiln has not yet fired. The forming room is still open, the Potter's hands still at work, the opportunity for reshaping still real.

Tomorrow the kiln may fire. Today the wheel still turns.

This is the pastoral weight of the kiln metaphor. It is not a threat but an invitation—a clarification of what is at stake while there is still time to respond. The believer who understands the deadline does not live in fear but in urgency. Every day is a day for formation. Every choice is a shaping pressure. Every moment of cooperation with grace is a preparation for the moment when the kiln fires.

Edwards, at nineteen, wrote resolutions precisely because he understood the deadline: "Resolved, that I will live so, as I shall wish I had done when I come to die." He was young and healthy. He had decades ahead of him. But he knew those decades were not infinite. The exam would come. And he wanted to spend the semester preparing.

Richard Baxter, the Puritan pastor, nearly died in his early thirties. During his illness, he contemplated the afterlife so intensely that he wrote *The Saints' Everlasting Rest* afterward—a book designed to help others contemplate heaven while they still had time to be shaped by the contemplation. Near his own death, years later, words attributed to his final days capture the settled soul: "I have pain—but I have peace, I have peace." The kiln was firing, and he knew what shape the clay had taken. He had peace.

What You Are Becoming

This is the continuity principle pressed to its conclusion. Everything else falls away. Career dissolves. Reputation evaporates. Wealth becomes irrelevant. What remains is the soul—and the soul that remains is the soul you have been forming all along.

The only thing you will carry out of your life is the person you will have become.

The kiln fires, and what emerges is you—sanctified, glorified, but *you*. The one who learned patience or failed to learn it. The one who cultivated love or neglected it. The one who grew in Christlikeness or resisted the shaping. The form you were becoming is the form you now are—perfected, yes, but recognizably continuous with what was forming in the interval.

This is why every moment matters. Not because a single moment can undo years of formation, but because years of formation are made of single moments. The habits are built one choice at a time. The grooves are carved gradually. The shape takes form slowly, almost imperceptibly—until the kiln fires, and what was soft becomes solid.

You are becoming someone. Right now. This moment. The wheel is turning, the clay is responding, the shape is emerging. And one day—perhaps many years from now, perhaps sooner than you expect—the kiln will fire.

What form will emerge?

The answer is being written, one day at a time, in the interval of grace.

CHAPTER 6
THE PATRISTIC WITNESS

We are not the first to see this.

The theology we have been building—the interval of grace, the two pillars, the kiln that fixes what has been forming—stands on ground tilled by hands far older than ours. We have already glimpsed some of these voices. Edwards on vessels of different sizes. Gregory on eternal progress into the infinite God. Aquinas on the fixity of the will. But these were glimpses, brief citations summoned to support an argument. Now we turn to face the witnesses directly.

The early church understood formation as the purpose of earthly existence. They were not moderns, embarrassed by supernatural claims and eager to reduce Christianity to ethical principles. Nor were they mere moralists, treating discipleship as self-improvement with religious vocabulary. They understood that human beings are destined for union with God—and that this union requires formation. Real formation. Formation that happens in time, through struggle, by grace, toward a destination that shapes how the journey must be walked.

They also understood what we have been circling throughout

these chapters: formation has a deadline. What is shaped here is what continues there. The interval matters because it closes.

The fathers were not speaking abstractly. They were reading the same Scriptures we read, facing the same questions we face, watching the same Spirit at work. Their witness is not antiquarian interest, the scholarly recovery of old opinions for academic cataloging. It is confirmation. It is the testimony of those who walked the road before us and left markers for those who would follow.

The Spirit Who Forms

Before we meet the individual fathers, we must name the agent they all assumed: the Holy Spirit.

The transformation we have been describing—the soul shaped toward God, the character formed through faithfulness, the becoming that persists through death into resurrection—is not self-generated. It is Spirit-wrought. Paul's teaching that we are "being transformed into the same image from one degree of glory to another" by the Spirit (2 Corinthians 3:18) anchors everything that follows. The Spirit is the agent. The transformation is real. The progression is from glory to glory—not instantaneous but gradual, not passive but responsive.

This is the framework within which the fathers worked. They did not imagine human beings hauling themselves toward God by moral effort, accumulating merit through gritted-teeth discipline. They saw something far more dynamic: the Spirit of God at work within human souls, enabling what we could never accomplish alone, inviting our cooperation in a transformation we did not initiate and cannot complete by ourselves.

Peter's second letter provides the seed from which the Eastern church's richest theology would grow: God's divine power "has granted to us all things that pertain to life and godliness, through the knowledge of him who called us to his own glory and excellence, by which he has granted to us his precious and very great promises, so that through them you may become partakers of the divine nature" (2 Peter 1:3-4).

Partakers of the divine nature. The phrase is stunning. The

Eastern fathers developed it into a comprehensive vision they called *theosis*—deification, divinization, the process by which human beings come to share in God's own life and character. This is not becoming God, as though creatures could somehow climb into the Creator's seat. It is becoming like God—participating in his nature, reflecting his character, embodying his love and holiness. And it is entirely the Spirit's work, received by grace, enabled by power not our own.

Yet it is also responsive. The fathers used a word that has sometimes been misunderstood: *synergy*. The term does not mean fifty-fifty partnership, as though God does his part and we do ours in equal measure. It means the Spirit enables what we could never accomplish alone, and we respond to what the Spirit makes possible. The clay does not shape itself. But neither is it passive. It yields to the Potter's hands. It cooperates with the pressure. It receives the form being given.

Dallas Willard, whose work has helped a generation recover these ancient insights, described grace as "God acting in our lives." This is the fathers' vision translated into contemporary idiom. The Spirit is everywhere present, everywhere active, the assumed power behind all formation. This is not a charismatic distinctive, not a theological emphasis peculiar to one tradition. It is the unanimous Christian confession: formation is the Spirit's work in us. Everything the fathers taught about becoming, about growth, about the soul's journey toward God, assumes this foundation. The Spirit is not a topic to be addressed and then set aside. The Spirit is the thread running through every witness we are about to hear.

Irenaeus on Maturation

Irenaeus of Lyon faced a question we might ask ourselves: Why didn't God simply create humanity perfect from the beginning? Why the long process of formation? Why the struggle, the failure, the slow and painful becoming? If God is omnipotent, he could have made Adam and Eve complete, incapable of falling, already arrived at their destination. Why didn't he?

The question pressed on Irenaeus because he faced opponents

who answered it wrongly. The Gnostics of the second century taught that the material world was a mistake, a prison created by an inferior deity, and that salvation meant escape from embodiment into pure spirit. Time was waste. The body was a cage. The goal was to flee creation, not to be formed within it.

Irenaeus saw the danger and answered it with a vision that reframes everything: formation is not the obstacle to God's purpose. Formation *is* God's purpose.

Writing around 180 AD, Irenaeus argued in his great work *Against Heresies* that humanity was created not as fallen from perfection but as young—infants who must grow toward capacity. "The child was not yet able to receive more substantial nourishment," he wrote, explaining why God did not simply deposit mature wisdom into Adam from the start. Maturation requires time. Growth requires process. The infant must learn to eat before it can digest solid food.

God could have made us complete immediately. He chose otherwise. This was not limitation but intention. The interval is not delay but design.

Irenaeus read the Genesis account differently than some later traditions would. For him, Adam and Eve were not fallen from a height they had occupied but interrupted in their growth toward a height they had not yet reached. Whether or not we follow Irenaeus in every detail, his central insight stands: formation is the point, not the obstacle. The interval of grace is not an unfortunate necessity caused by the fall. It is the arena God always intended for human maturation.

Consider what this means for the theology we have been building. In Chapter 2, we argued that brevity means intensity, not insignificance—that the short span of earthly life is not a waiting room but a crucible where formation happens under pressure. Irenaeus would recognize this vision. He saw the interval as the arena where growth occurs, where the infant soul learns to receive what it could not have received at the start.

And we are still on that journey. The interval of grace continues what was always intended. The Spirit who hovered over the waters at creation, who breathed life into Adam, who empowered the prophets and rested upon the Messiah—this same Spirit is at work in us, enabling the growth we were made for. Formation is the point. Not the obstacle to God's purpose. Not the unfortunate delay before glory. The point.

Irenaeus saw what we have been arguing from different angles: the doing and the becoming are how we mature. Faithfulness is the curriculum of growth. The soul that was created young is growing toward capacity for God—and the interval of grace is where that growth happens. The kiln will fire. But while the wheel turns, the clay is being shaped into something it could not have been at the start.

Augustine on Differentiated Glory

In Chapter 2, we encountered Jonathan Edwards on vessels of different sizes—small and large, both full, holding different volumes. Edwards was writing in the eighteenth century, but he was not innovating. He was harvesting what Augustine of Hippo had planted twelve centuries earlier.

Augustine stands as the most influential theologian in Western Christianity, a towering figure whose thought shaped Catholics and Protestants alike. Among his many contributions was a vision of heaven that refuses the modern assumption of undifferentiated equality. The saints in glory, Augustine taught, would shine with different degrees of radiance, proportioned to their earthly formation.

In the final book of *The City of God*, his masterwork completed in 426 AD, Augustine addressed the resurrection of the body and the life to come. His words are direct: "There will be degrees of honour and glory suitable to their various degrees of merit." The differentiation is real. Not all stars shine equally. Not all vessels hold the same volume.

But Augustine understood what might trouble us about this teaching. Does differentiation mean competition? Does variation mean envy? Will some in heaven look upon the greater glory of others and feel diminished?

No. Augustine's answer anticipates Edwards by more than a millennium. Perfect love will reign. Each will rejoice in the other's greater glory without any lessening of their own joy. The psychology of heaven is not the psychology of earth, where comparison breeds resentment and hierarchy breeds oppression. In the presence of God, where sin is purged and love is perfected, the greater glory of one becomes the joy of all. The thimble does not envy the ocean. Both are filled to capacity. Both overflow with gratitude.

Augustine offered another insight that connects directly to what we explored in Chapter 4 on the continuity principle. The wounds of martyrs, he taught, would persist in their resurrection bodies—not as disfigurements but as "badges of honor," marks of honor that tell the story of their faithfulness. The body carries its history forward. What happened in the interval is not erased in resurrection but transformed and glorified.

If the martyrs' wounds persist as badges of honor, what of the soul's formation? Augustine assumed what we have been arguing: the character shaped in the interval is the character that enters eternity. The differentiated glory is not imposed arbitrarily at judgment, as though God simply assigned ranks according to inscrutable preference. It is revealed. What was forming in secret becomes manifest. The shape the clay took while the wheel was turning is the shape that emerges from the kiln.

This is the historical root of Edwards' vessel metaphor. The lineage runs clear: Scripture teaches differentiation (star differs from star in glory); Augustine develops the theology (degrees of honor proportioned to merit, with perfect love eliminating envy); Edwards crystallizes the image (vessels of different sizes cast into an ocean of happiness, all full); Thérèse adds the homely precision of thimble and tumbler; and we inherit a tradition that refuses to flatten the glory of heaven into uniform grayness. Throughout this book, I combine Edwards' ocean with Thérèse's thimble into a single image—"thimble and ocean"—as shorthand for this tradition.

The interval matters. Augustine knew it. What you are becoming now shapes the capacity you will carry forever.

Gregory of Nyssa on Eternal Progress

We met Gregory briefly in Chapter 2, when we needed his vision to address the mathematics of forever. His teaching on *epektasis*—eternal progress into the inexhaustible God—resolved what might otherwise seem a contradiction at the heart of our argument. In Chapter 5, we argued that death fixes what has been forming. The kiln fires, and the shape becomes permanent. But we also affirmed, with Edwards and Gregory, that the saints continue growing forever. How can both be true? How can the soul be fixed at death yet continue advancing eternally?

Now we enter Gregory's thought more fully to understand the synthesis.

Gregory of Nyssa lived in the fourth century, one of the three great Cappadocian fathers alongside his brother Basil and their friend Gregory of Nazianzus. His *Life of Moses* is not biography in the modern sense but spiritual theology—a reading of Moses's journey as paradigm for the soul's ascent toward God.

The key insight is simple but staggering: God is infinite. Therefore, the soul can never exhaust him. There is always more of God to know, more of his beauty to behold, more of his love to receive. "Thus, no limit would interrupt growth in the ascent to God," Gregory wrote, "since no limit to the good can be found nor is the increasing of desire for the good brought to an end because it is satisfied."

Perfection, for Gregory, is not a destination at which the soul arrives and rests. Perfection is perpetual progress. The soul perfected is the soul that never stops advancing. "The perfection of human nature consists perhaps in its very growth in goodness."

This was a striking claim in Gregory's context. Greek philosophy had taught that perfection meant stasis—reaching a final state and remaining there unchanged, like a statue that achieves its form and then simply exists. Gregory reversed this entirely. The statue image is wrong. The soul is not marble but living flame, and living flame does not rest. It rises.

The term *epektasis* comes from Paul's language in Philippians 3:13 —"straining forward" toward what lies ahead. Paul had not arrived. He was pressing on. And Gregory saw in this not merely Paul's earthly posture but the eternal posture of every soul advancing into God.

Moses "always found a step higher than the one he had attained." So will we all.

Now we can synthesize what Chapter 5 established with what Gregory teaches.

At death, the soul's fundamental *orientation* is fixed. The direction of the will—toward God or away from him—is settled. For the believer, this orientation was secured by grace through faith during the interval. Death does not change it; death confirms it. The soul that was learning to bend toward God is now permanently inclined in that direction.

At death, the soul's *formed capacity* is established. The specific development that occurred in the interval—how much humility was cultivated, how deep the love grew, how expansive the generosity became—this persists as the foundation for eternal life. The thimble remains a thimble. The ocean remains an ocean.

But within that fixed orientation, from that established capacity, eternal growth continues. Not remedial growth, as though the soul were still battling sin and slowly overcoming it. Sanctification is complete at death; sin is purged; the struggle is over. What continues is *expansive* growth—glory upon glory, capacity enlarging forever, the soul advancing ever deeper into the inexhaustible riches of God.

Gregory's epektasis answers the question: What happens after the kiln fires?

The clay is fixed. The shape is permanent. But the fixed shape is not frozen in static existence. It is released into endless exploration of the God it was formed to know. The orientation determines the direction of travel; the formed capacity determines the starting point. From there, the journey continues forever.

Return to the image from Chapter 5: two runners at the starting line of an eternal race. One trained for decades—muscles developed, endurance vast, form perfected through years of discipline. The other barely trained—genuine faith, present at the starting line, but unprepared. The gun fires. Both run. Both improve. Both grow stronger forever, because the race is eternal and the God they are running toward is inexhaustible.

But they do not begin from the same place. The trained runner starts ahead. And that head start, established in the interval of grace, compounds eternally. Gregory's vision does not flatten differentiation; it extends it. The formed capacity is the starting point for endless advance—and starting points matter across infinite distance.

The Unanimous Voice

The fathers did not agree on everything. East and West diverged on significant points. Irenaeus wrote in Greek, in a church not yet scarred by the great schisms. Augustine wrote in Latin, shaping a Western tradition that would eventually divide again at the Reformation. Gregory worked within the Eastern framework that would develop its own distinctive emphases over the centuries to come.

They wrote in different centuries, different languages, different cultural contexts. They addressed different heresies and navigated different political pressures. They were not a monolith.

But on this they spoke with one voice.

You are being prepared for something. The interval of grace is not empty time between salvation and heaven. It is the arena of formation, the workshop where souls are shaped, the training ground where capacity for God is developed or neglected.

And the Spirit of God is doing the preparing.

The Spirit who enables, who transforms, who works within us both to will and to work for his good pleasure—this Spirit is the agent of all formation. Irenaeus's maturation is Spirit-enabled growth. Augustine's differentiated glory reflects Spirit-formed capacity. Gregory's eternal progress is Spirit-driven advance into the infinite God. The fathers assumed what we must recover: we are not self-made souls, hauling ourselves toward heaven by effort. We are clay on the wheel, responding to hands that shape with power and gentleness we could never generate ourselves.

The unanimous voice testifies:

Formation is the purpose of the interval—not merely moral improvement but ontological transformation. You are becoming something you were not at conversion. The infant is growing toward capacity for solid food.

The Spirit is the agent—not self-help with religious vocabulary but divine power at work within human souls. The transformation comes "from the Lord who is the Spirit."

Differentiation is real—not all arrive at the same capacity, the same glory, the same starting point. Thimble and ocean. Ten cities and five. Star differing from star.

Continuity is real—what is formed persists, transformed but recognizable. The wounds of martyrs become badges of honor. The scars of history are not erased but glorified.

The deadline is real—earthly life is the arena of formation. The kiln fires at death. What has been shaping becomes fixed.

This is the patristic witness. This is what the early church knew. This is the ground beneath our feet.

The Cloud of Witnesses

The writer of Hebrews summoned his readers to remember those who had gone before: "Therefore, since we are surrounded by so great a cloud of witnesses, let us also lay aside every weight, and sin which clings so closely, and let us run with endurance the race that is set before us" (Hebrews 12:1).

The cloud of witnesses is not merely watching. They are testifying.

Irenaeus testifies: you were created to grow. The interval is not obstacle but opportunity. Maturation takes time, and the time is given for a purpose.

Augustine testifies: your formation matters eternally. The capacity you develop is the capacity you carry. And perfect love will ensure that differentiation brings joy, not envy.

Gregory testifies: the journey never ends. What is fixed at death is not static but released—into endless advance, endless discovery, endless ascent into the God who cannot be exhausted.

And beneath all their voices, the Spirit testifies: you are not alone. The power at work within you is the power that raised Christ from the dead. The hands shaping the clay are the hands of grace. The transformation happening in you is coming "from the Lord who is the Spirit."

The ground beneath our feet is ancient. The vision we have been building was not invented in the modern era, recovered by Edwards, or popularized by Lewis. It runs back through Augustine and Gregory and Irenaeus to the apostles themselves, who spoke of transformation from glory to glory, of becoming partakers of the divine nature, of the imperishable crown awaiting those who run with endurance.

We stand in a great company. The witnesses are not silent. They are speaking still, across the centuries, to anyone with ears to hear.

The interval matters. The forming is real. The Spirit is at work. And what you are becoming now is what you will be forever.

The question is not whether the fathers were right.

The question is whether we will live as if they were.

CHAPTER 7
THE MYSTICAL VISION

The fathers gave us the theology of formation. Now we turn to those who mapped its inner landscape.

In Chapter 6, we heard the unanimous voice of the early church: formation is the purpose of the interval, the Spirit is the agent, differentiation is real, and the deadline is fixed. The fathers established what formation is and why it matters. But they were not the only witnesses. Others came after them—voices that explored not merely the doctrine of transformation but its experience. Not merely what is happening to the soul but what it feels like to be shaped, to enter darkness, to have Christ born within.

The mystics.

The word may conjure images of ecstatic visions and esoteric practices, of spiritual elites pursuing experiences beyond the reach of ordinary believers. This is not how we will encounter them. The mystics we are about to meet were theologians of the interior life—careful observers of the soul's journey toward God, cartographers of territory the fathers had named but not fully explored.

They did not abandon what the fathers taught. They inhabited it. And they left maps for those willing to follow.

The Spirit Still at Work

Before we enter mystical territory, we must remember what Chapter 6 established: formation is the Spirit's work. The mystics knew this. They were not teaching self-improvement techniques or esoteric methods of spiritual advancement. Like the fathers before them, they assumed the Spirit as agent.

But the mystics explored what cooperation with the Spirit looks like from the inside. The synergy Chapter 6 described—the Spirit enabling, the soul responding—here we see it from the human side. What does it feel like when the Potter's hands press into the clay? How does the soul experience the shaping? What happens in the darkness when God seems absent but is, in fact, working most deeply?

These are the questions the mystics addressed. Their answers do not replace the fathers' theology. They deepen it.

Maximus on Christ Formed in Us

Maximus the Confessor lived in the seventh century, a turbulent era when theological controversy threatened to tear the church apart. He defended the full humanity and divinity of Christ against those who would diminish either—and he paid for his convictions with his tongue and his right hand, cut off by imperial order. He died in exile in 662, a confessor in the truest sense.

But before his martyrdom, Maximus explored how Christ is formed within the believer. This was not metaphor for him. It was ontological reality.

"The Word of God," Maximus wrote, "wills always and in all things to accomplish the mystery of his embodiment." The incarnation was not a one-time event confined to first-century Palestine. Christ continues to take flesh—in us. He is "always willing to be born spiritually in those who desire him."

Consider what this means. In Chapter 4, we established that we are being "conformed to his image" (Romans 8:29). In Chapter 6, we saw the fathers develop this into the doctrine of theosis—participation in the divine nature. Maximus pressed deeper. The virtues we cultivate are not merely moral improvements. They are Christ taking shape within us. Each growth in love is Christ's love becoming incarnate. Each deepening of patience is Christ's patience being embodied. Each expansion of humility is Christ's humility gaining flesh.

The virtuous spiral we traced in Chapter 3—faithful action forming faithful character, enabling greater faithful action—Maximus understood as Christ being progressively fashioned in the soul. The becoming is not toward generic spiritual maturity. It is toward him. The form being shaped in the clay is his form.

And this formation is Spirit-wrought. Maximus never forgot the agent. The Spirit who formed Christ in Mary's womb forms Christ in our souls. The incarnation continues through the Spirit's work in willing hearts.

Eckhart on the God-Seed

Meister Eckhart was a fourteenth-century German Dominican, a preacher and theologian whose bold language sometimes brought him into conflict with church authorities. Some of his propositions were condemned after his death. But his central vision has nourished Christian souls for seven centuries, and his imagery connects directly to what we have been building.

"Pear seeds grow into pear trees," Eckhart wrote. "Nut seeds into nut trees. And God-seed into God."

In Chapter 4, we explored Paul's seed and plant metaphor from 1 Corinthians 15. The seed is sown; the seed dies; what rises is the seed transformed—not a different organism but the fullness of what the seed contained. The acorn becomes the oak. The wheat kernel becomes the stalk. Eckhart saw the same principle at work in spiritual formation, but with a startling claim: what has been planted in us is divine.

The God-seed. The divine life deposited in the soul at regeneration, growing toward its fullness. The becoming that persists through the interval of grace is the seed reaching what it was always meant to become.

This is not Eckhart teaching that we become God in essence. That would be heresy, and despite the condemnations, Eckhart consistently distinguished between the Creator and the creature. But something divine is planted, something real grows, and the growth is toward likeness to the One who planted it.

Consider the connection to the continuity principle. In Chapter 4, we argued that the self formed in the interval is the self that rises—transformation, not replacement. Eckhart's God-seed imagery captures the organic nature of this continuity. The oak does not replace the acorn. It is the acorn's destiny realized, its potential actualized, its identity fulfilled. So with the soul. What we are becoming is what the seed was always meant to become. The formation is not addition from outside but growth from within—the divine seed reaching its fullness.

And the interval is where this growth happens. The seed has been planted. The conditions for growth are present. But growth requires time, and the time is limited. The harvest comes.

John of the Cross on the Dark Night

John of the Cross was a sixteenth-century Spanish Carmelite, a reformer and poet whose writings on the soul's journey toward God remain among the most profound in Christian literature. He is best known for a phrase that has passed into common usage, often misunderstood: the dark night of the soul.

In popular parlance, the dark night means any period of suffering or depression. John meant something more specific. The dark night is God's purifying work in the soul—a work that feels like absence but is actually presence, that seems like abandonment but is actually surgery.

"The soul has to pass through two principal kinds of night," John wrote, "in order to attain to union with God." These are not punishments. They are necessary preparations. What God removes creates space for what God gives. The darkness is the operating room where the Great Physician cuts away what would prevent the soul from bearing more of him.

This connects directly to Chapter 5 and the kiln of death. We argued there that the clay is being shaped while the wheel turns, that every choice presses into the material, that death fires what has been forming. John saw that some of the most formative shaping happens in darkness—when God seems absent, when consolation withdraws, when the soul feels abandoned.

The dark night is perhaps *the* formative experience, not despite its pain but through it. The suffering is not an interruption of formation but its intensification. The soul learns to cling to God when there is no felt reward for clinging. The will is purified when there is no pleasure to sweeten obedience. The character is forged in the fire of apparent absence.

Chapter 18 will develop suffering as formation more fully. But John's witness belongs here, among the mystics who mapped the inner landscape. He saw what the activistic age often misses: that darkness serves light. That what feels like regression may be advance. That the Potter's hands work most deeply when we cannot see them working.

And even in the dark night, the Spirit is present. John never imagined the soul abandoned. The darkness is not God's absence but God's hidden presence—hidden from our feelings, not from reality. The Spirit who forms is forming still, even when we cannot perceive him. Especially then.

Böhme on the Fixity of the Will

Jakob Böhme was a German shoemaker of the early seventeenth century, an unlikely candidate for mystical insight. He had little formal education. He worked with his hands. But he experienced visions and devoted himself to understanding what he had seen. His writings are difficult, dense, often obscure. But on one point he achieved crystalline clarity—and it speaks directly to everything we have been building.

Böhme taught that the soul is essentially will—fire burning either in the light of God or in the wrath of darkness—and that as the will shapes itself in this life, so it remains shaped after death.

Let that sink in. The shape the will takes through earthly choices—the bending toward God or away, the habits of love or selfishness, the patterns of faithfulness or neglect—this is the shape that persists. The form you are becoming is the form you will be.

This is the kiln of death in mystical form. This is the continuity principle expressed with unsparing directness. In Chapter 1, we heard Dallas Willard say that the only thing we carry out of our lives is the person we have become. Böhme said the same thing three and a half centuries earlier. The will shapes itself through daily choices. Every act of love bends the will toward love. Every refusal of love bends it away. The shaping accumulates. The form takes hold. And when death comes, the form is fixed.

Böhme pressed further: "Every man carries heaven and hell within him in this world." The trajectory is not determined at death. It is established before death. The soul already oriented toward God carries that orientation into eternity. The soul bent away carries that bending. The interval is where the direction is set. Death confirms what has been forming.

This is what makes the interval so weighty. Not merely that we will face judgment—though we will. Not merely that rewards are being determined—though they are. But that the very self being formed is the self that will exist forever. The will shaping itself here is the will that remains shaped there.

Böhme understood the two pillars though he did not name them. The doing—each choice, each act, each turning—shapes the becoming. The becoming—the shaped will, the formed soul—determines capacity for eternal life. The doing is real. The becoming is real. And both carry through death.

The Mystical Testimony

Four witnesses. Six centuries of testimony. Different contexts, different languages, different emphases. And yet the same vision, the same reality, the same weight.

Maximus testifies: Christ is being formed in you. Not metaphor but ontology. The virtues you cultivate are his character taking flesh. The becoming is toward him.

Eckhart testifies: the God-seed is growing. What was planted at regeneration is reaching toward its fullness. The transformation is organic, continuous, the seed becoming what it was always meant to be.

John testifies: the dark night is formation. Suffering is not interruption but intensification. The Potter's hands work most deeply where we cannot see them.

Böhme testifies: the will shapes itself. Every choice forms. Every bending leaves its mark. And as the will shapes itself here, so it remains shaped after death.

The mystics mapped the territory the fathers had named. They explored what it feels like to be clay on the wheel, to enter the darkness, to have Christ born within. Their testimony confirms and deepens what Scripture teaches, what the fathers established, what the Spirit is doing in every willing soul.

Formation is real. It is happening now. The shaping is not abstract doctrine but lived experience. And the soul that cooperates—that responds to the Spirit's pressure, that allows Christ to be formed within, that endures the dark night as surgery rather than abandonment, that lets the will be shaped toward God—this soul is being prepared for what lies beyond the kiln.

The Witnesses Multiply

The cloud of witnesses grows. From Paul to Irenaeus to Augustine to Gregory to Maximus to Eckhart to John to Böhme—across fifteen centuries, the testimony is consistent. The interval forms. The Spirit enables. The soul responds. And what is formed is what persists.

But we have not yet answered all objections. The theology of becoming faces serious questions—questions about grace, about equality, about whether any of this is truly biblical or merely philosophical speculation dressed in Christian vocabulary. The questions deserve answers. To those we turn next.

Before we do, pause to consider where we stand. We have built a theology of becoming from Scripture. We have heard the fathers testify that this theology is ancient. We have listened to the mystics describe what formation feels like from within. The ground beneath us is solid. The company surrounding us is great. The vision is not innovation but recovery.

The interval matters. The forming is real. The Spirit is at work. The will is shaping itself.

The only question is whether you will cooperate—whether the clay will yield to the hands that shape, whether the seed will grow toward its fullness, whether you will endure the darkness as surgery.

You are becoming someone. The witnesses have told you what that means.

Now the objections must be answered.

CHAPTER 8
THE MODERN RECOVERY

Something was lost between the mystics and the moderns.
Perhaps it was the Enlightenment's rationalism, which reduced Christianity to moral philosophy and stripped eternity of its weight. Perhaps it was Protestant suspicion of Catholic spiritual practices, which inadvertently discarded the formation theology along with the abuses. Perhaps it was the activism of the industrial age, which valued production over becoming, or the distraction of the entertainment age, which made eternal stakes feel unreal compared to immediate pleasures.

Whatever the cause, by the twentieth century, the church had largely stopped teaching what fifteen centuries had known: that earthly life is formation for eternal existence. The vision of the fathers and mystics—*the interval of grace*, the soul shaped for glory, the becoming that persists—had faded from common Christian consciousness. Heaven became a vague destination rather than a differentiated kingdom. Salvation became fire insurance rather than the beginning of eternal life. Discipleship became moral improvement for temporal benefit rather than apprenticeship for eternal vocation.

But the vision was not entirely lost. Key voices in recent centuries recovered it, often against the grain of their contemporaries. We have glimpsed these witnesses throughout our journey—Edwards on vessels of different sizes, Lewis on choice-by-choice becoming, Willard on the person we will have become. Now we must hear them more fully. Their testimony forms a bridge between ancient wisdom and present urgency.

A.W. Tozer, the twentieth-century pastor whose devotional writings have shaped millions, saw the problem clearly. In *The Pursuit of God*, he wrote, "We have been snared in the coils of a spurious logic which insists that if we have found Him we need no more seek Him." The church had reduced the infinite God to a transaction completed and filed away. But Tozer knew what Gregory of Nyssa knew: finding God is not the end of seeking but its intensification. The infinite cannot be exhausted. The journey into God continues forever. And the capacity for that journey is being formed now.

This is the vision the modern voices recovered—not by innovation but by return. They read Scripture with fresh eyes and found what had always been there. They listened to the fathers and mystics and heard what the contemporary church had forgotten. And they spoke with urgency because they understood what was at stake.

Edwards on the Beauty of Differentiation

We have already encountered Jonathan Edwards on differentiated capacity—the vessels of different sizes, all filled to the brim, holding different volumes. But Edwards saw something beyond the fact of differentiation. He saw its beauty.

In his sermon series *Charity and Its Fruits*, Edwards devoted an entire discourse to what he called "Heaven, a World of Love." The title itself is significant. Heaven is not merely a world of reward, though rewards are given. It is not merely a world of rest, though toil ceases. It is a world of love—perfect, mutual, overflowing love between God and the saints and among the saints themselves. And this love transforms how differentiation is experienced.

"The saints in glory," Edwards wrote, "will have no desire to be higher than they are." This is not resignation. It is satisfaction. Each vessel is full. Each soul possesses all it can contain. The smaller vessel does not envy the larger because it lacks nothing—it is filled to the brim with the same infinite love that fills the greater.

But Edwards pressed further. The saints do not merely accept one another's different glories. They rejoice in them. "Those that are highest in glory, will be most full of love, and consequently the most happy; and those that are lowest in glory, will be most happy in seeing others above them in glory." The lowest in glory is most happy in seeing others higher. This is heavenly psychology—so foreign to earthly comparison, so liberating from the zero-sum competition that poisons human relationships.

How is this possible? Because perfect love has replaced the self-referential comparison that produces envy. In heaven, Edwards taught, the saints love God supremely and love one another perfectly. They see God's glory reflected in one another—and the greater the glory, the more there is to delight in. The saint with lesser capacity rejoices to see more of God's beauty displayed in the saint with greater capacity. The reflection is not rivalry but revelation.

This is why differentiation produces joy rather than hierarchy in the earthly sense. It is not that some are masters and others servants, as though heaven replicated the domination structures of fallen humanity. It is that all are lovers, and lovers delight in the beloved's excellence. The community of heaven is a community of mutual admiration, mutual celebration, mutual joy in one another's glorification.

Edwards saw what our egalitarian instincts miss: uniformity is not the highest good. A garden of identical flowers is less beautiful than a garden of varied blooms. A symphony of single notes is less magnificent than the interplay of different instruments. The differentiated glory of heaven is aesthetic—the beauty of harmony, not unison. Each saint contributes what only that saint can contribute. Each capacity reflects God from its unique angle.

And the capacity you bring—the vessel you have become through the interval of grace—determines what you contribute to that eternal symphony. The formation matters not merely for your own experience but for the beauty of the whole.

Lewis on the Weight of Glory

C.S. Lewis understood that eternal stakes change how we see everything—especially one another.

In his wartime sermon "The Weight of Glory," delivered at Oxford in 1941, Lewis pressed his listeners to feel the gravity of what Christianity actually claims about human destiny. "It is a serious thing," he said, "to live in a society of possible gods and goddesses, to remember that the dullest and most uninteresting person you talk to may one day be a creature which, if you saw it now, you would be strongly tempted to worship, or else a horror and a corruption such as you now meet, if at all, only in a nightmare."

The statement is staggering. The colleague who bores you. The neighbor who irritates you. The stranger on the street you pass without noticing. Each is becoming something—either a radiant being of unimaginable glory or a twisted creature of unspeakable corruption. The becoming is happening in everyone, everywhere, all the time.

There are no ordinary people.

Lewis drew the implication: "All day long we are, in some degree, helping each other to one or other of these destinations." Our interactions are not trivial. Every kindness, every cruelty, every encouragement, every discouragement plays some role in the formation happening in others—and in ourselves. The weight of glory is not merely personal. It is relational. We are shaping one another.

In *The Great Divorce*, Lewis dramatized this vision with unforgettable imagery. The ghosts who visit heaven from hell find the grass too solid, the light too bright, the reality too intense for their diminished selves. Heaven is not ethereal; it is more real than anything the ghosts have known. But they cannot bear it. They have become too insubstantial through their earthly choices. The solid people—those who have been formed for glory—walk easily on grass that pierces ghostly feet.

The metaphor captures what we argued in Chapter 5: formation determines capacity. The soul shaped for glory can bear glory's weight. The soul that refused formation cannot endure what it was made for.

Heaven would be hell for the unformed soul—not because God is cruel but because the soul lacks the capacity to receive what heaven offers. The kiln has fired. The shape is fixed.

One character in Lewis's story is particularly haunting: the apostate bishop who preferred his intellectual respectability to Christ, his reputation among scholars to truth. Given the opportunity to enter heaven's deeper reality, he declines. He has a paper to read to a theological society back in hell. He has become the kind of person who prefers the small satisfactions of his own importance to the overwhelming joy of God's presence.

The choice seems insane from outside. From inside his formed character, it is the only choice he can make. This is the vicious spiral reaching its terminus—the soul that preferred Christ's title to Christ himself, and so never belonged to him at all.

"Hell is a state of mind," Lewis wrote elsewhere in the same book. "And every state of mind, left to itself, every shutting up of the creature within the dungeon of its own mind—is, in the end, Hell." The soul that kept choosing itself has become a self—and nothing else. The dungeon is not imposed from outside. It is constructed choice by choice, until the prisoner cannot imagine wanting to leave.

But the reverse is equally true. Heaven is not merely a place but a capacity—the capacity to receive infinite love, to delight in absolute beauty, to participate in eternal joy. That capacity is being formed now.

Willard on Apprenticeship for Eternity

Dallas Willard spent his career recovering what the church had forgotten about discipleship. We have already heard his summation: "The only thing that you and I will get out of our lives one day when we die and stand before God, when everything is stripped away and who we really are is made known, is the person we will have become." But Willard's vision extended far beyond this single insight. He understood discipleship as apprenticeship—training for eternal vocation.

"The life we now have as the persons we now are," Willard wrote in *The Divine Conspiracy*, "will continue in the universe forever."

Notice what this means. Eternal life is not a different life given to us later. It is this life continuing. The person you are now—with your particular character, capacities, relationships, and history—is the person who will exist forever. Transformation will occur. Sin will be purged. Glory will be added. But it will be *you* who is transformed, *your* sin that is purged, *you* who is glorified.

This is the continuity principle we established in Chapter 4, expressed in Willard's characteristically direct prose.

This is why Willard insisted that discipleship is not optional for believers. Not because salvation depends on it—salvation is by grace through faith. But because the eternal self is being formed through it. The person who neglects discipleship does not merely miss blessings in this life. That person is failing to develop the capacities that will matter forever.

Willard described the Christian life as an "interactive relationship with God." This is the with-God life—not merely believing things about God but living in conscious cooperation with his presence and purposes. The Spirit is not an abstract force but a personal guide. Grace is not merely forgiveness of sins but "God acting in our lives to accomplish what we cannot accomplish on our own." Here is the synergy the fathers taught, translated into contemporary idiom.

And the kingdom of God, Willard taught, is available now. Jesus did not announce a kingdom that would arrive only after death. He announced a kingdom that was "at hand"—near, accessible, available to enter immediately. Eternal life has already begun. The interval of grace is not preparation for the kingdom; it is participation in the kingdom. What we do and who we become in this participation shapes what we will do and who we will be when the kingdom comes in fullness.

This is apprenticeship in the deepest sense. An apprentice learns a trade by practicing it under the master's guidance. A disciple learns eternal living by practicing it under Jesus' guidance—now, in the present, through the daily choices that shape the soul. The goal is not merely knowledge about the master but the master's own competencies formed within the apprentice.

Willard saw what many miss: heaven is not retirement. It is

promotion. The servant faithful over little is set over much. The apprentice who learned well takes on greater responsibilities. The skills developed in the interval—the patience, the love, the wisdom, the capacity to work with God—these are not discarded at death. They are deployed at a scale we cannot presently imagine.

Wright on Work That Lasts

N.T. Wright has done more than perhaps any contemporary theologian to recover the New Testament's vision of bodily resurrection and renewed creation. In *Surprised by Hope*, Wright argues against the Platonic distortions that imagine heaven as escape from the material world. He insists on the biblical hope: new heavens and new earth. Resurrection bodies. Physical existence transformed and glorified.

This vision has profound implications for the work we do now.

"What you do in the present—by painting, preaching, singing, sewing, praying, teaching, building hospitals, digging wells, campaigning for justice, writing poems, caring for the needy, loving your neighbor as yourself—will last into God's future." The claim is remarkable. Our work is not merely passing time until the real life begins. It persists. What is done in faith and faithfulness is somehow taken up into God's new creation.

This connects directly to the vision we explored in Chapter 4—the glory of the nations brought into the New Jerusalem (Revelation 21:24-26). Human cultural achievement, purified of sin, enters the eternal city. The work of civilization is not burned away as worthless but transformed and incorporated. Wright's contribution is to show that this applies not only to grand cultural achievements but to ordinary faithful work. The well you dig. The poem you write. The patient you heal. The child you teach. The neighbor you love.

It lasts.

Wright is careful to acknowledge mystery here. Scripture does not tell us the mechanics of how present work persists into future glory. But it tells us the principle: continuity. God's way is not to discard and replace but to redeem and transform. The new creation is not a second attempt after the first one failed. It is the first creation brought to its intended destination—including the work of human beings made in God's image to cultivate and create.

This vision dignifies every act of faithful work. The master returns and finds servants who multiplied the talents—and what they built is incorporated into his kingdom. The cultural mandate of Genesis 1—fill the earth, subdue it, exercise dominion—is not canceled by the fall or suspended until heaven. It continues. What is done faithfully now participates in what God is bringing about forever.

Wright also emphasizes what we have stressed throughout: the Spirit's role in this continuity. "What God does in the future," he writes, "is continuous with what he is doing in the present through the work of the Spirit." The Spirit who raised Jesus from the dead is at work now, in us, bringing about the transformation that will be completed at resurrection. Present formation and future glory are not separate programs. They are one continuous work of the same Spirit.

The Bridge to Now

The modern voices have spoken. Edwards, Lewis, Willard, Wright—and behind them, Tozer's reminder that finding God does not end seeking but intensifies it. They form a bridge between ancient wisdom and present urgency.

The bridge stands on common ground. Edwards read the fathers and built on their foundation. Lewis knew Augustine and learned from George MacDonald, the Scottish mystic who learned from the German mystics. Willard drew on the desert fathers and the medieval spiritual writers. Wright engages the full sweep of Christian tradition. They are not innovating. They are recovering. They are translating what the church has always known into language the modern mind can hear.

And their message is urgent because the modern church has largely forgotten it. We have reduced discipleship to behavior management. We have flattened heaven into uniform reward. We have treated the interval of grace as waiting room rather than forming room.

The modern voices call us back.

The witnesses are now assembled. From Paul through the fathers, through the mystics, to the modern recoverers—fifteen centuries of testimony, consistent in its central claims. Formation is real. The soul persists. Differentiation endures. The Spirit enables. The interval matters.

But objections remain. The theology of becoming faces serious questions—about grace, about equality, about how far Scripture warrants what we have been claiming.

The questions deserve answers. To those we now turn.

CHAPTER 9
OBJECTIONS ANSWERED

The witnesses have spoken.

Scripture, the fathers, the mystics, the modern voices—all testify to the same reality: the interval of grace forms what persists forever. The doing and the becoming carry eternal weight. The kiln fires, and what has been shaping becomes fixed. Across fifteen centuries, the cloud of witnesses has grown, and their testimony is consistent.

But objections press in. They always do when teaching carries weight. Some objections arise from theological concern—the fear that we are smuggling works-righteousness back into a gospel of grace. Others arise from pastoral concern—the worry that emphasizing stakes will crush sensitive souls. Still others arise from eschatological frameworks that assume discontinuity between this age and the next, or from the honest recognition that Scripture gives us principles rather than formulas.

Each deserves careful response. We do not claim certainty beyond what Scripture warrants, nor do we pretend that every question finds a tidy resolution. But if the vision we have been building is true, it should be able to withstand scrutiny. And we believe it can. The objections, when examined carefully, do not undermine the thesis. They may, in fact, clarify it.

"Doesn't This Contradict Grace Alone?"

The concern is understandable and must be taken seriously. If what we do and who we become matters eternally, have we not smuggled works-righteousness back into the gospel? Is this not the Galatian heresy dressed in new clothing—adding human effort to the finished work of Christ?

The objection rests on a confusion between salvation and reward, and it misunderstands the nature of grace-enabled formation. We must distinguish what Scripture distinguishes.

Salvation is by grace through faith, secured at conversion, never earned. This is the foundation on which everything else rests. Paul is unambiguous: "For by grace you have been saved through faith. And this is not your own doing; it is the gift of God, not a result of works, so that no one may boast" (Ephesians 2:8-9). This book has never suggested otherwise. The interval of grace presupposes grace—received, unmerited, sufficient.

But the very passage that establishes salvation by grace continues without pause: "For we are his workmanship, created in Christ Jesus for good works, which God prepared beforehand, that we should walk in them" (Ephesians 2:10). Grace creates workers. Grace prepares works. Grace enables the walking. The doing flows from the gift, not toward it.

Formation, too, is by grace—but grace that enables rather than replaces human response. This is the synergy we explored in Chapter 6: the Spirit enables; we respond; the response opens us to more enabling. Paul holds both realities together in a single breath: "Work out your own salvation with fear and trembling, for it is God who works in you, both to will and to work for his good pleasure" (Philippians 2:12-13). God works in; we work out. The formation is not self-generated achievement but cooperative reception of grace.

Reward is differentiated based on grace-enabled faithfulness. Paul makes this explicit when he describes works tested by fire: "If the work that anyone has built on the foundation survives, he will receive a reward. If anyone's work is burned up, he will suffer loss, though he himself will be saved, but only as through fire" (1 Corinthians 3:14-15). The person is saved either way. Salvation is not at stake. But reward varies based on what was built—and what was built was built by grace.

Dallas Willard captured the distinction with characteristic precision in *The Great Omission*: "Grace is not opposed to effort. It is opposed to earning." The effort of faithfulness is not earning salvation. It is cooperating with the grace that has already saved. The formation is entirely grace-enabled—but it is also real. The capacities developed are real capacities. The character formed is real character. And both persist.

If grace eliminated all significance from human response, the parables of Jesus would be meaningless. Why speak of talents multiplied and buried? Why speak of faithful servants and unfaithful ones? Why speak of ten cities and five cities, proportioned to faithfulness? Jesus assumed that what we do with grace matters. So does this book.

"Isn't This Speculation Beyond What Scripture Reveals?"

The concern deserves honest engagement. Scripture gives us principles, not formulas. It reveals enough for faith and practice, not a comprehensive manual for the mechanics of eternity. Epistemic humility is appropriate. We do not claim to know what we cannot know.

But the principles Scripture reveals are substantial, and the inferences we have drawn are modest.

Consider what Scripture clearly teaches. Resurrection involves transformation of the same person, not replacement—Paul's seed becomes the plant, not a different organism (1 Corinthians 15:35-44). Identity, memory, and relational bonds persist through death—Moses and Elijah were recognized at the Transfiguration, the rich man remembered his brothers, the disciples knew the risen Christ. Rewards are differentiated based on earthly faithfulness—ten cities for one servant, five for another;

star differing from star in glory. Character formed on earth has eternal significance—"the righteous still do righteousness; the holy still be holy" (Revelation 22:11). We are being transformed into Christ's image progressively—"from one degree of glory to another" (2 Corinthians 3:18). And there is a deadline to formation—"it is appointed for man to die once, and after that comes judgment" (Hebrews 9:27).

From these clear principles, what does the book infer? That the soul formed through earthly choices is the soul that enters eternity. That formation in the interval shapes capacity for eternal life. That different starting points yield different trajectories. These inferences follow directly from the biblical teaching. If the seed becomes the plant, then what the seed contained determines what the plant becomes. If rewards are differentiated, then something must ground the differentiation. If character persists, then character formed on earth is character carried forward.

We have not invented this framework. Irenaeus, Augustine, Gregory, Maximus, Eckhart, Böhme, Edwards, Lewis, Willard—across fifteen centuries, readers of Scripture arrived at the same vision. They were not importing Greek philosophy. They were exegeting the texts we have been exegeting. Their agreement does not prove the interpretation correct, but it suggests we are not innovating. We are recovering.

What we do not claim to know: the precise mechanics of eternal growth, the exact relationship between earthly formation and heavenly capacity, whether "levels of heaven" means spatial location or something else, how God evaluates what is possible for each soul. Where Scripture is silent, we remain silent. Where it speaks, we follow its testimony.

"What About 'All Things New'?"

Revelation 21:5 declares, "Behold, I am making all things new." If all things are made new, isn't the past—including the formation that occurred in it—swept away? Doesn't the new creation mean a fresh start for everyone?

The Greek word *kainos* does not mean replacement. It means renewal, restoration, transformation. The old is not discarded; it is redeemed.

This is God's consistent pattern. The new covenant did not erase the old; it fulfilled and transformed it. The new creation does not discard the old creation; it heals and glorifies it. The resurrection body is not a different body; it is this body transformed. God's way is redemption, not abandonment.

Revelation's own testimony confirms this. The very chapter that speaks of "all things new" also speaks of "the glory and honor of the nations" being brought into the New Jerusalem (Revelation 21:24-26). Human cultural achievement is not erased. It is purified and incorporated. If the glory of the nations enters the eternal city, how much more the glory of redeemed souls—formed by grace, carried through death, brought to completion in resurrection?

We established in Chapter 4 that the same self persists through death and resurrection—transformed but recognizable. Christ's wounds persisted in his glorified body. The martyrs' wounds become badges of honor, as Augustine taught. History is not erased; it is redeemed.

"All things new" does not mean all things replaced. It means all things healed, all things completed, all things brought to their intended glory. The soul formed in the interval is made new—not deleted.

"If Eternal Growth Continues, Why Does Earthly Formation Matter?"

This objection arose naturally from the tension we have been navigating. In Chapter 2, we followed Gregory of Nyssa into his vision of *epektasis*—eternal progress into the infinite God. The saints grow forever. There is always more of God to know, more of his glory to behold, more of his love to receive. The soul does not reach a plateau and stop.

But in Chapter 5, we established the kiln of death—the deadline that fixes what has been forming. The orientation is settled. The formed character is established. The starting point is determined.

If we all grow forever, won't the differences eventually become negligible? Why does the interval matter so much if eternity stretches endlessly before us?

The answer is twofold.

First, growth continues from fixed starting points. What the kiln establishes is not a ceiling but a foundation. The trajectory set in the interval extends into eternity; it is not erased by eternity. The two runners both run forever, but they do not begin from the same place.

But there is a deeper answer, and it is this: certain rewards and formations are only possible on earth.

The interval is not merely a head start on eternal growth. It is a unique window—the only window—for certain kinds of faithfulness that cannot occur afterward.

Consider faith itself. "Now faith is the assurance of things hoped for, the conviction of things not seen" (Hebrews 11:1). Faith operates in uncertainty, trusting what cannot yet be verified. But in glory, we will see face to face (1 Corinthians 13:12). Faith gives way to sight. The opportunity to trust God against appearances, to believe when evidence is ambiguous, to walk by faith and not by sight (2 Corinthians 5:7)—this opportunity exists only in the interval. In eternity, faith is no longer necessary. The reward for faith can only be earned now.

Consider perseverance. James writes: "Blessed is the man who remains steadfast under trial, for when he has stood the test he will receive the crown of life" (James 1:12). The crown of life is promised to those who endure trial. But trials of this kind—suffering, temptation, opposition—belong to the interval. In the new creation, there is no more mourning or crying or pain (Revelation 21:4). The conditions for perseverance will have passed. The crown for endurance can only be earned now.

Consider martyrdom. The martyrs under the altar cry out for vindication (Revelation 6:9-10). Their sacrifice was unrepeatable—you cannot be martyred in glory. The laying down of life for Christ's sake, the ultimate testimony, is possible only when death is possible. That window closes at death.

The pattern extends further. Generosity in the face of scarcity. Courage in the face of danger. Mercy when justice would be easier. Forgiveness when wounds are fresh. These are formations and faithfulnesses that require earthly conditions—conditions that will not exist in the new creation. The suffering that produces endurance, the endurance that produces character, the character that produces hope (Romans 5:3-4)—this progression requires the crucible of the interval.

The interval is irreplaceable, not merely preliminary.

This is why earthly formation matters so profoundly. Certain capacities can only be forged here. Certain rewards can only be earned here. Certain formations can only occur under conditions that will never exist again. When the kiln fires, the opportunity for faith-in-uncertainty closes. The opportunity for perseverance-under-trial closes. The opportunity for courage-against-death closes. What has been formed through these uniquely earthly conditions becomes the permanent foundation for eternal life.

"What About Fairness?"

Some believers live eighty years with access to Scripture, community, teaching, and opportunity. Others are converted on their deathbeds. Some grow up in spiritually rich environments. Others are born into spiritual deserts. If capacity formed on earth matters eternally, doesn't this favor those with more opportunity? Is God unfair?

The objection touches the mystery of divine sovereignty—territory where we must walk carefully.

"To whom much is given, much will be required" (Luke 12:48). The principle cuts both ways. Those with more opportunity bear greater responsibility. Those with less opportunity are not held to the same standard. God knows what was possible for each soul and judges according to what was given, not according to what was never received.

We do not know the calculus of eternal reward. We know rewards differ. We know faithfulness is evaluated. We do not know how God weighs circumstance, opportunity, starting point, and response. We do not know whether one hour of total surrender yields more than decades of half-hearted attendance. We suspect it might. The thief on the cross had hours, not years—yet Jesus said, "Today you will be with me in paradise" (Luke 23:43). God knows what is possible for each soul.

The parable of the laborers speaks to this (Matthew 20:1-16). Those who worked one hour received the same denarius as those who worked all day. The parable addresses salvation—all receive the gift regardless of when they came. But it also reveals something about divine generosity that transcends our calculations of fairness. God is not stingy with grace. He gives more than we deserve, more than we expect.

Some may wonder whether varying rewards will poison eternity with comparison and resentment. Augustine addressed this directly: the blessed in glory will rejoice in others' greater glory without any diminishment of their own joy. Perfect love will reign. Edwards captured this with his vessel metaphor—every vessel cast into the ocean of happiness is completely full, whether small or great. Both contain all they can hold. Neither lacks anything. Where sin has been purged and love perfected, another's gain is not your loss. It is your joy. "If one member is honored, all rejoice together" (1 Corinthians 12:26).

The appropriate posture is not anxiety about others' opportunities but faithfulness with our own. The question is not whether God will be fair—he will. The question is whether we are being faithful with what we have been given.

"Doesn't This Teaching Create Unbearable Pressure?"

The concern is pastorally significant. If the teaching produces paralysis rather than purpose, anxiety rather than action, it has been received wrongly. The problem may be the teaching, or it may be how the teaching is being heard. We must address both.

THE INTERVAL

The book's intention has never been to burden but to awaken. The goal is clarity, not anxiety. Knowing what matters allows us to release what does not. Understanding that the interval forms eternity frees us from chasing what will not last. The weight is meant to be clarifying, not crushing.

We introduced the phrase "the grace of now" in Chapter 5, and we return to it here. The clay is still soft. The wheel is still turning. The kiln has not yet fired. This is not threat but invitation. You have today. The Spirit is present. The hands of grace are at work.

Awareness is freeing, not paralyzing. A student who knows the exam is coming and knows what it covers is not crushed by this knowledge. She is equipped. She can prepare. The crushing thing would be to discover the exam only after it was over—to realize what was at stake when nothing could be done about it.

We can err in two directions. We can err toward presumption—assuming grace covers everything, effort is unnecessary, the outcome is guaranteed regardless of how we live. Or we can err toward anxiety—assuming we must earn what can only be received, that our effort must be sufficient on its own, that failure is final. Both errors misunderstand grace. Grace is not permission to coast. Grace is power to become. Grace is not opposed to effort. Grace enables effort.

The teaching of this book should produce urgency without despair. Not "I must do this or I am lost" but "I am invited to participate in something magnificent, and today's choices matter." Not pressure from outside but desire from within—the awakened soul eager to cooperate with what the Spirit is doing.

Consider the man who found treasure hidden in a field (Matthew 13:44). He sold everything he had to buy that field. But notice what the text says: "In his joy he goes and sells all that he has." In his joy. This is not a man crushed by obligation. This is a man who stumbled upon something so valuable that keeping anything else suddenly made no sense. He had walked past that field a hundred times, perhaps. He had lived ordinary days in ordinary places. And then one day he saw what had been there all along—treasure, hidden in the ordinary ground. The interval of grace is that field. It does not look spectacular. It looks like Monday mornings and mundane decisions and years that blur together. But there is treasure hidden in it—the opportunity to form an eternal soul, to lay up wealth that survives the fire, to become someone who will shine forever. Others walk past, not seeing. But if you see—if you truly see what is hidden in the ordinary field of your days—then the "selling" stops feeling like burden. It starts feeling like joy.

If you hear this teaching as burden, hear it again as invitation. The forming room is open. The Potter is at work. The clay can still be shaped.

"What About Wasted Years?"

The previous objection concerned those who feel crushed by the weight of the teaching. This one is more personal. It concerns those who feel they have already failed—not through lack of opportunity, but through neglect of the opportunity they had.

I hear what you are saying. I believe it. And it breaks my heart. Because I have wasted years—decades, perhaps. I was saved but asleep. I was justified but unformed. The interval has been passing, and I have not been cooperating with grace. Is it too late? Have I lost what cannot be recovered?

First, acknowledge the grief. If you feel genuine loss, do not rush past it. The years that were not invested cannot be re-invested. The formation that did not occur did not occur. We cannot pretend otherwise. The teaching of this book would be dishonest if it suggested that past neglect carries no consequence.

But the grief is not the whole story.

It is never too late to begin. The question is not "why didn't I start sooner?" but "will I start now?" The virtuous spiral can begin at any point. Today's faithfulness begins compounding today. The soul that awakens at seventy can still form in the years remaining. The soul that awakens on its deathbed still has moments—and moments can matter.

The thief on the cross had hours. Perhaps only an hour. He had lived an entire life in ways that merited crucifixion. His formation in the interval of grace was minimal by any human measure. Yet in those final hours, something happened. He rebuked the other criminal. He confessed his own guilt. He recognized Jesus as King when the King hung dying beside him. "Jesus, remember me when you come into your kingdom." And Jesus replied, "Truly, I say to you, today you will be with me in paradise" (Luke 23:42-43).

He was saved—genuinely, fully. What eternal capacity he carries, we do not know. But he was in paradise with Christ that very day. God knows what is possible for each soul, and God is both just and generous.

"Saved as through fire" is genuine salvation (1 Corinthians 3:15). The one whose works are burned up—who arrives with nothing, having built with wood and hay and stubble—is still saved. The salvation is real. The entrance into glory is real. The believer who wasted the interval does not forfeit heaven. They forfeit what might have been built. They forfeit the capacity that might have developed. But they do not forfeit Christ.

God restores what the locusts have eaten. Joel 2:25 speaks of restoration, of years redeemed. We do not know precisely what this means for eternal formation. But we know that God's grace exceeds our calculations. The widow's mite was small, but Christ praised it above the large donations. What looks like little to us may look like much to him. What feels like late may be exactly on time.

Grace can do more with little time fully surrendered than with much time halfheartedly offered. The soul that finally awakens and gives everything in the years remaining may develop more than the soul that drifted through decades of half-commitment. We do not know how God calculates. But we know he is just and generous.

The same grace that saves empowers the restarting. The Spirit who enables formation has not withdrawn. The hands of grace are still at work. The clay is softer than you think. Today's yes begins the ascent.

This book is not meant to condemn you for what you have not done. It is meant to awaken you to what you still can do. The interval is not yet closed. The kiln has not yet fired. This is the grace of now.

"Behold, now is the favorable time; behold, now is the day of salvation" (2 Corinthians 6:2).

The day of salvation—in every sense of that word. Salvation received. Salvation worked out. Salvation formed into eternal capacity.

Now is the day.

The Weight That Clarifies

The objections press in, and they deserve answers. But they do not overturn what Scripture, the fathers, the mystics, and the modern witnesses have established.

Grace remains the ground. The Spirit remains the agent. The formation remains real.

What we do and who we become matter eternally—not because we are earning salvation, but because salvation is shaping us for glory. The doing forms the being. The being enables the doing. The spiral ascends toward Christlikeness—or descends toward diminishment. The kiln fires at death, and what has been forming becomes fixed.

This is not burden. It is weight—the kind of weight that keeps you from floating away into insignificance. The kind of weight that makes life serious and substantial and worth living. The weight of glory.

We have now established the theology of becoming—the continuity principle, the kiln of death, the witnesses across fifteen centuries who testify that the soul formed here is the soul that continues there. But becoming is only one pillar. We have spoken of the two pillars throughout, and now we must turn to the other.

What we do. The stewardship dimension. The treasure laid up, the works tested by fire, the cities entrusted to the faithful. The theology of becoming explains who we are becoming; the theology of doing explains what that becoming qualifies us to receive and to give.

To that we now turn.

For readers who wish to explore the theological case for differentiated glory more fully—including objections regarding envy, grace, and eternal growth—see the Appendix.

PART THREE
THE THEOLOGY OF DOING
CHAPTERS 10–13

CHAPTER 10
THE DIFFERENTIATED KINGDOM

The Prize

In Chapter 3, we introduced two pillars—what we do and who we become. We traced their inseparability: doing shapes becoming; becoming enables doing. The virtuous spiral ascends through both, each reinforcing the other. We cannot separate them without distorting both.

But we can distinguish them. And Part II gave the becoming pillar sustained attention—the continuity principle, the kiln of death, the witnesses across fifteen centuries, the objections answered. We have established that the soul formed in the interval of grace is the soul that persists forever. The character shaped here is the character carried there.

Now we turn to the doing pillar. Not because it was absent from Part II—it was woven throughout, as it must be. But because it deserves focused treatment. The becoming pillar concerns who we are becoming. The doing pillar concerns what that becoming qualifies us for. Formation shapes the soul. Faithful action earns the assignment.

Part III gives the doing pillar sustained attention. And we begin with the prize—the differentiated kingdom that awaits the faithful.

Before we can understand the proving, the refining, or the alchemy of treasure transfer, we must see clearly what is at stake. The rewards are real. They differ. And they await those who finish well.

The Kingdom That Isn't Equal

Heaven is not communism. It is meritocracy by grace.

The statement will trouble some readers. We have been trained to imagine heaven as the great equalizer—everyone receives the same mansion, the same bliss, the same proximity to God. The faithful missionary and the nominal believer, the saint who suffered and the Christian who coasted, the martyred apostle and the deathbed convert—all arrive at the same destination, indistinguishable in glory. Any suggestion otherwise feels like introducing competition into paradise, hierarchy into the realm of love.

But Scripture does not present an egalitarian heaven. It presents a differentiated kingdom where reward corresponds to faithfulness, where responsibility is proportioned to proven stewardship, where glory varies as star differs from star.

We have touched on this reality throughout the book. In Chapter 2, we encountered Jonathan Edwards on vessels of different sizes—small and large, both full, holding different volumes. In Chapter 6, we heard Augustine testify that "there will be degrees of honour and glory suitable to their various degrees of merit." In Chapter 8, Edwards returned with his vision of heaven as a world of love where the lowest in glory rejoices to see others higher. In Chapter 9, we answered the objection that differentiation creates unfairness.

But we have not yet examined what the differentiation consists of. We have not yet explored the biblical vocabulary of reward—what Scripture actually promises to the faithful and how those promises vary. We have not yet asked what the Bema Seat accomplishes beyond mere evaluation.

That is the work of this chapter. This is where we see the prize.

THE INTERVAL

The Commissioning That Awaits

The judgment seat of Christ—the Bema Seat—appears in Paul's letters as the event where believers' works are assessed. "We must all appear before the judgment seat of Christ, so that each one may receive what is due for what he has done in the body, whether good or evil" (2 Corinthians 5:10). Chapter 1 introduced this reality. Every believer will appear. The evaluation is certain.

But what happens there?

The common imagination pictures a courtroom. The defendant stands before the Judge. Evidence is presented. A verdict is rendered. There is truth in this picture—works are tested, some survive the fire, some are burned. But the courtroom metaphor captures only part of what Scripture describes.

The Bema in Paul's world was not primarily a criminal court. It was the raised platform where magistrates rendered judgment, yes—but also where victorious athletes received crowns. It was the place of evaluation and the place of honor. The winner stood on the Bema to receive the wreath.

And in Jesus's parables, what follows the master's evaluation is not merely verdict but assignment. "Well done, good and faithful servant. You have been faithful over a little; I will set you over much. Enter into the joy of your master" (Matthew 25:21). The servant is not merely approved. The servant is promoted. The servant is given more.

The Bema Seat is not merely a courtroom. It is a commissioning ceremony. The evaluation leads to vocation. The faithful are not simply declared faithful and sent to enjoy their reward. They are assigned to responsibility commensurate with what they have proven.

"You shall have authority over ten cities" (Luke 19:17). This is not metaphor for increased happiness. It is governance. Real cities. Real authority. The servant who proved faithful with the mina is entrusted with a territory. The servant who proved faithful with less receives less territory—not as punishment, but as fitting assignment. Five cities for five minas' worth of proven faithfulness.

The Bema Seat, then, accomplishes two things at once. It evaluates what we built—the works tested by fire, some surviving as gold and silver, some burning as wood and hay. And it reveals who we became—the worker behind the works, the character that produced the fruit. Both dimensions matter. The evaluation issues in assignment. The commissioning follows the testing.

This is why the doing pillar cannot be separated from the becoming pillar. What we did reveals who we became. Who we became determines what we can be entrusted with. The servant faithful over little has become a faithful person—and a faithful person can be set over much.

The Prizes Scripture Names

Scripture does not speak of reward in vague generalities. It offers specific categories, each carrying distinct significance.

Crowns. The New Testament names at least four crowns available to believers.

The *imperishable crown* belongs to those who exercise discipline in the race. Paul writes: "Every athlete exercises self-control in all things. They do it to receive a perishable wreath, but we an imperishable" (1 Corinthians 9:25). The athletes at Corinth competed for a laurel wreath that would wither within days. The believer who disciplines body and soul competes for a crown that cannot decay. The crown is awarded for sustained effort, for the long obedience, for the race run with endurance.

The *crown of righteousness* belongs to those who love Christ's appearing. Paul, facing execution, wrote to Timothy: "There is laid up for me the crown of righteousness, which the Lord, the righteous judge, will award to me on that Day, and not only to me but also to all who have loved his appearing" (2 Timothy 4:8). This crown is not earned by moral perfection—Paul claims it while acknowledging his weakness. It is awarded to those whose hearts are oriented toward Christ's return, who live with eternal awareness, who love the Day that is coming.

The *crown of life* belongs to those who endure trial. James promises: "Blessed is the man who remains steadfast under trial, for when he has stood the test he will receive the crown of life, which God has promised to those who love him" (James 1:12). This is the crown for perseverance—the reward we explored in Chapter 9 as belonging exclusively to the interval. In the new creation, there will be no more mourning or pain. The conditions for earning this crown will have passed. It can only be won now, under trial, by steadfast endurance.

The *crown of glory* belongs to faithful shepherds. Peter writes to elders: "When the chief Shepherd appears, you will receive the unfading crown of glory" (1 Peter 5:4). This crown rewards those who tended the flock—not for shameful gain, not domineering over those in their charge, but as examples to the sheep. The shepherd who served faithfully receives a shepherd's crown.

Four crowns. Four distinct faithfulnesses. Four specific prizes for specific patterns of life.

And yet—a striking detail. In John's vision of heaven, the twenty-four elders 'cast their crowns before the throne, saying, "Worthy are you, our Lord and God, to receive glory and honor and power"' (Revelation 4:10-11). The crowns are not hoarded. They are laid before the throne—instruments of worship, trophies offered to the One who enabled their earning.

What does this suggest? Perhaps that reward in the kingdom is never finally about possession. The crown is earned, received, and offered—a cycle of grace, faithfulness, and worship. We do not hoard our rewards. We return them to their source. And in the returning, the joy is complete.

Cities. The parable of the minas in Luke 19 speaks of governance as reward. The servant whose mina earned ten more receives authority over ten cities. The servant whose mina earned five receives five cities. The proportion is exact. The reward matches the proven faithfulness.

These are not metaphors for happiness, as though "ten cities" meant "ten units of joy." The parable assumes actual governance, actual responsibility, actual work to be done in the kingdom. The new creation is not an eternal vacation. It is an eternal vocation. And the scope of that vocation is determined by what was proven in the interval.

We do not know precisely what governing a city in the new creation will entail. Scripture does not give us the organizational charts of heaven. But the principle is clear: faithful stewardship here qualifies for greater stewardship there. The doing matters because it is an audition. The master entrusts, departs, and returns to see what was done with what was given. Those who proved faithful receive more to be faithful with.

The Overcomer Promises. In Revelation 2-3, the risen Christ addresses seven churches, and to each he offers a specific promise to "the one who conquers"—the overcomer, the one who perseveres in faithfulness despite opposition.

To Ephesus, beset by false apostles but having abandoned first love: "To the one who conquers I will grant to eat of the tree of life, which is in the paradise of God" (Revelation 2:7). Access to the tree of life—the tree guarded since Eden, now opened to the faithful.

To Smyrna, facing persecution and poverty: "The one who conquers will not be hurt by the second death" (Revelation 2:11). To a church facing martyrdom, this promise carries particular weight. Those who may lose their lives for Christ are assured they will not face the second death—the lake of fire described later in Revelation (20:14). The assurance is framed in terms directly relevant to their suffering: you may face the first death, but the second holds no power over you.

To Pergamum, holding fast where Satan's throne is: "To the one who conquers I will give some of the hidden manna, and I will give him a white stone, with a new name written on the stone that no one knows except the one who receives it" (Revelation 2:17). Hidden manna—sustenance known only to the faithful. A white stone with a secret name—an intimacy with Christ so personal it cannot be shared.

To Thyatira, tolerating the false prophetess Jezebel yet also producing works of love and faith: "The one who conquers and who keeps my works until the end, to him I will give authority over the nations" (Revelation 2:26). Governance again—authority extending beyond cities to nations. The scope expands with the faithfulness.

To Sardis, the church with a reputation for life but actually dead: "The one who conquers will be clothed thus in white garments, and I will never blot his name out of the book of life. I will confess his name before my Father and before his angels" (Revelation 3:5). White garments of purity. A name confessed before the Father. Public honor in heaven for faithfulness on earth.

To Philadelphia, the church of little power that kept Christ's word and did not deny his name: "The one who conquers, I will make him a pillar in the temple of my God. Never shall he go out of it, and I will write on him the name of my God, and the name of the city of my God, the new Jerusalem which comes down from my God out of heaven, and my own new name" (Revelation 3:12). A pillar—permanence, stability, honor in God's dwelling. Inscribed with three names—belonging marked indelibly.

To Laodicea, the lukewarm church, wealthy but wretched: "The one who conquers, I will grant him to sit with me on my throne, as I also conquered and sat down with my Father on his throne" (Revelation 3:21). The most astonishing promise of all. Sitting with Christ on his throne. Sharing his reign. Participating in his sovereignty.

Seven churches. Seven conditions. Seven promises. Each tailored to the specific struggle, each rewarding the specific faithfulness required. This is not generic heaven. This is the differentiated prize.

Degrees of Glory. Paul, describing the resurrection, reaches for an analogy: "There is one glory of the sun, and another glory of the moon, and another glory of the stars; for star differs from star in glory. So is it with the resurrection of the dead" (1 Corinthians 15:41-42).

The differentiation is real. Not all stars shine equally. Not all resurrection bodies carry the same glory. The variation is established at death and becomes the starting point for eternal life.

Levels as Capacity

But what does differentiated glory mean in practice? Some have taught literal spatial proximity—the more faithful dwell closer to God's throne, the less faithful at greater distance. Dante's *Paradiso* portrays heaven as concentric spheres, each level nearer the Empyrean where God dwells. Medieval theology sometimes spoke of graduated proximity.

Scripture does not give us detailed maps of the new creation.

Whether there are areas of varied proximity to God's throne, we cannot say with certainty—nor should we dismiss the possibility. Perhaps those with greater capacity are able to dwell nearer the intensity of his presence. What we can observe from Scripture is that capacity varies: capacity to see God, capacity to steward, capacity to enjoy, capacity to glorify. Whether this capacity corresponds to placement, or whether location functions in the new creation as it does now, remains mysterious. What is not mysterious is that formation shapes capacity—and capacity determines how fully we can receive and reflect what God offers.

There is capacity to see God. "Blessed are the pure in heart, for they shall see God" (Matthew 5:8). The beatific vision—the direct apprehension of God himself—is promised to the pure. Purity is not merely the absence of sin; it is the presence of undivided devotion, the single eye, the heart that wants one thing. That purity creates capacity. The soul formed in singleness can see what the divided soul cannot bear.

There is capacity to steward. The faithful receive more to be faithful with. "To everyone who has will more be given" (Matthew 25:29). This is not arbitrary distribution but fitting assignment. The soul that developed faithfulness can handle greater responsibility. The soul that did not cannot. The capacity was formed—or not formed—in the interval.

There is capacity to enjoy. This is Edwards's insight: the formed soul has more receptors for joy. The person who cultivated love has more capacity to receive love eternally. The person who developed patience has more capacity to participate in God's patient purposes forever. The interval formed the receptors. The rewards fill what the receptors can hold.

There is capacity to glorify. Paul speaks of transformation "from one degree of glory to another" (2 Corinthians 3:18)—a progression that suggests varying capacities to reflect and radiate the Lord's image. Daniel was told that "those who are wise shall shine like the brightness of the sky above; and those who turn many to righteousness, like the stars forever and ever" (Daniel 12:3). The shining varies. The brightness differs. The soul that expanded in Christlikeness radiates more of

Christ—not from superior worth but from greater capacity, formed through faithfulness. Star differs from star in glory, and the differentiation is real.

Everyone in the new creation will be fully satisfied. No one will lack. No one will envy. This is the joy paradox we have addressed. But satisfaction does not mean uniformity. The thimble fully satisfied holds less than the ocean fully satisfied. The capacity varies. The fullness is the same.

It is ecology—an ecosystem of varied creatures, each fulfilling a unique role, each contributing what only it can contribute. A garden of different flowers. A symphony of different instruments. Edwards saw this clearly: the beauty of heaven is not uniformity but harmony. Each saint adds a note no one else can add. Each reflects an angle of God's glory no one else reflects. The differentiation is not competition. It is composition.

The Starting Point for Eternal Expansion

We established in Chapter 5 that the formation fixed at death becomes the foundation for eternal growth. Gregory of Nyssa's *epektasis*—eternal progress into the infinite God—means that the saints never stop growing. There is always more of God to know, more of his beauty to behold.

But growth continues from fixed starting points.

The reward earned in the interval is not a final lot, a static possession to hold forever unchanged. It is a starting point—a foundation from which eternal expansion continues. The five-talent servant and the two-talent servant both enter joy. Both grow. Both advance into God forever. But they do not grow from the same base.

This is why the doing matters so intensely. What faithful action earns is not merely a prize to be collected but a capacity to be expanded. The cities governed are not static assignments but growing responsibilities. The authority over nations is not a fixed territory but an expanding dominion. The rewards are not endpoints but beginning points.

And as Chapter 9 established, the interval is irreplaceable. Certain rewards can only be earned under earthly conditions. What could only be done here—the specific faithfulnesses that require earthly conditions—is either done or undone. The crown of life for endurance under trial cannot be earned where there is no trial. The crown of righteousness for loving an unseen appearing cannot be earned when he is visibly present.

Why the Prize Matters

If rewards are real—specific, differentiated, proportioned to faithfulness—then what we do in the interval is not optional for the serious believer. Not optional for salvation—that is settled by grace. But essential for vocation, capacity, eternal assignment.

This is not works-righteousness. Salvation remains by grace through faith. The threefold framework we established in Chapter 9 holds: salvation is gift, formation is Spirit-enabled cooperation, and reward is the fruit of grace-enabled faithfulness. We are not earning our entrance into the kingdom. We are determining our place within it.

But the differentiation must be rightly understood. Rewards are proportioned to faithfulness, not to raw capacity or visible platform. The five-talent servant and the two-talent servant received identical commendation—word for word—because both were equally faithful with what they were given. This is the only thing either servant could control. Neither chose his capacity. Neither determined his starting resources. The master distributed "to each according to his ability" (Matthew 25:15). What remained within each servant's control was whether to invest or bury—and both invested fully.

Both doubled what they were given. Both heard, "Well done, good and faithful servant." The commendation is identical because the faithfulness percentage is identical. But the servant who proved faithful with more is set over more. In Luke's parable, the principle becomes explicit: ten minas earned yields ten cities; five minas earned yields five. The commendation honors the faithfulness. The assignment reflects the scale of proven stewardship—not as punishment for the lesser, but as fitting entrustment for each.

THE INTERVAL

This distinction matters pastorally. The Sunday school teacher faithful over forty students is not competing against the evangelist faithful over millions. God does not evaluate her against the evangelist's gifts—only against her own. If she is fully faithful, she hears the same words he hears: "Well done, good and faithful servant." Her assignment will match what she proved she could steward. His will match what he proved. Both are "well done" in the Lord's eyes. The widow's two coins were counted by Jesus as "more than all" the wealthy contributed, because she gave everything while they gave from surplus (Mark 12:43-44). Heaven's ledger calculates proportionally. The differentiated kingdom is not rigged toward the prominently gifted. It honors the proportionally faithful.

We might call this works-significance rather than works-righteousness. The works do not save. But the works matter. They deposit treasure. They earn crowns. They qualify for authority. They shape the eternal vocation we will carry into the new creation.

The martyr who dies for Christ cannot have the same eternal vocation as the nominal believer who barely believed. If they arrive at the same capacity, the same responsibility, the same glory, then martyrdom loses meaning. Why lay down your life if the outcome is identical? But Scripture honors the martyrs precisely because their faithfulness cost everything—and that cost is not forgotten.

The differentiated kingdom makes sense of what Scripture emphasizes. The parables would be meaningless if the outcome were uniform. The crowns would be decorative if everyone received the same. The promises to overcomers would be empty if non-overcomers received identical blessing.

God is not egalitarian. He is generous—to all, freely, abundantly. But he is also just—rewarding faithfulness, recognizing sacrifice, proportioning assignment to proven stewardship. The kingdom operates by grace. And grace, in the kingdom, differentiates.

This chapter has established the prize—the differentiated kingdom, the varied crowns, the proportioned cities, the degrees of glory. The chapters that follow will trace how that prize is won.

The Invitation

The prize is not threat but invitation. You are being invited to earn crowns that will be cast before the throne. To qualify for cities that need governance. To develop capacity that can hold more of God.

The doing matters. The stewardship is being evaluated. The Bema Seat awaits—not to condemn, but to commission. What you do with what you have been given determines not whether you enter the joy, but the capacity with which you begin. Not whether you are saved, but what you are saved for.

The kingdom is differentiated. And the differentiation is beautiful. It is not the ugly hierarchy of earthly systems, where some dominate and others are diminished. It is the glorious ecology of heaven, where each contributes uniquely, where the lowest rejoices in the highest, where the symphony requires every instrument.

The soul being formed in you is unlike any other. The capacity you carry into eternity will be uniquely yours. What God will do with that uniqueness in the ages to come remains beyond our present knowing—but Scripture assures us the formation matters.

But how is the prize won? How does the King determine who can be trusted with ten cities and who with five? Not by arbitrary assignment. By proving. By refining. By the alchemy that converts temporal faithfulness into eternal treasure.

The prize awaits. The chapters that follow trace how it is obtained.

CHAPTER 11
THE STEWARDSHIP TEST

The Proving

The prize is established. The differentiated kingdom awaits—crowns for the faithful, cities for the proven, glory varying as star differs from star. But how does the King determine who can be trusted with such responsibility?

By proving. And the proving is already underway.

We have already encountered the training-ground logic of the parables. In Chapter 1, we traced Jesus's parable of the talents—the master who entrusts, departs, and returns for accounting. In Chapter 10, we saw the proportioned reward: ten cities for one servant, five for another. The principle is established: faithfulness in small things qualifies for stewardship of large things. "Well done, good and faithful servant. You have been faithful over a little; I will set you over much" (Matthew 25:21).

But Jesus did not leave us with the principle alone. He specified the test. And the specification reveals that the proving is happening not in dramatic spiritual moments but in the ordinary fabric of daily life.

The Test Under Invisible Lordship

The structure of the talents parable is significant. The master entrusts resources. The master departs. A period of absence follows—what Matthew calls "a long time" (25:19). Then the master returns for accounting.

The departure matters. During the master's absence, the servants are unsupervised. No one is watching—or so it appears. What they do with what they have been given is entirely up to them. The proving happens in the interval between entrustment and return.

This is precisely our situation. Christ has ascended. He will return. Between ascension and return stretches the interval of grace—the proving ground where we demonstrate what we will do with what we have been given. The Lord is not visibly present. The accounting has not yet come. What we do in this interval reveals what we are.

But there is a crucial difference the parable does not explicitly name: we are not unsupervised. The Spirit has been given. The One who "searches everything, even the depths of God" (1 Corinthians 2:10) dwells within the believer. The Father who "sees in secret" (Matthew 6:4, 6, 18) observes every choice. The interval is not abandonment. It is trust—the trust of a master who has provided everything needed for faithfulness and now watches to see what his servants will do.

The Spirit's presence transforms the test. We are not left to our own resources, straining to produce what we cannot generate. We are empowered. The same Spirit who raised Christ from the dead dwells in us (Romans 8:11). The proving is not "Can you succeed without help?" but "Will you cooperate with the help that has been lavishly provided?"

This is why faithfulness is possible for every believer. The test is not rigged against us. The Spirit empowers. Grace enables. The resources have been entrusted, and the Helper has been given. The only question is whether we will invest or bury.

The Three Tests

In Luke 16, Jesus specified what the proving examines. Three tests, each revealing a different dimension of trustworthiness.

"One who is faithful in a very little is also faithful in much, and one who is dishonest in a very little is also dishonest in much. If then you have not been faithful in the unrighteous wealth, who will entrust to you the true riches? And if you have not been faithful in that which is another's, who will give you your own?" (Luke 16:10-12).

Three tests. Three qualifications. Three dimensions of the proving.

The first test is scale. "One who is faithful in a very little is also faithful in much." The test of small things reveals what we would do with large things. The servant who cannot be trusted with a hundred dollars cannot be trusted with a million. The one who is careless with an hour will be careless with a decade. Scale changes nothing essential —it only reveals what was already true.

This is why God gives little before much. Not because he is stingy, but because he is wise. The small assignment is the proving ground for the large assignment. The obscure task is the audition for the significant task. Faithfulness in the very little qualifies for faithfulness in the much. Dishonesty in the very little disqualifies.

The implications are staggering. The way you handle today's small responsibilities is being observed. Not merely as moral evaluation— "Was this person good?"—but as vocational qualification: "Can this person be trusted with more?" The eternal assignment is being determined by the temporal proving.

The second test is currency. "If then you have not been faithful in the unrighteous wealth, who will entrust to you the true riches?" Jesus draws a contrast between two kinds of wealth. There is "unrighteous wealth"—the mammon of this present age, the currency that rusts and moths destroy and thieves steal. And there is "true riches"— the wealth of the age to come, the currency that endures forever.

The test: What do you do with the lesser currency? The money in your bank account is not true riches. It is training riches. It is the Monopoly money of the kingdom—real enough in this game, worthless when the game ends. But how you play with it reveals whether you can be trusted with the currency that never devalues.

The one who hoards unrighteous wealth has failed the test. The one who uses unrighteous wealth for kingdom purposes—generosity, justice, mercy, gospel advance—has passed. Not because the giving earned heaven, but because the giving revealed a heart already oriented toward heaven's values. The currency test is a heart test.

The third test is ownership. "And if you have not been faithful in that which is another's, who will give you your own?" Everything you currently possess belongs to another. Your money is God's money, entrusted for a season. Your time is God's time, allocated for a purpose. Your gifts are God's gifts, distributed for his ends. You are not an owner. You are a steward—managing another's resources.

The test: How do you handle what belongs to someone else? The employee who works faithfully when the boss is away reveals character. The child who cares for borrowed items reveals maturity. The steward who manages the master's estate as if it were his own—with diligence, wisdom, and care—reveals qualification for ownership.

The promise embedded in the test is remarkable: faithfulness with another's qualifies you for your own. There is something coming that will be yours—not borrowed, not entrusted, but given as permanent possession. What that looks like in the new creation, we cannot fully know. But the principle is clear: stewardship precedes ownership. Faithfulness with the temporary qualifies for the permanent.

Three tests. Three dimensions of the proving. And all three are being administered right now, in the ordinary decisions of ordinary days.

According to His Ability

But we must pause here to address what might otherwise become a crushing misunderstanding. If the proving determines eternal reward, and if some are given greater platforms, greater gifts, greater opportunities—does this mean the Billy Grahams of the world are destined for greater eternal glory while the faithful Sunday school teacher is consigned to lesser reward?

THE INTERVAL

The answer is nuanced, and getting it right matters.

Billy Graham may indeed have greater glory in heaven—and rightly so. He was given much. If he was faithful with that much, he will be rewarded accordingly. The scope of his gift was vast; the scope of his faithfulness, if proportional, would yield vast reward. Scripture does not teach that all rewards are equal. It teaches that rewards are proportioned to faithfulness.

But here is the crucial truth: the Sunday school teacher is not disadvantaged. She is not competing against Graham's gifts. She is being evaluated on her own faithfulness with her own gifts. And if she is faithful with what she was given—fully faithful, holding nothing back—she too will hear "well done." Her reward will be proportioned to her faithfulness, not measured against someone else's platform.

Both realities are true. Graham's greater scope of faithfulness may yield greater scope of reward. And the widow's two coins, given from her poverty, were counted by Jesus as "more than all" the wealthy contributed (Mark 12:43). Both are true because heaven's ledger calculates proportionally.

Return to the parable of the talents. Before the master departed, he distributed resources "to each according to his ability" (Matthew 25:15). The distribution was unequal by design. Five talents to one, two to another, one to a third. The master knew his servants. He knew their capacities. He calibrated the entrustment accordingly.

And here is the crucial detail: when the master returned, the five-talent servant and the two-talent servant received *identical* commendation. Word for word. "Well done, good and faithful servant. You have been faithful over a little; I will set you over much. Enter into the joy of your master" (Matthew 25:21, 23). The master did not say to the five-talent servant, "Well done, you produced more." He said, "You have been faithful." Both servants doubled their investment. Both were equally faithful *relative to what they were given*. Both heard the same words.

The five-talent servant is set over more in the kingdom—five talents' worth of proven faithfulness is more than two talents' worth. But the commendation was identical. The "well done" was the same. The proportional faithfulness was equal. This is crucial: God evaluates what we can control. Neither servant chose his capacity. Neither determined his starting allocation. What each controlled was whether to invest or bury. Both invested fully—and both heard "well done." The different assignments that follow reflect demonstrated capacity, not superior approval. Ten cities for one, five for another—each fitted to what was proven. But the Master's pleasure in both servants is identical, because both were faithful with everything they had.

This is the governing principle: evaluation is proportional to what was given, not absolute in output.

Jesus made this explicit at the temple treasury. The wealthy contributed large sums. A widow put in two small copper coins—worth perhaps a few cents. By any absolute measure, she gave less. By heaven's measure, she gave more: "Truly, I say to you, this poor widow has put in more than all those who are contributing to the offering box. For they all contributed out of their abundance, but she out of her poverty has put in everything she had" (Mark 12:43-44).

The widow's mite is not a charming story about small gifts. It reveals how heaven calculates. The question is not "How much did you give?" but "How much did you give relative to what you had?" The wealthy gave from surplus. The widow gave everything. By proportional measure, she gave more—and will be rewarded accordingly.

This principle cuts in two directions.

First, it liberates. You are not competing with Billy Graham. You are not disadvantaged by your small platform, your limited resources, your obscure assignment. The country pastor who faithfully shepherds forty people for forty years is not being compared to the evangelist who fills stadiums. Each is evaluated on faithfulness to their own gift, their own calling, their own capacity. God knows what he gave you. He knows what was possible for you. And he will evaluate you—not against someone else's gifts, but against your own.

Paul understood this. "All these are empowered by one and the same Spirit, who apportions to each one individually as he wills" (1 Corinthians 12:11). The distribution is sovereign. The foot is not inferior to the hand. The hidden member is not less honorable than the visible one. Different function, equal dignity, proportional accountability.

But the principle also increases the weight. You cannot hide behind "I didn't have his platform." You cannot excuse unfaithfulness by pointing to what you were not given. The one-talent servant tried this defense: "Master, I knew you to be a hard man... so I was afraid, and I went and hid your talent in the ground" (Matthew 25:24-25). He blamed the master's severity. He implied the game was rigged against him. He refused to risk because the odds seemed unfair.

The master did not accept this defense.

The one-talent servant had everything he needed to be faithful. One talent was a fortune—twenty years of wages. He could have invested, traded, put it to work. He chose to bury. And the evaluation was devastating: "You wicked and slothful servant!"

"To whom much is given, much will be required" (Luke 12:48). The one given much faces greater accountability, not automatic greater reward. Billy Graham will be evaluated against Billy Graham's gifts. You will be evaluated against yours. And the widow will be evaluated against hers—and her everything may outweigh another's surplus.

This is the proportional evaluation. The proving is customized to you. Your test is not another's test. Your capacity is not another's capacity. But your test is real, and your capacity must be stewarded.

What will you do with what *you* have been given?

What Counts as "Little"

The "little" you are given is unique to you. It encompasses every dimension of your life where faithfulness is possible. Jesus said we would be tested in "a very little." But what constitutes the little? Where is the proving ground?

Time is given. Every day contains the same twenty-four hours for everyone. But what you do with those hours—especially the discretionary hours, the margins, the moments no one else sees—this is proving ground. The hour spent in prayer when you could have scrolled. The evening invested in your children when you could have checked out. The years given to a calling that pays little but matters much.

Money is given. Whatever amount—much or little by the world's measure—it is entrusted. The tithe. The offering beyond the tithe. The spontaneous generosity when need appears. The financial margin maintained so that giving is possible. The refusal to let lifestyle expand to consume every increase. Money is the most measurable dimension of the test. The records exist. The patterns are traceable.

Influence is given. For some, influence extends to millions. For others, to a handful. But influence exists for everyone—family, friends, coworkers, neighbors. The words spoken that shape how others see God. The example set that others consciously or unconsciously follow. The doors opened, the introductions made, the platforms shared.

Opportunity is given. Doors open and close. Moments arise and pass. The conversation that could turn toward the gospel. The suffering neighbor who needs presence. The wrong that could be righted. The gift that could be given. Opportunity is often time-sensitive—today's door may not open tomorrow.

Relationships are given. Every person in your life is an entrustment. Spouse, children, parents, friends, colleagues, the stranger whose path crosses yours. Each relationship is an arena of faithfulness—an opportunity to love, to serve, to invest in an eternal soul.

Suffering comes. This may seem strange to list as stewardship. Suffering arrives through many channels — the brokenness of a fallen world, the malice of others, the consequences of our own choices, the mysterious providences we cannot fully explain. For some suffering — particularly persecution for Christ's sake — Paul even says it has been "granted" to us (Philippians 1:29). But whatever its source, suffering is something to steward. What you do with pain, loss, disappointment, betrayal — this too is proving ground. The suffering that produces endurance, character, and hope (Romans 5:3-4) is suffering faithfully stewarded. James understood: "Count it all joy, my brothers, when you meet trials of various kinds" (James 1:2). Not joy for the suffering, but joy in the opportunity to steward it toward formation.

Words are given. The tongue is small but powerful. Every word spoken is a use of entrustment—to build up or tear down, to speak truth or falsehood, to encourage or discourage, to bless or curse. Jesus said we would give account for every idle word (Matthew 12:36). Words are currency in the proving.

Attention is given. What you focus on, you feed. What you feed, you become. The attention given to Scripture or to entertainment. The attention given to prayer or to worry. The attention given to eternal things or to passing things. Attention is the rudder that steers everything else.

Each dimension is a proving ground. Each is being tested. And the One who sees in secret is watching—not to condemn, but to evaluate. Not to catch you failing, but to catch you faithful.

The Audition You Didn't Know You Were Taking

Most believers do not realize they are being tested. The three unready figures in Jesus's parables share this blindness.

The one-talent servant did not know his burial would be exposed. He assumed the master's absence meant the master's ignorance. He calculated that inaction was safe. He was wrong.

The five foolish virgins did not know the bridegroom would delay until their oil ran out. They assumed there would be time to prepare later. They were wrong.

The goats in Matthew 25 did not know that their treatment of the hungry, the thirsty, the stranger, the naked, the sick, and the imprisoned was treatment of Christ himself. "Lord, when did we see you hungry or thirsty or a stranger or naked or sick or in prison?" (Matthew 25:44). They didn't know the test was happening. They failed it anyway.

This is perhaps the most sobering dimension of the proving. The test is not announced. The audition does not post a schedule. The evaluation happens in real time, in real life, in moments that feel ordinary rather than momentous.

The way you speak to your spouse this morning is part of the proving. The decision you make about your bonus this quarter is part of the proving. The response you give to the difficult colleague, the time you spend with your aging parent, the attention you pay to the person no one else notices—all proving. All being recorded in a ledger that will be opened.

This is not meant to paralyze but to awaken. The sleepwalking believer who drifts through days without awareness is failing the test without knowing it. The awakened believer who sees clearly—who understands that every moment is proving ground—can cooperate with the Spirit in real time, making choices that qualify for the commendation to come.

The Test That Forms What It Reveals

The two pillars cannot be separated, even here. The proving is not merely revealing what we are. It is forming what we are becoming.

Every time you pass a small test—choosing faithfulness when unfaithfulness would be easier—you become a more faithful person. The choice forms the character. The repeated choice becomes the settled disposition. The test that you pass shapes you into someone who passes such tests.

This is the integration we traced in Chapter 3. The doing shapes the becoming. The servant who faithfully invested the talents did not merely produce a return; he became a faithful servant. The character that qualified for ten cities was formed through the faithful action that produced the ten minas.

Edwards's vessel metaphor appears again. The tests are sizing the vessel. Every act of generosity expands the generous soul. Every discipline of patience deepens the patient character. Every choice to steward well forms a steward who can be trusted with more.

You are not merely being evaluated in the proving. You are being shaped. The test itself is the formation.

This is why the proving cannot be crammed. You cannot coast for years and then cram faithfulness into the final weeks before the master returns. The five foolish virgins tried this—rushing to buy oil when the bridegroom appeared. The door was already shut. The vessel had already been sized. The time for formation had passed.

The proving is happening now. The formation is happening now.

THE INTERVAL

The vessel is being sized now. And the master may return at any time—or death may end your proving before his return. Either way, the interval closes. And what you have become through the proving is what you carry into eternity.

The Accounting That Is Coming

The master will return. The accounting will come. Every servant will stand before him, and the ledger will be opened.

For some, the accounting will be glory. "Well done, good and faithful servant. You have been faithful over a little; I will set you over much. Enter into the joy of your master." The words will be worth more than all the treasures of earth. The five-talent servant heard them. The two-talent servant heard them—the same words, the same commendation. Both were faithful with what they were given. Both entered joy.

For others, the accounting will be loss. The one-talent servant heard no commendation. His talent was taken and given to another. Interpreters debate whether his severe fate—"outer darkness," "weeping and gnashing of teeth"—describes one who merely professed faith, exposed as never truly belonging, or a genuine believer facing consequences beyond mere loss of reward. What cannot be debated is the seriousness of the warning: stewardship matters, and the master will not be indifferent to what was done with what he entrusted.

The proving is underway. The tests are being administered. The Spirit empowers. Grace enables. The resources have been entrusted. The evaluation is proportional—not comparing you to others, but measuring your faithfulness against your gifts.

The question is not whether you will be tested. You are being tested now.

The question is whether you will be found faithful.

Not everything we build in the proving carries equal weight. Some works will survive the fire; others will burn. To the refining we now turn.

CHAPTER 12
THE FIRE THAT TESTS

The Refining

The proving is underway. Every believer is being tested in the ordinary moments of life—time, money, relationships, opportunity. The Spirit empowers. Grace enables. The evaluation calculates proportionally, measuring faithfulness against what was given.

But not everything we build in the proving carries equal weight.

Some works will survive the fire. Others will burn. The builder is saved either way—but the difference between arriving with the "well done" and arriving singed is significant beyond our present ability to measure. This chapter turns to the refining: the fire that will test what sort of work each one has done.

The Day Will Disclose

Paul's first letter to the Corinthians presents this reality with unsparing clarity. The passage has been referenced throughout our journey—Chapter 1 introduced the one "saved as through fire,"

Chapter 9 developed the distinction between salvation and reward. But we have not yet unpacked the passage itself. Now we must.

"According to the grace of God given to me, like a skilled master builder I laid a foundation, and someone else is building upon it. Let each one take care how he builds upon it. For no one can lay a foundation other than that which is laid, which is Jesus Christ" (1 Corinthians 3:10-11).

The foundation is non-negotiable. Christ alone. No other foundation is possible for the believer. The question is not whether we have the right foundation—if we are in Christ, that is settled. The question is what we are constructing on it. And Paul's warning—"let each one take care"—suggests that carelessness is possible. We can build poorly on the right foundation. We can construct hay on the rock.

"Now if anyone builds on the foundation with gold, silver, precious stones, wood, hay, straw—each one's work will become manifest, for the Day will disclose it, because it will be revealed by fire, and the fire will test what sort of work each one has done" (1 Corinthians 3:12-13).

Two categories of material. The first—gold, silver, precious stones—are refined by fire, not destroyed by it. These materials do not merely survive the flames; they emerge purified, proven, more glorious than before. Fire is their friend. It burns away impurity and reveals their true worth.

The second category—wood, hay, straw—cannot endure the test. They are consumed entirely. Nothing remains. What seemed solid proves to be kindling. What looked impressive collapses into ash.

The Day will disclose. There is a Day coming—the day of evaluation, the Bema Seat we examined in Chapter 10. On that Day, fire will reveal what each person has built. What was hidden will be manifest. What seemed impressive may prove to be kindling. What seemed insignificant may prove to be gold.

"If the work that anyone has built on the foundation survives, he will receive a reward. If anyone's work is burned up, he will suffer loss, though he himself will be saved, but only as through fire" (1 Corinthians 3:14-15).

The outcomes diverge dramatically. One builder receives reward —the prize we traced in Chapter 10, the crowns and cities and commendation. Another builder suffers loss—not loss of salvation, but loss of what might have been. The work is burned. The builder escapes, but as one fleeing a burning house with nothing but the clothes on his back. Singed. Empty-handed. Saved, but barely.

Both are saved. Paul is not describing believers and unbelievers. He is describing two kinds of believers—both on the same foundation, both genuinely in Christ. But one arrives with reward. The other arrives with little to show for a lifetime of building.

This is not about salvation. It is about what survives.

Quality, Not Quantity

Notice what the fire tests. Paul says it will reveal "what sort of work" each one has done. The Greek asks "what sort"—what kind, what quality. The fire is not measuring volume. It is testing substance.

This is the proportional evaluation extended into new territory. In Chapters 10 and 11, we established that heaven's ledger calculates proportionally—the widow's two coins counted as more than the wealthy's large sums because she gave everything while they gave from surplus. The same principle applies to the fire. A small work of gold survives. A massive work of hay burns. Scale is irrelevant. Substance is everything.

The mega-church built on prideful self-promotion may burn while the faithful prayer closet shines. The bestselling book written primarily for acclaim may be consumed while the obscure letter of encouragement proves to be gold. The ministry empire constructed mainly for legacy may collapse into ash while the single life poured out in hidden service gleams in the flames.

This is not an argument against large ministries or visible platforms. It is a warning against assuming that size equals substance. The fire does not care about metrics. The fire tests material.

The widow at the temple treasury built with gold. Two small coins, given from poverty, offered without fanfare. That was gold— pure, enduring, precious in God's sight.

The Pharisee who trumpeted his giving built with something else. Jesus' verdict: "They have received their reward" (Matthew 6:2). Paid in full. Nothing left for the fire to honor.

Same action—giving. Different material. The difference was not in the amount. It was in something deeper, something the fire would reveal.

What Makes Work Survive?

If the fire tests quality, we must ask: What determines quality? What distinguishes gold from hay?

Scripture suggests four characteristics of work that endures. But we must hold these with humility. Only God fully knows what survives the fire. We see dimly. We aspire toward gold while acknowledging that our self-assessment is imperfect and our motives are rarely pure.

First, work built on Christ rather than self.

Paul established the foundation: Christ alone. But having Christ as foundation means more than initial conversion. It means Christ as source, aim, and pattern. Work built on Christ flows from him, points to him, resembles him.

Work that flows primarily from self—my need for significance, my hunger for legacy, my drive to prove my worth—may be in danger of burning, regardless of how religious it appears. We cannot always discern where Christ ends and self begins in our own motivations. But the aspiration matters: to build for him rather than for ourselves. The direction of our intention shapes the material of our work.

Second, work empowered by the Spirit rather than mere human effort.

In Chapter 6, we traced the fathers' teaching on synergy—the Spirit enables, we respond. Formation is Spirit-wrought. The same is true of the work we build.

Paul distinguished between the works of the flesh and the fruit of the Spirit (Galatians 5:19-23). Work can appear virtuous—disciplined, productive, impressive—and still be powered primarily by self-effort. Flesh-powered work may achieve temporal results. But it risks proving to be hay when the fire tests it.

This is why prayerlessness is dangerous. Not because prayer is merely a religious duty, but because prayerlessness often reveals self-reliance. The one who does not pray may be building impressively. They may also be building with combustible materials—trusting their own strength rather than the Spirit's power.

Third, work done for God's glory rather than human praise.

Jesus addressed this directly: "Beware of practicing your righteousness before other people in order to be seen by them, for then you will have no reward from your Father who is in heaven" (Matthew 6:1).

The warning is specific: practicing righteousness "in order to be seen." The motive is the issue. The same act—giving, praying, fasting—can be gold or hay depending on the audience it seeks to please.

"When you give to the needy, sound no trumpet before you, as the hypocrites do... Truly, I say to you, they have received their reward" (Matthew 6:2). The transaction is complete. The human applause was the payment. Nothing remains for the Day.

But "when you give to the needy, do not let your left hand know what your right hand is doing... and your Father who sees in secret will reward you" (Matthew 6:3-4). This is gold stored for the fire—given in secret, witnessed only by the Father, awaiting the Day when hidden things are revealed.

Fourth, work aligned with eternal values rather than only temporal ones.

"Do not lay up for yourselves treasures on earth, where moth and rust destroy and where thieves break in and steal, but lay up for yourselves treasures in heaven" (Matthew 6:19-20). Two orientations. One survives the fire. The other does not.

Investment in people, in character, in kingdom advance—this is investment in what lasts. Investment in comfort alone, in status alone, in temporary acclaim alone—this is investment in what passes. Not evil, necessarily. But combustible.

The Complexity of Motive

Here we must pause and acknowledge what every honest soul knows: our motives are rarely pure.

We give—and something in us hopes to be noticed. We serve—and something in us craves appreciation. We sacrifice—and something in us wants credit. The gold and the hay are often mixed in the same act. The Christ-centered and the self-centered coexist in the same heart.

This is the human condition. We are not yet glorified. Sin still clings. Even our best works are tainted by the imperfection that marks everything we do this side of resurrection.

What, then, can we hope for? That the fire will be more merciful than we deserve? That grace will somehow cover even the mixed motives of our building?

Scripture does not resolve this tension neatly. It holds both realities: the fire will test, and God knows we are dust. The same Lord who warned of works burning is the Lord who remembers that we are but flesh. Scripture elsewhere assures us that "love covers a multitude of sins" (1 Peter 4:8).

Perhaps the fire is more surgical than we imagine—burning away the hay while preserving whatever gold was genuinely present. Perhaps a work done with mixed motives yields partial reward, the gold separated from the dross. Perhaps God, who alone sees the heart, weighs the genuine aspiration alongside the impure admixture.

We do not know the mechanics. What we know is the call: build with gold. Aspire toward purity of motive even while acknowledging we never fully achieve it. Aim for Christ as foundation, Spirit as power, God's glory as goal, eternity as orientation—even while confessing that self intrudes at every turn.

The fire will sort what we cannot sort. Our task is not to achieve perfect purity but to pursue it. Not to guarantee that every work is gold but to build in the direction of gold. Not to eliminate mixed motives but to increasingly subordinate them to the one motive that matters: love for God and neighbor, flowing from the grace that first loved us.

Self-Examination Before the Fire

We need not wait for the Day to consider what we are building. Paul urged: "Let each one take care how he builds" (1 Corinthians 3:10). The command assumes we can examine, at least partially, the direction of our construction.

But self-examination is limited. We cannot see our own hearts as God sees them. The prophet warned that "the heart is deceitful above all things" (Jeremiah 17:9). We are capable of self-deception at depths we cannot fully fathom. The Pharisee in Jesus' parable thanked God that he was not like other men—and walked away unjustified. He could not see himself truly.

So we examine—not with the confidence that we can render final verdict, but with the humility of those who know they see dimly. We ask questions not to achieve certainty but to cultivate direction:

Does this work flow primarily from Christ, or primarily from my need for significance?

Does this work depend on the Spirit, or mainly on my own energy and determination?

Does this work seek God's glory, or mainly my reputation and advancement?

Does this work invest in what lasts, or only in what impresses now?

The questions are aspirational. They reveal direction more than destination. We may not be able to answer them with certainty—but we can notice which direction we are leaning. We can catch ourselves building for the wrong audience. We can pause, repent, and reorient.

And the grace is this: we can still adjust our building. The Day has not yet come. Today's choice of material influences what survives tomorrow's test. The one who has been building carelessly can begin, today, to build more carefully. The foundation is secure. The opportunity remains.

Paul's command is present tense: "Let each one take care how he builds." Not past tense, fixed, unchangeable. But present—ongoing, still within our power to influence. The wheel is still turning. The construction is still underway.

Better to examine now, however imperfectly, than to discover then.

With Reward or As Through Fire

The fire will fall. The Day will come. Every work will be tested. And the outcomes will diverge.

One builder arrives with reward. The work survives. Gold, silver, precious stones emerge refined, more glorious than before. The "well done" is spoken. The crowns and cities and glories traced in Chapter 10 are distributed. The faithful steward enters the joy of the master, carrying what was built.

Another builder arrives as through fire. The work is consumed. What seemed impressive proves to be kindling. The builder escapes—genuinely saved, genuinely on the foundation—but having suffered loss. Saved, but singed. Present in the kingdom, but with less than might have been.

Both are saved. This cannot be emphasized enough. Paul is not warning of hell. He is warning of loss—not loss of salvation but loss of reward. Not loss of eternity but loss of what might have filled eternity.

And yet the loss is real. The difference between the two outcomes is not trivial. It is the difference between hearing "well done, good and faithful servant" and hearing... we do not know what. Perhaps the Lord's gentle acknowledgment that more was possible. Perhaps simply the absence of commendation where commendation might have been.

The stakes are real even though salvation is secure. This is the tension the book has been holding from the beginning. Salvation by grace alone. Reward proportioned to faithfulness. Both true. Both biblical. Both pressing upon us.

The question is not whether you are building. You are. Every day, with every choice, you are constructing something on the foundation of Christ. The only question is with what materials. Are you building with gold—work that flows from Christ, depends on the Spirit, seeks God's glory, and invests in what lasts? Or are you building carelessly, without attention to what survives?

The fire will reveal what we cannot fully discern. But the aspiration shapes the building. The direction matters even when the destination remains uncertain. And God, who sees not as man sees, knows the difference between the heart that aims for gold and misses, and the heart that never aimed at all.

There is still time—still opportunity to build more carefully, still grace to begin again. And there is a mechanism: a way to convert temporal resources into eternal treasure. What we hoard here, we leave behind. What we release in faith, we may find waiting. To that alchemy we now turn.

CHAPTER 13
THE TREASURE TRANSFER

The Alchemy

The prize is clear. The proving is underway. The refining will come. One question remains: What does it look like to lay up treasure that endures? What does it look like to store wealth in heaven rather than on earth?

Chapter 12 established that the fire tests quality—only works built on Christ, empowered by the Spirit, done for God's glory, and aligned with eternal values survive. But how, practically, do we build with gold? What moves treasure from the realm that is passing to the realm that endures?

This chapter examines the alchemy—the mysterious transfer that stores treasure where it cannot be lost.

The Actual Transaction

Jesus did not speak of heavenly treasure as metaphor. He spoke of it as mechanism.

"Do not lay up for yourselves treasures on earth, where moth and rust destroy and where thieves break in and steal, but lay up for yourselves treasures in heaven, where neither moth nor rust destroys and where thieves do not break in and steal. For where your treasure is, there your heart will be also" (Matthew 6:19-21).

The command assumes the possibility. "Lay up for yourselves treasures in heaven" only makes sense if such laying up is actually possible—if there is a way to store wealth in the realm that lasts. Jesus is not offering poetic sentiment. He is describing an actual transaction.

Two locations. Two outcomes. Treasure stored on earth faces moth, rust, and thieves—the slow decay and sudden loss that mark everything in the passing age. Treasure stored in heaven faces none of these. It endures. It remains. It waits.

The logic is simple, even if the mechanics remain mysterious. What we grip here, we leave behind. Everything stored on earth stays on earth when we depart. The bank accounts, the properties, the portfolios, the possessions—all of it passes to other hands or simply passes away. We arrive at death with nothing we accumulated here.

But what we release in faith, we find waiting. The treasure stored in heaven precedes us. It is there when we arrive. The transfer happened while we were still in the interval, and the treasure accumulated in the realm where we will spend eternity.

"Where your treasure is, there your heart will be also." This is not merely observation; it is invitation. The heart follows the investment. Store treasure in heaven, and your heart will orient toward heaven. The alchemy transforms not only the treasure but the one who transfers it.

From Joy to Mechanism

In Chapter 9, we met the man who found treasure hidden in a field. We noted his joy—he was not crushed by obligation but delighted by discovery. "In his joy he goes and sells all that he has and buys that field" (Matthew 13:44). The selling was not loss. It was exchange—the lesser for the greater. He had seen what was hidden, and everything else paled in comparison.

But what did he actually do? He sold. He released. He let go of what he had in order to obtain what he had found. The joy was real, but so was the mechanism. Without the selling, the treasure remained hidden in someone else's field. The release was how the treasure became his.

This is the alchemy in miniature. The man did not lose his possessions; he converted them. He exchanged what he could not keep for what he could not lose. The treasure was already in the field—already real, already valuable, already waiting. The selling was simply how he took possession of it.

The interval of grace is that field. There is treasure hidden in the ordinary ground of our days—treasure that survives the fire, treasure that awaits in the realm that lasts. The question is whether we see it, and whether, seeing it, we are willing to exchange the lesser for the greater.

The Miscalculation

Not everyone who sees the treasure is willing to make the exchange.

A man came to Jesus with the right question. "Teacher, what good deed must I do to have eternal life?" (Matthew 19:16). He was earnest. He was seeking. He had kept the commandments from his youth. He was, by every external measure, a righteous man.

Jesus looked at him and loved him. And then Jesus named the alchemy:

"If you would be perfect, go, sell what you possess and give to the poor, and you will have treasure in heaven; and come, follow me" (Matthew 19:21).

The mechanism could not be clearer. Sell. Give. And you will have treasure in heaven. The transfer was offered explicitly. The rich young ruler was invited to exchange earthly wealth for heavenly treasure—to convert the currency of the passing age into the currency of the age to come.

He refused.

"When the young man heard this he went away sorrowful, for he had great possessions" (Matthew 19:22).

The tragedy is not that he was wealthy. The tragedy is that he chose visible treasure over invisible treasure. He kept what he could not keep—for his possessions would pass from his hands at death, whether he willed it or not. And he lost what he could not lose—for the treasure in heaven would have endured forever.

His calculation was backwards. He thought he was preserving wealth by keeping it. In fact, he was forfeiting wealth by refusing to transfer it. The treasure in heaven was offered. He walked away from it, clutching treasure on earth that was already slipping through his fingers.

The contrast with the man in the field is stark. Both were offered treasure. Both faced the same mechanism—release here to possess there. But the man in the field sold everything in joy because he had seen what was hidden. The rich young ruler walked away in sorrow because he could not—or would not—see it. He looked at his great possessions and could not imagine that something greater was being offered.

We cannot judge his eternal destiny. Scripture does not tell us whether he returned later, whether the sorrow eventually broke him open, whether he reconsidered and released. What Scripture records is the moment of refusal—the choice to grip the lesser rather than receive the greater. The story is preserved as warning, not as verdict on his soul.

But the warning is serious. The treasure in heaven was explicitly offered. The mechanism was named. And still he walked away. Great possessions can blind us to greater treasure.

Storing Up for the Future

Paul addressed those with great possessions directly. His instruction was not condemnation but redirection:

"As for the rich in this present age, charge them not to be haughty, nor to set their hopes on the uncertainty of riches, but on God, who richly provides us with everything to enjoy. They are to do good, to be rich in good works, to be generous and ready to share, thus storing up treasure for themselves as a good foundation for the future, so that they may take hold of that which is truly life" (1 Timothy 6:17-19).

The wealthy are not condemned for being wealthy. They are charged not to be haughty, not to set their hopes on uncertainty. Riches in this present age are uncertain—subject to the moth, rust, and thieves that Jesus named. The one who sets hope on uncertain riches builds on sand.

But there is another option. Be generous. Be ready to share. Do good. Be rich in good works. And in so doing, store up treasure—"a good foundation for the future."

The alchemy is named again. Generosity here becomes foundation there. The transfer is real. Something is being stored. The mechanism is the same one Jesus described: release in the present age, accumulate in the age to come.

And the purpose is profound: "so that they may take hold of that which is truly life." The treasure stored in heaven is connected to life itself—not mere existence, but the fullness of life in the presence of God. The alchemy is not about accumulating possessions in another realm. It is about positioning ourselves to receive what God offers eternally.

Paul does not explain the mechanics. He does not tell us how a generous act here becomes treasure there. He simply names the reality and invites participation. The wealthy—and all of us who have anything to give—are invited to store up treasure as a good foundation for the future.

The Alchemy of Release

The pattern is consistent across the passages. What we hoard, we leave behind. What we release in faith, we find waiting. The mechanism is release—selling, giving, loosening the grip, opening the hand.

Jesus called earthly wealth "unrighteous mammon" (Luke 16:9)—not because money is evil, but because it belongs to the present age, the age that is passing away under judgment. It is the currency of a world that will not last. The wise steward converts it before it's too late. The kiln fires. The opportunity closes. What was not transferred remains behind.

But the alchemy extends beyond money. In Chapter 11, we traced the dimensions of the proving: time, money, influence, opportunity, relationships. Each of these can be hoarded or released. Each can be stored on earth or transferred to heaven.

Time given to eternal purposes—prayer, service, discipleship, presence with those who need it—is time stored in heaven. Time consumed entirely by temporal pursuits, with no margin for kingdom investment, remains behind.

Talent deployed for God's glory—the gift exercised in faith, the skill offered in service, the ability used to build others up—becomes treasure that endures. Talent buried or used only for self-advancement stays in the ground where it was hidden.

Influence directed toward eternal ends—the platform used to point others to Christ, the relationship leveraged for someone's spiritual good, the voice raised for what matters forever—transfers to the realm that lasts.

The alchemy is not only for the wealthy. The proportional evaluation we established in Chapter 11 applies across every dimension. The widow's two copper coins—everything she had—were counted by Jesus as more than all the large sums the wealthy contributed. Heaven's ledger calculates proportionally. The question is not "How much did you give?" but "How much did you give relative to what you had? How much did you keep?"

The widow kept nothing. The wealthy kept much. By heaven's measure, she stored more treasure than they did.

This means the alchemy is available to everyone—not only those with financial margin, but anyone with time to give, talent to deploy, influence to direct, or relationships to invest in. The one with little can transfer as surely as the one with much. The proportional faithfulness matters more than the absolute amount. We cannot see the ledger. We cannot calculate another's proportion. But we can attend to our own.

And the complexity of motive applies here as well. In Chapter 12, we established that the fire tests quality—and motive is part of what determines quality. The Pharisees who gave to be seen by others received their reward in full: human applause, and nothing more. "Truly, I say to you, they have received their reward" (Matthew 6:2). The transaction was complete. The payment was rendered. Nothing remained for the fire to honor.

But the one who gives in secret, seeking God's glory rather than human recognition, stores treasure that survives the fire. "Your Father who sees in secret will reward you" (Matthew 6:4). The motive determines whether the giving is gold or hay. The same act—generosity with time, talent, or treasure—can be stored in heaven or consumed at the judgment, depending on whether it was done for God or for applause.

We acknowledged in Chapter 12 that our motives are rarely pure. The gold and hay are often mixed in the same act. We give—and something in us hopes to be noticed. We release—and something in us wants credit. This is the human condition, not yet glorified.

But the aspiration matters. Building in the direction of gold, even imperfectly, is different from building carelessly with no thought of motive at all. The heart that aims for purity and misses is not the same as the heart that never aimed. We examine ourselves, we repent where we find corruption, we ask the Spirit to purify our giving—and we trust that the fire will be more surgical than we fear, burning away the hay while preserving whatever gold was genuinely present.

We do not fully understand how the alchemy works. How does money given here become treasure stored there? How does time invested in prayer become foundation for eternity? Scripture does not explain the mechanics. The transfer remains mysterious—which is perhaps why we call it alchemy rather than transaction.

But we trust the Teacher who promised it. We give, we release, we believe something is being stored that we cannot yet see. This is faith—the conviction of things not seen. The man who bought the field could not carry the treasure home that day. He had to trust it was there, hidden beneath the ordinary ground. We trust that our giving is storing something real, even though we cannot see the ledger, cannot verify the balance, cannot confirm the transfer until we arrive and find what is waiting.

The Invitation

How, then, should we live?

The answer is not a formula. It is a posture—one of listening, releasing, and trusting.

The Spirit leads differently in different seasons and circumstances. Some are called to radical divestment—to sell all and follow, as the rich young ruler was invited to do. Others are called to faithful stewardship of ongoing resources, with generous giving woven throughout their lives. The Macedonians gave "beyond their means" (2 Corinthians 8:3). The Philippians sent support to Paul again and again (Philippians 4:16). Barnabas sold a field and laid the proceeds at the apostles' feet (Acts 4:37). Lydia opened her home (Acts 16:15). Dorcas made garments for widows (Acts 9:39). Each expressed the alchemy differently. Each was faithful.

The question is not "What is the right percentage?" or "What is my number?" The question is "What is the Spirit saying? How is he leading me to steward what he has entrusted? Where is he inviting me to release?"

Good stewardship matters. The one who provides nothing for his household has denied the faith (1 Timothy 5:8). The one who fails to plan leaves chaos for those who remain. As Proverbs teaches, wisdom builds the house while folly tears it down. The alchemy is not recklessness. It is not financial irresponsibility dressed in spiritual language.

But good stewardship is not the same as anxious accumulation. The rich fool was not condemned for having a good harvest. He was condemned for building bigger barns to hoard it, for saying to his soul "relax, eat, drink, be merry," for being rich toward himself and not toward God (Luke 12:21). The line between prudent provision and hoarding is not always clear. It requires discernment. It requires listening.

Some have found it helpful to set a lifestyle threshold—a level beyond which increases are redirected toward eternal investment. Others practice proportional giving that grows as income grows. Still others hold all resources loosely, making major decisions prayerfully as needs and opportunities arise. The expressions vary. The posture is the same: holding loosely, listening carefully, releasing freely.

The heart that grips tightly—whether gripping much or little—is not practicing the alchemy. The heart that holds loosely and releases as the Spirit leads—whether from abundance or from poverty—is storing treasure in heaven.

The invitation stands for everyone. The alchemy is not reserved for the wealthy. It is offered to anyone who has anything to give—which is everyone. Time, attention, encouragement, service, presence, prayer, talent, influence, and yes, money—all of it can be released, all of it can be transferred, all of it can become treasure stored where moth and rust do not destroy.

What Will You Store?

The alchemy is real. What we release in faith, we find waiting. What we grip in fear, we leave behind.

The man in the field sold everything and obtained the treasure. The rich young ruler kept everything and forfeited what could have been his. The same mechanism was offered to both. The difference was whether they could see what was hidden—and whether, seeing it, they were willing to exchange the lesser for the greater.

The treasure is hidden in the ordinary field of your days. The interval does not look spectacular. It looks like bank accounts and budgets and decisions about how much is enough. It looks like hours that could be given or consumed. It looks like abilities that could be deployed or buried. It looks like opportunities to give that arise and pass, and hands that could open or remain closed.

But there is treasure to be stored. Treasure that moth and rust cannot destroy. Treasure that thieves cannot steal. Treasure that fire cannot burn.

The alchemy is available. The mechanism is release. The invitation stands.

Part III has traced the theology of doing: the prize that awaits, the proving that qualifies, the refining that tests, the alchemy that transfers. The doing matters. It matters eternally. What we do with what we have been given shapes what we will have forever.

But a question remains. We have spoken throughout this book of the two pillars—doing and becoming. Part II traced the theology of becoming: who we are being formed into across the interval. Part III has traced the theology of doing: what we do with what we have been given. But how do these pillars relate? Are they parallel tracks, or something more?

The answer is integration. The doing shapes the becoming. The one who gives generously is becoming a generous person—forming the soul that will steward eternal treasure. The one who releases freely is becoming free—loosening the grip that would otherwise bind. The one who serves faithfully is becoming faithful—developing the character that qualifies for greater entrustment.

And the becoming enables the doing. The generous soul finds the next act of generosity easier, more natural, more joyful. The faithful character can be trusted with more. The servant heart delights in serving. Character enables action; action forms character. The spiral ascends.

This is not two separate processes running side by side. It is one integrated reality. The alchemy transforms not only the treasure but the one who transfers it. The doing and the becoming are woven together in every faithful act.

The prize awaits. The proving is underway. The refining will come. The alchemy is available. And the two pillars—doing and becoming—are not parallel tracks but a single ascending spiral, each enabling the other, both shaping the soul that will live forever.

But we have not yet asked how heaven calculates the value of all this faithfulness. We have spoken of treasure stored, of works tested, of character formed. But by what measure does heaven weigh these things? The answer may surprise us: heaven's economy operates by laws entirely different from earth's. What looks small here may prove immense there. What impresses the world may register as nothing in the eternal ledger. And the currency that transfers most fully is not gold or achievement but something far more precious.

To that economy we now turn.

PART FOUR
HEAVEN'S ECONOMY
CHAPTERS 14–17

CHAPTER 14
THE GREAT INVERSION

Jesus Christ our Lord surrendered in order that He might win; He destroyed His enemies by dying for them and conquered death by allowing death to conquer Him. — A. W. Tozer

Every kingdom operates by laws. Drop an object in this kingdom and it falls. Release heat and it rises. Plant a seed and, given water and sun, it grows. These are not arbitrary rules imposed from outside. They are the physics of how reality operates here.

The Kingdom of Heaven also operates by laws. But they are not ours.

In heaven's kingdom, what you release, you keep. What you cling to, you lose. The way up is down. The path to fullness runs through emptying. Death is the mechanism of life. These are not paradoxes designed to puzzle the mind or moral exhortations meant to humble the proud. They are the physics of how reality operates there—and increasingly here, as heaven's rule breaks into the present age.

We have arrived at Part IV of this book: Heaven's Economy. The phrase itself suggests something transactional—investments, returns, ledgers, calculations. And there is indeed a ledger. There are indeed returns. But before we can understand heaven's accounting, we must grasp something more fundamental: heaven's economy isn't a reward system layered on top of earthly reality. It is the actual operating system of the universe, temporarily obscured by sin, fully revealed in Christ, and now to be learned and lived during the interval of grace.

The inversions Jesus taught are not exceptions to the rules. They are the rules.

Heaven Has Different Physics

We stood at the temple treasury in Chapter 11, watching the widow drop her two copper coins. There we saw proportional evaluation—God measuring her faithfulness against her capacity, not against the wealthy donors beside her. But look again at Jesus' words, and see something more.

He did not say her gift was "proportionally equivalent." He said she gave more: "Truly, I say to you, this poor widow has put in more than all those who are contributing to the offering box" (Mark 12:43).

More. Two copper coins outweigh the accumulated gold. This is not poetry. It is accounting. Heaven has a different ledger.

Chapter 11 asked: "How does God evaluate?" The answer was proportional faithfulness—each measured against their own capacity. This chapter asks a different question: "What does heaven's ledger actually record?" And the answer is inversion. The widow's coins did not merely equal the wealthy donors' gold when adjusted for capacity. They exceeded it. In earthly calculation, their gifts were larger by every measurable standard. In heaven's calculation, hers was larger by the only standard that matters.

Consider another scene. Jesus is sending out his disciples, warning them of the hardships ahead, and then offers this assurance: "Whoever gives one of these little ones even a cup of cold water because he is a disciple, truly, I say to you, he will by no means lose his reward" (Matthew 10:42).

A cup of cold water. An act so small it registers nowhere on any earthly ledger. No monument commemorates it. No biography records it. Perhaps even the giver forgets it by evening. Yet Jesus guarantees—"by no means"—that the reward is secure. What is invisible to earth is visible to heaven. What is negligible here is weighty there.

And then there are the Beatitudes, that strange catalog of blessings pronounced over the last people the world would call blessed. "Blessed are the poor in spirit, for theirs is the kingdom of heaven. Blessed are those who mourn, for they shall be comforted. Blessed are the meek, for they shall inherit the earth" (Matthew 5:3-5). The grammar matters: Blessed *are*—not "will be," but "are." Present tense. The poor in spirit are blessed now, even if their circumstances suggest otherwise. Heaven's verdict has already been rendered, and it contradicts the verdict of the world.

Earth says: acquire, ascend, assert. Heaven says: release, descend, surrender. Earth honors the powerful, the prominent, the prosperous. Heaven honors the poor in spirit, the mourning, the meek. "The last will be first, and the first last" (Matthew 20:16)—not as occasional reversal but as governing principle.

These are not scattered sayings. They form a pattern. And the pattern points to a principle: heaven calculates differently because heaven *operates* differently. The question is: why?

The Christological Center: Kenosis as the Master Pattern

The inversions are not arbitrary. They reflect the very character of God as revealed in Jesus Christ. To understand why heaven's physics work the way they do, we must look to the One in whom heaven's reality became flesh.

Paul captures it in what scholars call the "Christ hymn" of Philippians 2: "Have this mind among yourselves, which is yours in Christ Jesus, who, though he was in the form of God, did not count equality with God a thing to be grasped, but emptied himself, by taking the form of a servant, being born in the likeness of men. And being found in human form, he humbled himself by becoming obedient to the point of death, even death on a cross. *Therefore* God has highly exalted him and bestowed on him the name that is above every name." (Philippians 2:5–9)

The word translated "emptied" is the Greek *ekenōsen*—from which we get "kenosis." It means to pour out, to empty, to make void. Christ Jesus, who existed in the form of God, did not cling to the prerogatives of deity but poured himself out, taking the form of a servant, accepting the humiliation of human flesh, submitting even to death on a cross.

But the crucial word is "therefore." *Therefore* God has highly exalted him. The exaltation is not compensation for the emptying—as if God felt sorry for what Jesus endured and decided to make it up to him. The exaltation is the *result* of the emptying. It is the consequence, the fruit, the inevitable outcome when reality operates as it was designed to operate. Christ emptied himself, and *therefore* he was exalted. The emptying was not the price of exaltation. It was the *mechanism*.

This is not unique to the incarnation. It is the pattern of divine operation. The incarnation itself: God becoming human is not subtraction from deity but its supreme expression. The cross: apparent defeat is actual victory. The resurrection: death is the mechanism of life. These are not exceptions to normal reality, special cases where God suspended the usual rules. They are revelations of how reality actually works under God's rule—how it always worked, how it was designed to work, how it will work forever.

Theologians debate the precise meaning of kenosis—what exactly Christ "emptied" himself of, whether divine attributes were laid aside or merely veiled. But the essential point is this: God's power is qualitatively different from human power. Christ did not relinquish his divine power; rather, he expressed this power in the weakness of his humanity.

The emptying *was* the power. The descent *was* the victory. The death *was* the life.

And here is the implication that presses upon us: "Have this mind among yourselves, which is yours in Christ Jesus." We are not merely told to admire the pattern. We are called to adopt it. The inversions are not demands laid upon us from outside, imposed by a God whose ways are simply inscrutable. They are invitations to operate by the logic that governs ultimate reality—the logic revealed in Christ, written into the fabric of creation, destined to govern the new heavens and new earth forever.

The Philosophical Depth: Simone Weil and the Art of Decreation

The kenosis of Christ illuminates the pattern. But certain thinkers have traced its implications further than most. One voice in particular—largely unknown to evangelical readers—saw with unusual clarity what self-emptying means for the human soul.

Simone Weil was a French philosopher and mystic who lived only thirty-four years, dying in 1943 during the Second World War. Jewish by birth, she was drawn irresistibly to Christ yet never formally joined the church—standing at the threshold, she said, because she could not bear to leave anyone outside. She wrote in the margin between philosophy and theology, with a rigor that unsettles comfortable categories. And she coined a term that illuminates the inversion from an unexpected angle: *décréation*—decreation.

Weil observed that God created by withdrawing. The universe exists because God made space for it—limiting himself, as it were, so that something other than God could be. Creation is an act of divine self-limitation, a kenosis before the kenosis of Christ. And human beings participate in God's nature by imitating this withdrawal—by "decreating" the grasping self that wants to expand, to consume, to fill every available space with its own presence.

In her notebooks, published posthumously as *Gravity and Grace*, Weil captured it starkly: "We possess nothing in the world—a mere chance can strip us of everything—except the power to say 'I.' That is what we have to give to God—in other words, to destroy."

The "I"—the grasping ego, the self that asserts and acquires and clings—this is what must be surrendered. Not destroyed, as if we were to disappear into nothingness. But yielded. Released. Offered back to the One who gave it. This is decreation: making room for God by unmaking the self that crowds God out.

And here is the inversion at its sharpest: "We only possess what we renounce. What we do not renounce escapes from us."

Read that again. We only possess what we renounce. The thing grasped slips away; the thing released remains. What feels like loss is actually the precondition of possession. What feels like diminishment is actually the mechanism of enlargement. The inversions are not compensations for sacrifice, as if God rewards those who give things up with equivalent goods in return. They are revelations of how reality actually works. Renunciation *is* possession, rightly understood. Emptying *is* filling, rightly perceived.

Weil offers one more insight that cuts to the heart of our situation: sin itself is an inversion. We have the order upside-down. We are born into a world where the hierarchy is reversed—grasping when we should release, ascending when we should descend, clinging when we should surrender.

Sin itself is an inversion. We have the order upside-down. We grasp when we should release. We cling when we should surrender. We ascend when we should descend. The Kingdom inversions that feel so counterintuitive to us are not strange at all. They are reality restored. They are things set right. What feels backward is actually forward. What feels like losing is actually finding. We are the ones who are inverted; Christ comes to turn us right-side up.

The eighteenth-century German mystic Gerhard Tersteegen, a man who gave up worldly success to live in radical simplicity and service, drew the contrast starkly: "An ungodly person is one who is detached from God and cleaves to himself and the creature; a godly person is one who is detached from himself and the creature, and adheres to God with all affection. His whole heart says to all that is not God, 'I am not for you, and you are not for me.'"

Detached from God, cleaving to self: this is the inverted life. Detached from self, cleaving to God: this is reality restored. And the movement from one to the other is what happens during the interval of grace.

THE INTERVAL

The Mechanism: The Grain of Wheat

Philosophy and theology illuminate the pattern. But Jesus offered an image so simple that a child could grasp it—and so profound that the wisest have not exhausted its meaning.

Greeks have come to Jerusalem seeking Jesus. The Gentile world is arriving at his doorstep. Rather than welcoming them with a speech or a miracle, Jesus offers a strange announcement: "The hour has come for the Son of Man to be glorified" (John 12:23). And then, immediately: "Truly, truly, I say to you, unless a grain of wheat falls into the earth and dies, it remains alone; but if it dies, it bears much fruit" (John 12:24).

A grain of wheat. His first-century hearers knew this viscerally. A grain kept in a jar remains a single grain indefinitely—preserved, intact, but sterile. The same grain planted in the soil—buried, broken open, destroyed as a grain—becomes a stalk, multiple heads, dozens of grains per head. One seed yields eighty or a hundred.

The multiplication is not despite the death. It is *through* the death. The death is not the price of new life, paid reluctantly and then compensated. The death is the *mechanism* of new life, the process by which multiplication occurs. Without the dying, the grain "remains alone." Through the dying, it "bears much fruit."

Jesus is speaking of himself. He is the grain of wheat. His death is not tragedy but mechanism—the process by which the harvest of human salvation becomes possible. He could have chosen not to die. He could have entered heaven by his own perfect righteousness, alone in his glory. But then no sinner could have followed. The harvest required the dying.

But Jesus does not stop with himself. The very next verse extends the logic to his followers: "Whoever loves his life loses it, and whoever hates his life in this world will keep it for eternal life" (John 12:25). The pattern that governs Christ governs those who belong to him. We too must be planted. We too must die to ourselves. The grain of wheat that insists on remaining intact—on preserving its form, protecting its boundaries, maintaining its self-sufficient existence—remains alone.

The grain that falls into the ground and dies becomes fruitful beyond measure.

A. W. Tozer captures what this means in practice: "The man with a cross no longer controls his destiny; he lost control when he picked up his cross. That cross immediately became to him an all-absorbing interest, an overwhelming interference. No matter what he may desire to do, there is but one thing he can do; that is, move on toward the place of crucifixion."

The cross is not a decoration or a metaphor. It is an instrument of death—and therefore, in heaven's economy, an instrument of life. The way of the cross is the way of the grain of wheat: falling into the ground, dying to what we were, and bearing fruit we could never have imagined while we clung to our intact, sterile, solitary existence.

The Master Inversion: Lose Your Life to Find It

The grain of wheat illustrates the mechanism. But Jesus stated the principle in its starkest form elsewhere—the master inversion that governs all others.

Peter has just confessed Jesus as the Christ, the Son of the living God. Jesus has blessed him for this revelation. And then, for the first time, Jesus begins to tell his disciples what being the Christ will mean: suffering, rejection, death, resurrection. Peter rebukes him—"Far be it from you, Lord! This shall never happen to you." And Jesus turns on Peter with words that still shock: "Get behind me, Satan! You are a hindrance to me. For you are not setting your mind on the things of God, but on the things of man" (Matthew 16:22-23).

The things of man. Peter was thinking in earthly physics—where suffering is to be avoided, death is defeat, and self-preservation is wisdom. Jesus was operating by heavenly physics—where the path to glory runs through the cross. To reject the cross was to think like men, not like God. It was to be aligned with Satan, not with the Father.

And then comes the teaching that presses upon everyone who would follow: "If anyone would come after me, let him deny himself and take up his cross and follow me. For whoever would save his life will lose it, but whoever loses his life for my sake will find it. For what will it profit a man if he gains the whole world and forfeits his soul?" (Matthew 16:24-26).

This is the master inversion. It encompasses all the others. The widow's mite? She lost her livelihood to gain eternal treasure. First becoming last? Those who seek position lose it; those who release it receive it. The kenosis? Christ emptied himself and was therefore exalted. All are instances of this single pattern: *life through death, fullness through emptying, finding through losing.*

The word translated "life" is the Greek *psyche*—soul, self, the whole person. This is not merely about physical survival. It is about selfhood—who you are, your identity, your being. The paradox cuts to the deepest level: grasping for self destroys self; releasing self for Christ's sake discovers self. The one who clutches their identity, protecting it, defending it, building it on their own terms, will find it slipping away. The one who surrenders their identity to Christ will find it given back—but transformed, enlarged, established on foundations that cannot be shaken.

Tozer described the Christian as one who "empties himself in order that he might be full, admits that he is wrong so he can be declared right, goes down in order to get up." The logic of heaven runs counter to every instinct formed by life in a fallen world. And yet it is the only logic that leads to life.

"What will it profit a man if he gains the whole world and forfeits his soul?" The question hangs in the air. Earth says: gain the world. Acquire, accumulate, achieve. Heaven says: the whole world is not worth your soul—and the way to gain your soul is to lose it for Christ's sake. The accounting is so different that what looks like profit on one ledger appears as loss on the other. And only one ledger endures.

The Formation: Learning Eternal Physics Now

We have traced the inversion through Scripture, christology, philosophy, and image. But one question remains: What does all this mean for us now, in this brief span called the interval of grace?

The answer is formation. The inversions are not merely principles to understand but a way of being to inhabit. Each act of surrender, each choice to release rather than grasp, each decision to go down rather than up, forms us. We are not simply learning about heaven's physics. We are *becoming* people who naturally operate by them.

This formation can only happen here—in the interval, where the inversions cost something. In eternity, everyone will see that emptying leads to fullness. The reality will be self-evident. But here, in this age, we must believe it without seeing. We must act on kingdom physics while still feeling the pull of earthly physics. We must release while every instinct screams to grasp.

This is why the interval is irreplaceable. Faith, as we have seen in earlier chapters, can only be exercised in conditions of uncertainty. Trust requires circumstances where the outcome is not guaranteed. Surrender costs something only when what is surrendered feels valuable. The very difficulty of living by heaven's physics in an earthbound world is what makes this time formative. We are becoming people for whom the inversions will feel natural—not because we have figured them out intellectually, but because we have practiced them until they have become second nature.

Those who have practiced kingdom physics here will be at home when they arrive there. The logic will be familiar. The economy will make sense. They will not arrive as strangers trying to learn a foreign language but as citizens returning to their native land.

Those who have spent their earthly lives operating by earthly physics will arrive disoriented. Everything will be backward from what they learned. First will be last. The poor in spirit will be rich. The servant will be greatest. They will be saved—if they belong to Christ, they will be saved. But they will arrive as foreigners to an economy they never learned to navigate.

C. S. Lewis captured the weight of this in a passage from *The Weight of Glory*: "The load, or weight, or burden of my neighbour's glory should be laid daily on my back, a load so heavy that only humility can carry it, and the backs of the proud will be broken." The proud—those who operate by earthly physics, who grasp and ascend and assert—will find the weight of glory crushing. The humble—

those who have learned to empty and descend and surrender—will carry glory the way they were made to carry it.

Tersteegen wrote a hymn that has been called "The Pilgrim Song," and in it he captures what it means to live by kingdom physics now:

> *O children, was it sorrow?*
> *Though thousand worlds be lost,*
> *Our eyes have looked on Jesus,*
> *And thus we count the cost.*

A thousand worlds lost—and no sorrow. Because our eyes have looked on Jesus. Because we have seen the One who emptied himself and was therefore exalted. Because we have understood that loss is gain, death is life, surrender is victory. We count the cost and find it no cost at all—or rather, a cost so swallowed up in gain that it ceases to register as loss.

> *To speed, unburdened pilgrims,*
> *Glad, empty-handed, free;*
> *To cross the trackless deserts,*
> *And walk upon the sea.*

Glad, empty-handed, free. This is the fruit of decreation—the soul that has released its grip and found, to its astonishment, that empty hands can hold more than full ones ever could. This is life lived by kingdom physics, where the unburdened pilgrim travels faster than the one weighed down with possessions, where empty hands are free to receive what clutching hands could never grasp.

The Law Established

The law has been established. Heaven's economy operates by inversion —what is released is kept; what is grasped is lost; death is the mechanism of life; emptying is the precondition of fullness. This is not moral paradox but operating principle. It is how reality works when eternity governs.

Heaven's economy isn't a reward system layered on top of earthly reality. It is the actual operating system of the universe, temporarily obscured by sin, fully revealed in Christ, and now to be learned and lived during the interval of grace.

The remaining chapters of Part IV apply this principle to specific domains. What does heaven's economy value most highly? What does its ledger record? How does eternal return compound over time?

We begin with the investment that yields the most striking return. If the inversion is true—if we only possess what we renounce—then what actually persists through death? Not gold or accomplishment or legacy in the ordinary sense. Material wealth stops at the threshold. But there is one earthly reality that shares heaven's permanence: persons. The people we invest in—discipled, encouraged, served, loved toward Christ—cross over with us. They are not merely the fruit of our labor. They are, Paul says, our crown. Our glory and joy. The treasure that has faces and names.

To that currency we now turn.

CHAPTER 15
THE CURRENCY OF SOULS

The Only Treasure That Comes With Us

Everything material stops at death's door.

Egyptian pharaohs filled their tombs with gold, chariots, servants' statues, even boats for the celestial journey. None of it accompanied them anywhere. The elaborate preparations only enriched whoever eventually opened the tomb. What the kings clung to, they lost. What they hoarded, they left behind for strangers.

The same law governs every human crossing. Portfolios stay behind. Property stays behind. The carefully constructed empire of possessions dissolves at the threshold no one avoids. "Naked I came from my mother's womb, and naked shall I return" (Job 1:21). The billionaire and the beggar cross over equally unburdened by material wealth.

And yet Jesus speaks of treasure that transfers: "Lay up for yourselves treasures in heaven, where neither moth nor rust destroys and where thieves do not break in and steal" (Matthew 6:20). Some currency works in both economies. Some investment survives the crossing. The question is not whether treasure can transfer but what kind.

The answer emerges through elimination. Not material wealth—moth and rust consume it. Not earthly accomplishments—fame fades faster than memory. Not even good works as such—the deeds themselves are temporal acts in temporal space, however lasting their record. What remains is the only thing on earth that shares heaven's immortality: transformed persons. Human souls. People brought into righteousness, redirected toward God, made alive in Christ.

This is the currency that crosses over. This is the only export from earth to heaven.

You Are Our Crown

The claim sounds familiar—invest in people, not things. But Scripture says something more startling than that worn counsel suggests.

Paul writes to the Thessalonians with an intensity that strains language: "For what is our hope or joy or crown of boasting before our Lord Jesus at his coming? Is it not you? For you are our glory and joy" (1 Thessalonians 2:19-20). The construction demands careful attention. Paul does not say the Thessalonians will *bring* him a crown. He does not say they will *earn* him reward. He says they *are* his crown. They *are* his glory and joy.

The Greek *stephanos* was the victory wreath—the crown given to athletes, soldiers, and honored citizens. In Macedonia, these crowns were woven from oak leaves. The victor didn't receive a crown *in addition to* his achievement; the crown *was* the visible form of his achievement. Paul borrows this image and transforms it: when I stand before Christ at his appearing, you are the oak leaves. You are the trophy. The reward is not *for* the souls I helped bring home. The souls themselves *are* the reward.

This is not transactional but relational. The treasure we lay up in heaven isn't stored in celestial vaults. It walks, speaks, worships alongside us forever. Our eternal wealth isn't counted in units of heavenly currency but measured in the presence of those we helped bring home. The crown has faces. The treasure has names.

Paul makes the same astonishing claim to the Philippians:

"Therefore, my brothers, whom I love and long for, my joy and crown, stand firm thus in the Lord, my beloved" (Philippians 4:1). Joy and crown. The believers themselves constitute his eternal wealth—not a representation of it, not a symbol pointing toward it, but the thing itself.

Richard Baxter would have understood. When Baxter arrived in Kidderminster in 1641, the small English town showed little evidence of spiritual life. "There was about one family in a street that worshiped God," he later recalled. He preached with ferocious urgency: "I preached as never sure to preach again, and as a dying man to dying men." He spent two days each week, seven hours each day, meeting with families one hour at a time—systematic, relentless investment in souls. By the time he was ejected in 1661, the town had transformed. "There were some streets where there was not one family that did not worship God."

Those families—those transformed households that worshiped God where before they had been indifferent—constitute Baxter's eternal wealth. They are his crown. They crossed over with him.

Shining Like Stars Forever

Daniel saw this principle blazing across the eschatological horizon.

"And those who are wise shall shine like the brightness of the sky above; and those who turn many to righteousness, like the stars forever and ever" (Daniel 12:3).

The Hebrew repays attention. *Zohar* means radiance, splendor, brilliant shining—not reflected light but intrinsic luminosity. This word became the title of the most influential mystical Jewish text, the *Zohar*, suggesting depths of divine illumination beyond ordinary comprehension. Those who are wise will possess this radiance, shining like the vast brightness of the sky itself.

But a second category receives specific attention: "those who turn many to righteousness." The Hebrew phrase *matsdike harabim* is causative—those who *cause* many to become righteous, who actively participate in others' transformation. These don't merely shine; they shine *like the stars forever and ever.*

The astronomical distinction matters. Stars don't shine equally. The sun is a star, but so is Rigel, which burns a hundred thousand times brighter. Those who turn many to righteousness receive individual, distinctive, eternal radiance. The souls they influenced become embedded in their glory.

And the duration is emphasized with the strongest Hebrew idiom for permanence: *le'olam va'ed*—forever and ever, perpetuity without end. This isn't temporary recognition at a celestial ceremony. It is permanent luminosity. The radiance never dims. The stars never fade. What was gained through investment in souls remains gained across all the ages that follow.

Here is the great inversion we established in the previous chapter, applied to its most potent form. In earthly economy, expending yourself for others depletes you. In kingdom physics, expending yourself for others multiplies your glory. The more you pour out, the brighter you shine—forever.

The Chain That Extends

Paul compressed four generations into a single verse.

"What you have heard from me in the presence of many witnesses entrust to faithful men, who will be able to teach others also" (2 Timothy 2:2).

Four links in the chain: Paul, Timothy, faithful men, others. The investment doesn't terminate in the person directly reached. It flows through them to the next generation, and through that generation to the next. The soul-winner participates in every link of the chain that extends from their investment.

C.T. Studd understood this extension. He was one of England's most famous cricketers—a celebrated Test player whose name was known throughout the country. He gave away his entire inheritance (equivalent to several million pounds today) and spent his life on mission fields in China, India, and finally the heart of Africa. "Some wish to live within the sound of Church or Chapel bell," he wrote. "I want to run a rescue shop within a yard of hell."

Studd grasped what his contemporaries missed. Cricket championships stay behind. Batting records fade from memory within a generation. But souls travel forward. Each person he reached who reached another who reached another extended a chain that continues still. His crown continues to grow oak leaves.

The principle is not complicated: invest in what perishes, and your investment perishes with it. Invest in what endures, and your investment endures with it. Human souls are the only earthly reality that shares heaven's permanence. Investment in souls is therefore the only investment that transcends the grave.

George Whitefield preached with this clarity burning in his chest. He delivered over eighteen thousand sermons to an estimated ten million hearers across Britain and America. "If your souls were not immortal, and you in danger of losing them, I would not thus speak unto you," he cried. "But the love of your souls constrains me to speak: methinks this would constrain me to speak unto you forever." He rode sixty miles in a day, preached two or three times, then rode through the night to his next stop. His body was wracked with illness his entire ministry. When friends urged him to slow down, he had a ready answer: "I would rather wear out than rust out."

The urgency was not anxiety but clarity. Whitefield saw what his comfort-seeking contemporaries could not: the stakes were eternal, the window was brief, and souls were the only currency that would cross over.

Companions for Eternity

But there is a dimension to this investment that most treatments miss. The familiar framework suggests we give and others receive. The biblical vision is more reciprocal: we become *companions* for eternity. We don't just help them arrive; we travel together forever.

The "with" language saturates Scripture's vision of eternal life. "And so we will always be with the Lord" (1 Thessalonians 4:17). Jesus prays "that they also, whom you have given me, may be with me where I am" (John 17:24). The souls we influence aren't notches on a heavenly belt or entries in a celestial ledger. They are the people we will worship alongside, work alongside, explore alongside across endless ages. The relationship that began in temporal investment becomes eternal companionship.

This transforms how we see the people around us. C.S. Lewis caught the weight of this in his famous meditation: "There are no ordinary people. You have never talked to a mere mortal. Nations, cultures, arts, civilizations—these are mortal, and their life is to ours as the life of a gnat. But it is immortals whom we joke with, work with, marry, snub, and exploit."

Every person is a potential eternal companion. The annoying coworker, the difficult neighbor, the seemingly insignificant stranger—each one an immortal being whose trajectory might be influenced by our investment. If even one of them crosses over because of something we said, something we did, something we were, they become part of our eternal community. They are not merely beneficiaries of our generosity but companions in our glory.

The Investor Is Formed

And here is the deeper truth that completes the circle: investing in souls forms the investor.

The familiar framework suggests we form others through our investment. True enough. But the deeper reality is that investing in souls *transforms us*. The teacher learns more than the student. The discipler is shaped by discipling. The one who pours out is filled in the pouring.

When you invest in a soul, several things happen to *you*. You learn to see people as God sees them—eternal beings rather than interruptions. You learn to value what God values—the one sheep becomes worth leaving the ninety-nine. You learn to expend yourself without calculating return. You practice heaven's economics *now*, making yourself fluent in the language of the coming kingdom.

This is itself eternal formation. Those who develop the capacity to value souls, to invest in persons, to see with heaven's eyes—they are being formed into the kind of people who will thrive in a kingdom where every relationship carries eternal weight.

Baxter was transformed by his years of systematic soul-care.

THE INTERVAL

Whitefield was shaped by his eighteen thousand sermons into someone who could honestly say "the love of your souls constrains me to speak." The decades of soul-labor formed *them* into people utterly at home in a kingdom where souls are the only currency that matters.

The *interval of grace* accomplishes this work. Here, in this brief window, we have opportunity to develop capacities that cannot be developed elsewhere. In eternity, the value of souls will be self-evident. Everyone will see clearly. But here, in this age, investing in souls costs something. It requires faith. It means choosing invisible eternal return over visible temporal comfort. Those who make that choice repeatedly, who discipline themselves to value what heaven values when the valuation is not yet obvious, are being formed into people prepared for their eternal home.

Those who never develop this capacity—who spend their earthly years accumulating what cannot cross over while neglecting what can—will arrive in heaven disoriented. Saved, yes. Present, certainly. But foreign to an economy they never learned, unfamiliar with a currency they never handled, strangers to the companions they might have traveled with forever.

Living as People Who Believe This

The application is not complicated, however challenging its execution.

If souls are the only currency that transfers, every person becomes an eternal opportunity. The conversation at the coffee shop, the patience with a difficult family member, the witness to a skeptical colleague, the investment in a young believer's formation—each one carries potential eternal weight. Not every investment will yield visible return. Some seeds fall on rocky soil. But the faithful investor keeps planting because the one seed that takes root in good soil produces a harvest that outlasts the stars.

If souls are our eternal crown, accumulation of assets must serve that larger purpose. Money is not evil, but it is temporary—a tool for eternal purposes rather than an end in itself. Studd gave away his fortune not from ascetic self-denial but from clear-eyed eternal accounting. He calculated what his wealth could accomplish for souls and concluded that no earthly use could match that return.

If souls are our eternal companions, urgency is appropriate. Not anxiety—the work is God's, and he will accomplish his purposes. But clarity about what matters. Baxter preached "as a dying man to dying men" because he grasped what his casual contemporaries missed: time is brief, souls are eternal, and the window for investment will close.

The mature Christian who has heard these truths for decades may wonder what remains to be learned. Perhaps this: knowing the principle and living the principle are separated by a vast chasm that only practice can bridge. It is one thing to affirm that souls matter eternally. It is another to structure your life, your time, your resources, your attention around that affirmation. The interval of grace exists precisely for that practice—not merely to inform us of eternal realities but to form us into people who live as though we believe them.

The Ledger Beyond Our Sight

Chapter 14 established that heaven operates by inverse logic—the upside-down physics of a kingdom where emptying leads to fullness and losing leads to finding. This chapter has named the currency that matters in that economy: transformed souls. People brought into righteousness. Companions for eternity. The living treasure that crosses death's threshold with us.

But a question presses forward. If souls are the currency, what determines the *value* of our contribution? Two people might invest in souls with equal hours and apparent effort. Yet Jesus suggests their eternal credit differs dramatically. The widow's two coins outweighed the wealthy donors' gold. A cup of cold water given in Jesus' name earns eternal remembrance while elaborate gifts may be forgotten.

Heaven's ledger records something other than observable metrics. It weighs not just what we do but *why* we do it—the hidden motives, the unseen faithfulness, the secret sacrifices that no human eye notices but God sees with perfect clarity.

To that hidden ledger we now turn.

CHAPTER 16
THE HIDDEN LEDGER

The Double Books

Every major organization maintains multiple ledgers. The public financial statements display one set of numbers for stakeholders—the polished figures suitable for annual reports and investor presentations. The internal books record another set entirely—the actual operations, the adjustments, the complexities invisible to outside observers. Auditors know the two rarely match perfectly. Sometimes the discrepancy reveals fraud. More often it simply reveals reality that external observers cannot access.

With eternal matters, the discrepancy is more radical still. Earth keeps one ledger. Heaven keeps another. And the two accounting systems operate by principles so different that their results diverge dramatically.

Earth's ledger records the visible metrics: donations logged, hours volunteered, services rendered, platforms built, followers accumulated, recognition received. These are the numbers we can count, the achievements we can measure, the contributions that appear in newsletters and on donor walls. Heaven's ledger records something else entirely: motive weighed, sacrifice measured, heart examined, relationship cultivated. The same transaction that registers impressively in one system may barely appear in the other—or may register with inverted valuations.

Jesus once sat opposite the temple treasury and watched people deposit their offerings. The wealthy gave large sums that registered impressively on earth's ledger—the kind of contributions that fund building projects and earn naming rights. A widow approached and dropped in two copper coins. The amount was negligible. In any annual report, her gift would round to zero. No temple administrator would have recorded it as significant.

But Jesus rendered a verdict that exposed the discrepancy between ledgers: she gave more than all of them combined.

Same treasury. Same day. Same observable transactions. Radically different valuations.

We established in the previous chapter that souls are the currency that transfers into eternity—that our investment in people is the treasure we are storing in heaven. But two people can invest in souls with equal hours and apparent effort, yet receive dramatically different eternal credit. Heaven weighs not just what we do but why we do it, not just what we give but what it costs us, not just how we serve but who we are when no one sees—and who we are becoming in the hidden relationship with God that shapes everything else.

This chapter opens the hidden ledger.

Paid in Full

Matthew 6:1-18 is usually read as ethical instruction: don't show off when you give, pray, or fast. The teaching seems straightforward enough—avoid religious performance, practice sincere devotion. But Jesus uses a term that reveals mechanism, not mere morality. Understanding that term transforms the entire passage.

Three times Jesus says of those who practice righteousness publicly: "They have received their reward." The phrase sounds like a simple statement of fact. But the Greek verb—*apechousin*—was a technical term from commercial transactions. *Apecho* was the word written on receipts to indicate "paid in full." When a debt was settled completely, when nothing remained outstanding, the creditor wrote *apecho* across the account. The balance was zero. The transaction was closed.

Jesus is not merely cautioning against hypocrisy. He is describing a mechanism. Human praise literally functions as payment. When you receive applause, recognition, admiration for your religious performance—the transaction is complete. The account is closed. Nothing transfers to heaven's ledger because earth's ledger already shows "paid in full."

This is not metaphor. It is mechanism.

The Pharisee who prays loudly on the street corner and receives admiring glances has cashed his check. The donor who gives with fanfare and receives public recognition has collected his return. The faster who wears suffering on his face and earns a reputation for piety has already been compensated. *Apecho*—paid in full. The account is settled. Nothing remains to transfer.

Jesus traces this pattern through giving, praying, and fasting—the three core expressions of Jewish piety. In each case, the dynamic is identical. Those who "sound the trumpet" when they give, who pray "standing in the synagogues and at the street corners to be seen," who disfigure their faces to display their fasting—these have received their reward. The verb is emphatic: they have it in full. There is no outstanding balance.

But for those who give in secret, who pray behind a closed door, who fast with anointed head and washed face so that no one knows—for these, a different verb applies. "Your Father who sees in secret will reward you." The verb here is *apodidomi*—He will repay, He will render what is owed. This is future payment pending, an account still open, a transaction not yet complete.

Two entirely different economies. *Apecho* for those who collect human approval: paid in full, account closed, nothing pending. *Apodidomi* for those who wait for the Father's reward: payment coming, account active, transaction ongoing.

One payment terminates at death. The other commences at resurrection.

Notice Jesus' repeated phrase: "Your Father who sees in secret." The hiddenness is not ultimately about location—it is about audience. The Father sees what no camera captures, records what no observer notices, weighs what no metric can measure. And His payments are rendered in currency that survives the grave.

This is the hidden ledger—the accounting system only God operates.

The Heart the Lord Sees

When Samuel arrived in Bethlehem to anoint one of Jesse's sons as the next king of Israel, he expected the selection to be obvious. When tall, impressive Eliab walked in—commanding presence, leadership material, kingly stature—Samuel thought: "Surely the LORD's anointed stands here."

God's response exposes the ledger discrepancy: "Do not look on his appearance or on the height of his stature, because I have rejected him. For the LORD sees not as man sees: man looks on the outward appearance, but the LORD looks on the heart."

Seven sons passed before Samuel—each evaluated, each rejected. Finally, almost as an afterthought, Jesse mentioned the youngest was in the fields tending sheep. So overlooked was David that his own father had not invited him to the selection ceremony. Earth's ledger didn't record him at all. Heaven's ledger had already circled his name.

The principle extends beyond this single story. God's selection criteria are hidden from human assessment. What impresses us may not impress Him. What disqualifies someone in our eyes may be irrelevant to His. Samuel saw commanding presence; God saw a heart He could not use. Samuel overlooked the shepherd boy; God saw the king.

Luke 16:15 states the inversion bluntly: "What is exalted among men is an abomination in the sight of God." This is not hyperbole. The value systems are not merely different—they are inverted. What impresses people may repel God. What people ignore may be precisely what God celebrates.

The anonymous prayer warrior in the back pew. The faithful mother whose investment in her children's souls will never appear on any platform. The quiet believer who does ordinary work with extraordinary love. Earth's ledger may not record them at all. Heaven's ledger may record them above those whose names everyone knows.

We cannot read hearts. Only God sees with perfect clarity. But we can attend to our own hearts—and trust that the One who evaluates knows the full truth we cannot even tell ourselves.

The Calculus of Sacrifice

The widow's mite principle we traced in Chapter 11 applies here with fresh force—but now we see the mechanism behind it. Jesus said her two copper coins exceeded all the large sums the wealthy contributed. Not proportionally greater. Absolutely greater. The Greek word is *pleion*: more. By heaven's mathematics, negligible coins outweighed bags of gold.

Why? The wealthy gave from surplus—from abundance, overflow, what they would never miss. She gave from lack—from deficiency, want, what she could not spare. They gave what cost them nothing. She gave what cost her everything. Heaven weighs sacrifice, not sum. Cost to the giver, not impact in the world.

But here we must be careful. This principle does not mean poverty is spiritually superior to wealth. Scripture honors those called to generate resources and deploy them strategically for the kingdom. Some are given the gift of giving—Romans 12:8 lists it alongside prophecy, teaching, and mercy as a genuine spiritual endowment. Lydia used her wealth to host the early church in her home. Barnabas sold his field and laid the proceeds at the apostles' feet. The Macedonians gave "beyond their means," but Paul also commended believers who gave generously from their means. Both are honored.

Strategic giving has kingdom value. The believer who funds Bible translation in an unreached language, who underwrites church planting in closed countries, who supports the long-term formation of pastors where they are scarce—this is not less spiritual than the widow's two coins. It is a different calling, evaluated by the same principle: faithfulness to what was entrusted, sacrifice relative to capacity, motive known only to God.

The wealthy person who lives simply and gives the majority away may be making sacrifice equal to the worker who tithes from genuine hardship. The hidden ledger records what no external audit can calculate: the cost in the heart of the giver.

What we cannot see—and must not presume to calculate—is another's sacrifice. We don't know their full resources, their competing obligations, their internal struggles, their motives. We see the gift; God sees the giver. We see the amount; God sees the cost. We record the transaction; He records the heart.

This is precisely why the ledger remains hidden. We would calculate wrongly. We would honor the wrong people and overlook the right ones. The widow's coins would be forgotten; the wealthy donors' gold would be inscribed on donor walls. Only God sees truly—and His ledger will stand when all earthly records have dissolved.

The Secret Place

The hidden ledger records more than our hidden acts toward others. It records our hidden communion with God Himself. The relationship cultivated behind the closed door is not merely preparation for service—it is itself an entry in the eternal account.

"But when you pray, go into your room and shut the door and pray to your Father who is in secret. And your Father who sees in secret will reward you."

The secret place is not merely a strategy for avoiding hypocrisy. It is the foundation of everything else. Before we serve in secret, we commune in secret. Before the hidden ledger records our faithfulness to others, it records our faithfulness to Him. What happens behind the closed door shapes everything done in the open.

This is about relationship, not merely discipline. The secret place is where we come to know God—not know about Him, but know Him. Hear His voice. Learn His ways. Become His friend.

THE INTERVAL

Scripture uses that language deliberately. Abraham was called "the friend of God"—and God shared His plans with Abraham as one discusses decisions with an intimate. "Shall I hide from Abraham what I am about to do?" the LORD asked before revealing His intentions for Sodom. Moses spoke with God "face to face, as a man speaks with his friend"—direct communication, not mediated through ritual alone. And Jesus told His disciples: "No longer do I call you servants, for the servant does not know what his master is doing; but I have called you friends, for all that I have heard from my Father I have made known to you."

Friendship with God is not presumption. It is invitation. The Creator of the universe desires to share His heart with those who will take time to listen. He reveals His thoughts to those who linger in His presence. He speaks—and those who cultivate the secret place learn to recognize His voice.

"My sheep hear my voice," Jesus said, "and I know them, and they follow me." This hearing is developed in hidden communion. The capacity to discern God's leading, to sense His pleasure and displeasure, to know His heart on a matter—this comes from hours accumulated in the secret place that no one else observes. The friendship deepens through time spent together, through conversation sustained across years, through intimacy that grows precisely because no audience witnesses it.

The hidden communion with God serves both pillars of this book's thesis. It deposits treasure in the eternal account—the Father who sees in secret rewards. This is not merely spiritual refreshment or personal enrichment. It is kingdom work that registers in heaven's ledger. Time spent in prayer, in fasting, in hidden generosity—Jesus explicitly names these as seen and rewarded by the Father. And if these, why not the hours of worship, of Scripture, of listening, of resting in His presence? The principle suggests that the Father who sees in secret sees all that is offered to Him in secret. The hours of communion are themselves acts of faithfulness that the Father sees—shaping who we become.

We become like those we spend time with. The one who lingers in God's presence takes on something of His character. Moses descended from the mountain with a face that shone—the hidden encounter produced visible transformation. The disciples were recognized as men who "had been with Jesus." Something about their manner, their confidence, their words betrayed hours of invisible communion.

Here is what makes this essential to understanding the interval of grace: the relationship cultivated in the secret place is not merely preparation for eternity. It is the eternal life that has already begun. When we commune with God now—knowing Him, hearing Him, walking with Him as friend—we are not practicing for something that will start later. We are living the life that will continue forever.

The friendship with God that we develop during the interval of grace is the friendship we will enjoy for endless ages. Every hour in the secret place is an hour of the eternal life we have already entered. The hidden ledger records not just what we do for God but what we are with Him—and that communion is itself the treasure.

The Final Vindication

First Corinthians 4:5 is typically read as threat—exposure of hidden sins, revelation of shameful secrets. The verse warns that the Lord will "bring to light the things now hidden in darkness and will disclose the purposes of the hearts." This sounds ominous. Who wants their hidden motives exposed?

But look at how Paul ends the verse: "Then each one will receive his commendation from God."

The Greek word is *epainos*—praise, commendation, approval. Paul does not end with warning but with hope. The revealing is for vindication, not shame.

Consider what this means for those who have served faithfully in obscurity. The secret prayers no one heard? Finally recognized. The anonymous gifts no one tracked? Finally credited. The hidden sacrifices—the early mornings, the quiet intercessions, the kindness that cost something and received no thanks—all will be brought to light. Not to expose but to honor.

The hours in the secret place that seemed to accomplish nothing visible? Recorded. Rewarded. Revealed—the foundation that sustained everything else. The friendship with God that no one witnessed? Displayed as the greatest treasure of all.

Paul writes with confidence: "It is the Lord who judges me." Human evaluation is incomplete, often wrong. The Corinthians were evaluating Paul against flashier apostles, judging by metrics that impressed them—eloquence, showmanship, visible results. Paul refused to be troubled by their assessment. He knew something they didn't: only God sees the full ledger.

And when God reveals that ledger, the faithful will receive what their faithfulness deserved. Not condemnation but commendation. Not shame but praise. Not exposure but honor.

You may have invested decades in quiet faithfulness. The world may never have noticed. Your service may be unrecorded in any earthly archive. Your hours with God may have seemed to produce nothing anyone could measure.

But the hidden ledger has recorded every entry. And when all books are opened, what was done in secret will be proclaimed from the rooftops—not as accusation but as commendation.

This is not primarily warning. It is promise.

Historical Witnesses

Nicholas Herman of Lorraine was converted at eighteen when he saw a bare winter tree and contemplated how God would bring it to life again. He joined a Carmelite monastery in Paris, took the name Brother Lawrence, and spent thirty years in the kitchen—work for which, he admitted, he had "naturally a great aversion."

But he practiced offering every task as worship, every moment as communion. He cultivated friendship with God amid pots and pans, in the noise and clatter of ordinary labor. "The time of business does not differ with me from the time of prayer," he later wrote. "In the noise and clatter of my kitchen, while several persons are at the same time calling for different things, I possess God in as great tranquility as if I were upon my knees."

His most famous observation captures this chapter's thesis: "We ought not to be weary of doing little things for the love of God, who regards not the greatness of the work, but the love with which it is performed."

And this: "I make it my business only to persevere in His holy presence, wherein I keep myself by a simple attention, and a general fond regard to God, which I may call an actual presence of God; or, to speak better, an habitual, silent, and secret conversation of the soul with God."

A habitual, silent, and secret conversation. This was the hidden relationship that formed everything else. No one witnessed it. No audience observed his interior communion while he turned cakes in the pan or washed dishes in the sink. Yet his letters and conversations were compiled after his death as *The Practice of the Presence of God*— a small book that has shaped Christian spirituality for three centuries. The hidden ledger recorded what no human eye saw. And that record continues to bear fruit in lives transformed by his witness.

Thérèse Martin entered a Carmelite convent at fifteen and died of tuberculosis at twenty-four. She held no position of influence, performed no miracles during her lifetime, wrote no theological treatises. Her "Little Way" was exactly about hidden faithfulness: "I can prove my love only by scattering flowers, that is to say, by never letting slip a single little sacrifice, a single glance, a single word; by making profit of the very smallest actions, by doing them for love."

Her fellow sisters saw nothing remarkable in her. Sister Anne of the Sacred Heart, who lived with Thérèse for seven years, was often asked about her after she became famous. She invariably answered: "There is nothing to say about her, she was very good and very self-effacing, one would not notice her, never would I have suspected her sanctity."

One would not notice her. The woman who would become one of the most beloved saints in Christian history was invisible to those who knew her best. Earth's ledger recorded nothing extraordinary. Heaven's ledger recorded everything.

Near the end of her life, Thérèse wrote something that illuminates the deepest truth of the hidden ledger: "It would not disturb me if (supposing the impossible) God himself did not see my good actions.

THE INTERVAL

I love him so much, that I would like to give him joy without his knowing who gave it."

This is hiddenness that transcends even reward—faithfulness so pure it would continue even if no ledger recorded it at all. Love for its own sake. Relationship as its own treasure. The friendship with God valued not for what it earns but for what it is.

The Formation of Integrity

The word "integrity" comes from Latin *integer*—meaning whole, complete, undivided. A mathematical integer is a whole number, not a fraction. A person of integrity is not fragmented. What they are in public, they are in private. What they profess, they practice. The inner life matches the outer.

Public performance creates the opposite. The person who acts one way when observed and another way when alone is divided—a self for the audience and a self for solitude. This is duplicity in its literal sense: *duo* (two) + *plicare* (to fold). A double-folded self. A fractured identity that must be managed rather than simply lived.

Hidden faithfulness creates a unified self. The person who prays the same whether alone or observed, who gives the same whether recorded or anonymous, who serves the same whether noticed or invisible—this person is being formed into wholeness. There is no gap between the public persona and the private reality because there is no performance to maintain.

And the one who cultivates genuine relationship with God in the secret place—not for reward, not even for formation, but because they love Him—this person is becoming who they will be forever.

Both pillars are served in hidden faithfulness. It deposits treasure in the account only God sees—this is the doing pillar, laying up treasure in heaven through acts that transfer into eternity. But it also forms integrity—this is the becoming pillar, developing unified character that will persist forever. Who you are when no one watches is who you really are. And who you really are is who you will be for eternity.

The kiln of death we traced in earlier chapters applies here. The hidden moments are where the real formation happens. The public moments merely reveal what was forged in private. The person who serves faithfully in obscurity for decades and then receives public responsibility does not suddenly become someone different. They simply display what was shaped in the hidden years. The character developed when no one was watching becomes the character that everyone eventually sees.

This formation can only happen under earthly conditions—where faith is required, where reward is delayed, where no one but God sees. Those who never develop the capacity for hidden faithfulness—who require an audience to sustain their effort, who need recognition to continue serving—will arrive at eternity with fragmented selves. Saved, yes. But formed for visibility rather than integrity. Prepared for platforms rather than for the one-audience life that eternity actually is.

The interval of grace is when this integration happens. It cannot be manufactured later. The capacity for hidden faithfulness, cultivated now, becomes the capacity for eternal joy—the ability to find God Himself sufficient, to need no applause but His, to be whole in His presence alone.

Living as Those Who Believe This

If heaven operates a different accounting system, the implications are practical.

We stop tracking the metrics that impress—followers, platform size, public recognition, visible impact. These may or may not appear in heaven's ledger. Their presence in earth's ledger proves nothing about their eternal weight. The person with millions of followers may have already received their reward in full. The person with none may be accumulating treasure that will never diminish.

We start valuing the hidden investments—prayers offered at five in the morning when no one knows, generosity given anonymously, service rendered without recognition, faithfulness maintained in obscurity, hours spent in the secret place with the Father. These may appear nowhere on earth. But the hidden ledger records every entry.

We evaluate success differently. Not by visibility but by faithfulness. Not by applause but by integrity. Not by the size of the audience but by the truth of the heart. Not by what we accomplish for God but by who we become with Him.

We live in an age of unprecedented visibility. Cameras monitor public spaces. Social media invites constant self-presentation. We carry devices that tempt us to document and share every experience. Many of us have internalized an imaginary audience, curating our lives for observers real and imagined even when we are alone. We have become performers by default.

In this context, true hiddenness is radical. Doing something that will never be known, never be posted, never generate content—this is countercultural in ways previous generations could not have imagined. The hidden prayer, the anonymous gift, the secret act of kindness that will never appear on any feed: these are acts of resistance against the tyranny of visibility.

Brother Lawrence turned cake in the pan for the love of God and rose from the task, as he put it, "happier than a king." The hidden ledger recorded what the world never saw. And his joy was independent of any audience but One.

The hidden ledger operates on heaven's accounting system—valuing what earth overlooks, weighing what humans cannot see, recording what no camera captures. At its heart is the hidden relationship with God Himself: the secret place where friendship is cultivated, where we learn to hear His voice, where we become who we will be forever.

But there is another dimension to heaven's mathematics that we have not yet traced.

If hidden faithfulness matters—if motive determines value, if sacrifice outweighs sum, if what is done in secret carries eternal weight—then what happens when these hidden acts are multiplied by time?

The widow's coins were given once. But what of the widow who gives sacrificially year after year for decades? The prayer warrior who intercedes faithfully for forty years? The parent who invests in a child's soul day after day until the days become decades? The believer who spends an hour in the secret place this morning, and tomorrow morning, and every morning for a lifetime?

Small faithfulness, multiplied by time, does not merely add up. It compounds. The cup of cold water given today, repeated tomorrow and the day after, produces not linear growth but exponential return.

This is the mathematics of faithfulness—the compound effect that transforms small deposits into eternal wealth.

To that mathematics we now turn.

CHAPTER 17
THE COMPOUND EFFECT

The Long Obedience

Eugene Peterson borrowed the phrase from an unlikely source. Friedrich Nietzsche, no friend of Christianity, nonetheless recognized something about sustained effort that most people miss: "The essential thing 'in heaven and earth' is... that there should be a long obedience in the same direction; there thereby results, and has always resulted in the long run, something which has made life worth living."

Nietzsche meant it philosophically. Peterson saw the spiritual truth hiding in plain sight and made it the title of his book on discipleship: *A Long Obedience in the Same Direction*. Formation happens not through dramatic moments but through sustained direction. Not through intensity but through consistency. Not through the sprint but through the marathon run at walking pace.

Our age prizes the breakthrough—the revival, the transformation, the sudden turn that changes everything. Heaven prizes something quieter: the long obedience. The prayer offered this morning that will be offered again tomorrow. The discipline maintained this year that will be maintained next decade. The small faithfulness repeated until the repetition itself becomes the achievement.

In Chapter 2, we traced the mathematics of forever—how the interval's brevity, far from diminishing its significance, amplifies it. Now we apply that mathematics to the smallest acts of faithfulness. What happens when hidden deposits are multiplied by time?

They compound.

The Mathematics of Accumulation

The experience of compounding defies intuition. The early deposits seem to accomplish nothing. The returns appear negligible. Only time reveals what was actually happening beneath the surface.

Consider a simple illustration. A modest sum invested monthly for forty years at reasonable rates of return yields far more than double that sum invested monthly for twenty years. The mathematics are not linear. The final years produce the largest returns—but only because the early years laid the foundation. Remove the early years and the later abundance never materializes.

The spiritual application is direct. The person who prays faithfully for forty years possesses something the person who prays intensely for forty days cannot approximate. Not because length earns merit, but because certain formations require time as their medium. Depth cannot be rushed. Roots cannot be hastened. The oak that has weathered decades of storms has a stability the sapling cannot imagine.

Scripture understood this. "Cast your bread upon the waters," the Preacher wrote, "for you will find it after many days" (Ecclesiastes 11:1). Not immediately. After many days. The return requires patience. The investment requires faith that what is cast will somehow, eventually, return—though the mechanism remains invisible and the timing remains unknown.

The early deposits of faithfulness—made when no one notices, when results are invisible, when the account seems to hold nothing— these become the foundation on which everything else compounds.

The Conditional Promise

Paul understood the compound effect. He also understood what threatens it.

"Let us not grow weary of doing good," he wrote to the Galatians, "for in due season we will reap, if we do not give up" (Galatians 6:9).

Note the conditional. The harvest is certain—but not unconditional. "In due season" implies waiting. The temptation is to stop sowing when the ground shows nothing, when the investment seems to disappear into soil that never responds. Due season is not immediate season.

And then the hinge: "if we do not give up."

The compounding depends on continuation—but breaks do not destroy what came before. The person who serves faithfully for ten years, drifts for five, and then returns does not lose the first ten years. Those deposits remain. What is lost is what might have been deposited during the wandering—and that loss is real. The years cannot be recovered. But the restart is immediate. Today's faithfulness begins compounding today. The grace of the interval is that the account remains open until the kiln fires.

The writer of Hebrews pressed the same point: "You have need of endurance, so that when you have done the will of God you may receive what is promised" (Hebrews 10:36). Endurance is not passive waiting. It is active continuation—the long obedience, the sustained direction, the repeated faithfulness when results remain invisible.

Chapter 5 established that the kiln of death fixes what has been forming. Our active compounding ends when the interval closes—we can no longer make new deposits or become something other than what we have become. But the fruit of what was faithfully planted may continue to yield returns long after the planter has gone. What we carry into eternity is what we have accumulated and who we have become. What may continue accumulating is the harvest from seeds sown during the interval. This creates the urgency: the window for planting will close. What grows from those seeds is in God's hands.

George Müller: Sixty Years of Recorded Faithfulness

George Müller is famous for his orphanages. Over the course of his life, he cared for more than ten thousand children in Bristol, England—without ever directly asking anyone for money. He prayed. He trusted. And provision came, year after year, in amounts that could not be explained by coincidence.

Less famous is what he kept: records. Meticulous, specific records of prayers offered and prayers answered. By the time he died in 1898 at the age of ninety-two, he had documented over fifty thousand specific answers to prayer.

Fifty thousand. Documented. Recorded. Specific requests and specific provisions, accumulated across six decades of faithful asking.

What made Müller extraordinary was not intensity but consistency. He prayed. He recorded. He continued. Year after year, decade after decade, the ledger grew. His journal entries from year forty look remarkably like his entries from year four—the same humble requests, the same quiet confidence, the same faithful recording. No dramatic shifts. No seasons of spiritual fireworks. Just the long obedience in the same direction.

By the end, the compound effect was staggering. Not merely in provision received—though that was remarkable enough—but in faith formed. The man who had trusted God fifty thousand times was not the same man who had trusted Him the first time. Each answered prayer built capacity for the next. Each deposit of faith earned returns that funded larger deposits still.

Both pillars were served across those sixty years. Treasure was deposited—provision for orphans, a legacy of faith that continues to inspire. And the soul was formed—a man who had become trust, who had been shaped by sustained faithfulness into someone whose very nature was confident dependence on God.

THE INTERVAL

William Wilberforce: Sixteen Years in the Wilderness

William Wilberforce introduced his first bill to abolish the slave trade in 1791. It failed.

He introduced it again in 1792. Defeated or stalled. Year after year—1793, 1797, 1798, 1799, 1804, 1805. Failed, failed, failed.

The Slave Trade Act finally passed in 1807. Sixteen years of parliamentary defeat before victory.

But Wilberforce did not stop at abolition of the trade. He continued pressing for abolition of slavery itself throughout the British Empire. Three days after the bill passed the House of Commons, Wilberforce died. The Slavery Abolition Act became law a month later.

What sustained him? Not visible results—there were almost none for two decades. Not public acclaim—he was mocked, vilified, exhausted. What sustained him was conviction that the direction was right, and that faithfulness in that direction would eventually yield what faithfulness always yields.

The defeats were not wasted. They were deposits. Each failed bill built coalitions, shifted opinions, prepared ground. The compounding was invisible until it wasn't. When the harvest finally came, it came abundantly—but only because he had not grown weary, had not given up, had cast his bread upon waters that seemed to swallow everything and return nothing.

The long obedience. The sustained direction. The small faithfulness multiplied by time.

The Soul Being Formed

The compound effect operates on the becoming pillar as powerfully as the doing pillar.

Chapter 3 established that what we do shapes who we become. Now we see the mechanism. Repeated choices form grooves. Grooves deepen into habits. Habits solidify into character. Character becomes the fixed self that enters eternity.

The person who chooses patience today finds patience slightly easier tomorrow. The person who chooses generosity this week finds generosity more natural next month. The choices are small. The daily difference is imperceptible. But small choices, repeated across decades, produce a soul that has *become* patient, generous, faithful—not as effort but as identity.

This is why the long obedience matters more than the dramatic moment. The dramatic moment reveals what the long obedience has formed. Müller could trust God for thousands of pounds because he had trusted God for shillings, day after day, until trust became reflexive. Wilberforce could endure year twenty because he had endured years one through nineteen, until endurance became who he was.

Chapter 9 named the interval "irreplaceable, not merely preliminary." Certain formations are only possible under earthly conditions—where faith is required because sight is denied, where endurance is forged because opposition is real, where the long obedience costs something because shortcuts constantly tempt. The compounding that shapes eternal capacity happens here, in the interval, or it does not happen at all.

Who you are becoming through the small repeated choices is who you will be forever.

Part IV has traced heaven's economy—its inversions that overturn earthly assumptions, its true currency of transformed souls, its hidden ledger that records what no human observer sees, and now its compound mathematics that multiply small faithfulness into eternal weight.

But there are specific investments that accumulate in this economy—currencies whose true value remains hidden until eternity reveals it.

The first of these currencies may be the most counterintuitive of all. We would not choose it. We need not seek it. But when it comes, it qualifies us for what ease never could.

The currency is suffering. And to that crucible we now turn.

PART FIVE
THE HIDDEN CURRENCIES
CHAPTERS 18–19

CHAPTER 18
THE CRUCIBLE OF CHARACTER

How Suffering Produces What Ease Cannot

Why would Scripture call suffering a gift?

Paul wrote to the Philippians with a claim that should stop us cold: "It has been *granted* to you that for the sake of Christ you should not only believe in him but also suffer for his sake" (Philippians 1:29). The verb is *echaristhe*—from *charis*, grace. Suffering has been graced to you. Given. Bestowed. The same word Paul uses for the gift of faith he uses for the gift of suffering. Both are granted.

This is not the language of punishment or accident. It is the language of bestowal.

The claim unsettles our categories. We think of suffering as something to be eliminated, avoided, or at best endured until it passes. But Paul saw something different. He saw suffering as currency—one of the hidden currencies that accumulates eternal weight when all the ledgers are opened. Chapter 17 traced how small faithfulness compounds over time. Now we turn to a currency that looks like loss and proves to be gain, that appears to interrupt formation and actually accelerates it.

Suffering is not the interruption of formation. It is formation's most potent crucible—producing what ease cannot produce, qualifying us for what comfort could never qualify.

And this crucible is available only now. In the new creation, where every tear is wiped away and mourning has ceased, the conditions for suffering-forged character will no longer exist. The crown of life belongs exclusively to those who endure trial. That window closes at death.

The chapter ahead does not celebrate suffering—that would be masochism. It does not minimize suffering—that would be denial. It reveals what suffering does when received as formation rather than accident. And it presses the question that matters for eternity: What is being formed in you through what you are enduring?

The Chain That Cannot Be Bypassed

Paul traced a sequence that has no shortcuts.

"We rejoice in our sufferings," he wrote to the Romans, "knowing that suffering produces endurance, and endurance produces character, and character produces hope, and hope does not put us to shame, because God's love has been poured into our hearts through the Holy Spirit" (Romans 5:3-5).

Note the chain: suffering produces endurance. Endurance produces character. Character produces hope. Each link generates the next. The grammar is present tense—this is ongoing, active production. Suffering is *working*. Formation is *happening*. Right now, in the crucible you may be enduring as you read these words.

The chain cannot be jumped. There is no shortcut from suffering to hope that bypasses the middle links. You cannot purchase endurance at the store. You cannot shortcut character. These are forged capacities—developed through the very pressure that seems designed to destroy them. The *thlipsis* (pressure, tribulation) produces *hupomone* (patient steadfastness under load). The steadfastness sustained over time produces tested character—the self that has been through the fire and emerged. And tested character produces hope that does not disappoint, because it has been proven, not merely professed.

James confirms the same pattern. "Count it all joy, my brothers, when you meet trials of various kinds, for you know that the testing of your faith produces steadfastness. And let steadfastness have its full effect, that you may be perfect and complete, lacking in nothing" (James 1:2-4). The word is *teleios*—perfect, mature, complete. This is formation language. The suffering is not an obstacle to maturity but an instrument of it. Without the testing, faith remains untested—theoretically present but unproven.

The crucible completes what ease leaves unfinished.

In Chapter 3, we established that what we do shapes who we become—the virtuous spiral of doing and becoming in perpetual motion. Now we see the spiral's dark counterpart. Suffering presses into the soul. The soul either hardens into bitterness or softens into depth. The pressure either crushes or forms. And the response—enabled by grace, empowered by the Spirit—determines which.

The Crown That Closes

"Blessed is the man who remains steadfast under trial," James wrote, "for when he has stood the test he will receive the crown of life, which God has promised to those who love him" (James 1:12).

The crown of life. A specific reward for a specific faithfulness. Promised to those who endure trial.

In Chapter 9, we established that the interval is *irreplaceable, not merely preliminary*—certain formations require conditions that will not exist in eternity. Now we apply that insight to suffering directly. Consider what Revelation promises about the new creation: "He will wipe away every tear from their eyes, and death shall be no more, neither shall there be mourning, nor crying, nor pain anymore, for the former things have passed away" (Revelation 21:4).

No more mourning. No more crying. No more pain. This is a glorious promise. It is also a closing window.

The conditions for perseverance-under-trial will have passed permanently. Faith will give way to sight—we will see him as he is (1

John 3:2). Courage-against-death will become meaningless when death itself is destroyed. The endurance that required suffering will no longer be necessary when suffering has ceased. The crown of life, promised to those who stand the test, can only be won now, in this interval, under these earthly conditions.

Paul pressed this urgency in his letter to Timothy: "If we endure, we will also reign with him" (2 Timothy 2:12). Reigning requires endurance. Endurance is formed through suffering. The qualification cannot be obtained after the conditions for suffering have ended.

This is not threat. It is reality. Just as certain minerals can only form under extreme pressure—diamonds from carbon subjected to forces that would destroy lesser substances—certain character can only form under suffering's weight. The easy path may be the impoverished path. The comfortable life may be building a soul too shallow to hold the weight of glory.

What remains unformed when the kiln fires remains unformed. The window for earning the crown of life is closing—not in threat but in the nature of things. The conditions are temporary. The character forged is permanent.

Learning Obedience

The writer of Hebrews made a claim that should stagger us: "Although he was a son, he learned obedience through what he suffered" (Hebrews 5:8).

Pause on this. The eternal Son. The one through whom all things were made. The Word who was with God and was God. He *learned* something through suffering that could not be learned otherwise.

This does not mean Jesus was previously disobedient—he was without sin (Hebrews 4:15). But there is a dimension of obedience that can only be understood experientially through the furnace of suffering. Obedience in comfort is one thing. Obedience when obedience costs everything is another. The obedience learned through suffering is obedience in its fullest, most complete form—the obedience that says, in Gethsemane, through sweat like drops of blood, "Not my will, but yours be done" (Luke 22:42).

The writer continues: "For it was fitting that he, for whom and by whom all things exist, in bringing many sons to glory, should make the founder of their salvation perfect through suffering" (Hebrews 2:10). The word is *teleiōsai*—to complete, to bring to the goal, to perfect. The pioneer of our salvation was completed through suffering. Not morally improved—he was already sinless. But humanly completed. Experientially perfected. Made complete in a way that only suffering could accomplish.

If Jesus—fully God, fully human, sinless from conception—was perfected through suffering, what does this say about us?

It says we follow the path the pioneer blazed. Our formation follows his pattern. In Chapter 4, we traced the continuity principle—the self formed here is the self that continues there. Now we see that the formation follows Christ's own pattern: suffering as completing agent, as the means by which the goal is reached. Paul understood this. His desire was to know Christ and "the fellowship of his sufferings" (Philippians 3:10)—not masochism but participation. To share in Christ's suffering is to be formed by the same process that formed him.

The interval is where this pattern operates. The suffering we receive here is forming us by the same mechanism that formed our Lord.

The Surgery of the Soul

John of the Cross was a sixteenth-century Spanish Carmelite, a reformer and poet whose writings on the soul's journey toward God remain among the most penetrating in Christian literature. He was imprisoned by his own order in a stifling cell where he endured darkness, weekly lashings, near-starvation, and extremes of heat and cold—nine months of deprivation and suffering that would have broken most men.

From that darkness he wrote some of the most luminous theology ever produced.

His phrase *the dark night of the soul* has passed into common usage, often misunderstood. In popular parlance, it means any period of depression or spiritual dryness. John meant something more specific. The dark night is God's purifying work in the soul—a work that feels like absence but is actually presence, that seems like abandonment but is actually surgery.

John distinguished between suffering as punishment and suffering as surgery. The dark night is not God's anger but God's scalpel. What God removes creates space for what God gives. The removal is painful; the result is capacity.

"The soul has to pass through two principal kinds of night," John wrote, "in order to attain to union with God." The nights—of the senses and of the spirit—strip away attachments that prevent the soul from bearing more of God. His teaching is clear: no matter how much we do through our own efforts, we cannot purify ourselves enough for divine union. God must take over and purge us in a fire that is dark to us.

In Chapter 7, we met John briefly among the mystics who mapped the inner landscape of formation. Now we see why his testimony belongs here. John understood what the activistic age often misses: that darkness serves light, that what feels like regression may be advance, that the Potter's hands work most deeply when we cannot see them working. The dark night is perhaps *the* formative experience—not in spite of its pain but through it.

The surgery affects both pillars. It strips away attachments to false treasures—the doing pillar, recalibrated toward what actually lasts. It forms the soul for greater capacity—the becoming pillar, enlarged to hold more of God. The darkness is temporary; the formation is permanent. The surgery ends; the healing remains.

Witnesses from the Crucible

The theology requires witnesses—not to prove what Scripture establishes but to show what it looks like when Scripture is lived.

Alexander Solzhenitsyn: The Maturity of the Soul

Alexander Solzhenitsyn spent eight years in Soviet labor camps. The Gulag system was designed to destroy—physically, psychologically, spiritually. What emerged in Solzhenitsyn was not destruction but transformation.

He entered prison as a decorated Soviet artillery captain: young, successful, arrogant. His own words describe who he was before the crucible: "In the intoxication of youthful successes I had felt myself to be infallible, and I was therefore cruel. In the surfeit of power I was a murderer, and an oppressor. In my most evil moments I was convinced that I was doing good, and I was well supplied with systematic arguments."

The man who entered prison was self-assured, blind to his own evil, convinced of his own righteousness. The crucible changed everything.

"And it was only when I lay there on rotting prison straw," he wrote, "that I sensed within myself the first stirrings of good. Gradually it was disclosed to me that the line separating good and evil passes not through states, nor between classes, nor between political parties either—but right through every human heart."

The suffering stripped away self-deception. It revealed what ease had hidden. And then came the astonishing benediction:

"Bless you prison, bless you for being in my life. For there, lying upon the rotting prison straw, I came to realize that the object of life is not prosperity as we are made to believe, but the maturity of the human soul."

The very instrument of his suffering became the object of gratitude. Not gratitude for the cruelty—Solzhenitsyn never romanticized the evil of the system. Gratitude for what the crucible produced. "The maturity of the human soul." This is our thesis in different words. The soul formed here is the soul that continues there. And Solzhenitsyn discovered, on rotting prison straw, that suffering forms what ease never could.

Both pillars were served. Solzhenitsyn emerged to write works that exposed Soviet tyranny and shaped the conscience of the twentieth century—*The Gulag Archipelago, One Day in the Life of Ivan Denisovich*—treasure deposited, the doing pillar. And he *became* the man capable of writing them—humble where he had been arrogant, clear-eyed where he had been self-deceived, prophetic where he had been complicit—the becoming pillar. Neither would have existed without the suffering. The crucible produced both the work and the worker.

Joni Eareckson Tada: The Limited Window

A diving accident at age seventeen left Joni Eareckson Tada paralyzed from the shoulders down. After two years of rehabilitation and deep spiritual struggle, she emerged to a ministry reaching millions. Over fifty years in a wheelchair—fifty years of chronic pain, dependency, and limitation—has produced not bitterness but a theology of suffering forged in lived experience.

She speaks of her wheelchair as a "gift"—a term she did not use lightly or arrive at quickly. "I never would have chosen this gift," she testifies, "but since God chose it for me, I'll take it as a gift, hard as though it may be at times."

Most striking is her awareness of the interval—the very reality this book has been tracing:

"This is the only time in history when I get to fight for God. This is the only part of my eternal story when I am actually in the battle. Once I die, I'll be in celebration mode in a glorified body in a whole different set of circumstances. But this is my limited window of opportunity, and I'm going to fight the good fight for all I'm worth."

Joni understands viscerally what the theology teaches abstractly. The interval is irreplaceable. The conditions for fighting exist only now. The character formed in the fight continues forever. The crown of life, promised to those who endure trial, can only be won while the trial lasts.

She has also discovered the paradox of capacity: "To believe in God is to empty myself; and to empty myself is to increase the capacity—the pond area—for God." The suffering has enlarged her. In Chapter 2, we met Edwards's image of vessels cast into an ocean of happiness—

different sizes, all filled to capacity. Joni's testimony reveals how suffering expands the vessel. What comfort keeps small, the crucible enlarges.

Fifty years of paralysis. Fifty years of pain. And a soul large enough to hold it all.

The Enlargement of the Soul

The witnesses confirm what the theology establishes: suffering stretches capacity.

How does capacity increase? Not through comfort. Through stretching. Through pressure that expands rather than crushes. Through suffering that carves out space, removes what fills without satisfying, creates room for more.

This explains a paradox that observers have noted across centuries: the saints who have suffered most often display the greatest capacity for joy. Not joy despite their suffering but joy somehow because of it—because the suffering enlarged them. The shallow soul, never tested, never stretched, can hold only shallow joy. The deep soul, forged in the crucible, can hold oceanic joy.

Ease produces comfort. Suffering produces capacity. The easy life may be the impoverished life—not in material terms but in soul terms. This is not to romanticize suffering or seek it. It is to understand what it produces when it comes.

And here both pillars unite in their deepest form. The enlarged soul *is* the becoming pillar in action—the character formed that will persist forever. The enlarged capacity to enjoy God forever *is* the treasure, the doing pillar in its highest expression. Suffering serves both simultaneously: forming the soul and expanding what it can hold. What ease could never produce, the crucible forges.

Receiving What Comes

A word of wisdom is required before we close.

We do not manufacture suffering. That is presumption at best, masochism at worst. God supplies sufficient crucibles without our engineering. We need not court unnecessary suffering. But we cannot escape the suffering God permits. It finds us. The question is not whether it will come but what we will do when it arrives.

We receive what comes as formation, not accident.

This does not mean we understand it. Suffering often defies explanation in the moment—and sometimes forever, on this side of glory. The book of Job exists precisely because suffering's meaning is not always disclosed. But we can receive what we do not understand. We can trust what we cannot trace. We can believe that the crucible is producing something, even when we cannot see what.

Two people face the same suffering; one emerges bitter, one emerges transformed. The suffering did not determine the outcome. The response did. And the response is grace-enabled. The Spirit empowers the receiving. The same grace that saves equips the suffering. "Count it all joy" (James 1:2) is not natural capacity but supernatural gift—the ability to see what suffering is producing even when the suffering produces pain.

Some readers are in the crucible right now—not seeking fresh theology but survival. For them, the word is this: what you are enduring is forming something. The darkness is not meaningless. The pain is producing. The character being forged will shine when the fire relents. The interval is irreplaceable, and what is being formed in you through this suffering is being formed for eternity.

Hold on. The crucible will not last forever. But what it produces will.

The Currency That Compounds

Suffering is the crucible where character is forged that ease cannot produce. It is one of the hidden currencies—looking like loss, actually being gain; looking like interruption, actually being acceleration. The Father who sees in secret sees the tears shed in private, the perseverance no one witnessed, the faith held when evidence argued against it. The hidden ledger records what human observers miss.

But suffering, like all formation, requires a medium. Time. The hours and days and years we are given cannot be stored, cannot be recovered, can only be redeemed—converted from mere passing into eternal investment. The crucible operates within time. The compounding Chapter 17 traced requires time. Every investment we have examined—the souls we influence, the suffering we steward, the faithfulness we sustain—operates within the unrepeatable resource of time.

Once passed, moments cannot be recalled. What could have been formed in them is either formed or lost.

Time is the unrepeatable resource. To that we now turn.

CHAPTER 19
THE UNREPEATABLE RESOURCE

Time as the Medium of Eternal Investment

Everything we have examined operates within time.

The hidden currencies of Chapter 17 compound within time. The crucible of Chapter 18 operates within time. The souls we influence, the suffering we steward, the faithfulness we sustain—all require time. The interval of grace *is* time—the numbered days between conversion and death.

Time is not one investment among many. It is the container within which all investments occur. Without time, there is no formation. Without the interval, there is no becoming. Without becoming, there is no differentiated glory.

This chapter is the arrival point. Everything has been building toward the recognition that what we do and who we become happens here, within the unrepeatable resource of time.

Your time. Not time in the abstract—yours. The hours you have lived are gone. The hours that remain are finite, numbered, closing. What will you do with what is left?

The Container Was Sanctified

Before Christ, time was simply passing—the arena of mortality, the measure of decay.

Then the eternal entered time. "When the fullness of time had come, God sent forth his Son" (Galatians 4:4). The Greek is *pleroma*—fullness, completion, the filling up of what was empty. Time itself became full when eternity entered it.

The incarnation sanctified temporality. The eternal Son submitted to sequence, to growth, to the passing of days. He was a child before he was a man. He learned obedience through what he suffered, as we explored in Chapter 18. He lived within the container he had created.

Now every moment within the interval can participate in this sanctification. Time is no longer mere duration—it is opportunity for eternity to enter. The hours are not simply passing; they are being offered, moment by moment, as occasions for eternal weight.

This transforms everything. We are not merely "using time wisely"—that is productivity advice. We are inhabiting moments where temporal and eternal intersect. Every choice, every action, every response occurs at a junction point where what we do can carry weight into forever.

The container was sanctified. What fills it now is up to us.

The Arrow That Does Not Return

Time flows in one direction. What passes does not return.

Augustine saw this clearly: the past exists only as memory, the future only as expectation. Only the present is real—and it is constantly slipping into the past. We cannot step into the same river twice. The moment you inhabited while reading the previous sentence is gone.

This is not merely physics. It is the architecture of formation. You cannot become before you decide. You cannot reap before you sow. You cannot form the soul before you live the life. Sequence is required because becoming requires sequence.

Unlike money, which can be earned again. Unlike reputation, which can be rebuilt. Unlike health, which is sometimes restored. Time never returns. The hours spent cannot be unspent. The days passed cannot be relived. What was not formed in those hours remains unformed.

Moses learned this. After forty years of faithful leadership, he asked God to let him enter the promised land. The answer was no. "Enough from you; do not speak to me of this matter again" (Deuteronomy 3:26). The window had closed. What remained undone would remain undone.

The arrow does not return.

The Moment That Holds Eternity

Søren Kierkegaard, the Danish philosopher-theologian, saw something most miss.

He called it *Øjeblikket*—"the moment," or literally, "the blink of an eye." In his analysis, the moment is not merely a unit of passing time. It is where time and eternity touch.

"The moment is that ambiguity in which time and eternity touch each other," Kierkegaard wrote, "and with this the concept of temporality is posited, whereby time constantly intersects eternity and eternity constantly pervades time."

Nothing is as swift as a blink of the eye, he observed, and yet it is commensurable with the content of the eternal. The moment passes instantly—yet it can hold infinite weight. Every moment is a potential intersection. Every instant is a decision point where the temporal can receive the eternal.

Kierkegaard called such moments "the fullness of time"—echoing Galatians 4:4. Time can be *full* or *empty*. The question is not merely whether we use our moments, but whether our moments have fullness—weight, substance, eternal content.

This transforms how we see the interval. We are not managing a depleting resource, though we are. We are inhabiting a series of intersection points where eternity can enter, where formation can occur, where the eternal self is being shaped through temporal decisions.

Every moment in the interval is a moment touching eternity.

The soul reading these words right now is at such an intersection. What you do with this moment—and the next, and the next—is not merely time management. It is eternal investment. The moment holds more than it appears to hold.

Redeeming the Kairos

Paul understood the stakes.

"Look carefully then how you walk, not as unwise but as wise, making the best use of the time, because the days are evil" (Ephesians 5:15-16).

The phrase "making the best use" translates *exagorazomenoi*—a market term meaning "buying up" or "redeeming." Paul pictures a merchant in a closing market, purchasing everything of value before the opportunity passes. The wise person sees the market closing and acts accordingly.

The word for time here is *kairos*, not *chronos*. *Chronos* is clock time—the steady tick of seconds. *Kairos* is opportune time—pregnant moments, windows that open and close, occasions ripe for action. Paul is not merely saying "use your hours well." He is saying: discern the *kairos* moments, the decisive opportunities, and purchase them before they pass.

"Because the days are evil." The context is opposition, difficulty, a world that does not encourage eternal investment. The market is not friendly. But the wise merchant sees opportunity within opposition, purchasing power within difficulty.

To the Colossians, Paul writes the same: "Walk in wisdom toward outsiders, making the best use of the time" (4:5). Same verb. Same urgency. The opportunities for influence, for witness, for soul-shaping investment are available now—but the market is closing.

What are you purchasing? What opportunities pass unpurchased because you did not see their value? What *kairos* moments slip into the past while you wait for more convenient occasions?

The market will close. For each of us, at a time we do not know, the final opportunity will pass. What is bought before then is bought. What is left unpurchased is lost.

The Prayer for Vision

"So teach us to number our days that we may get a heart of wisdom" (Psalm 90:12).

This is Moses's prayer—the same Moses whose window closed, who saw Canaan but could not enter. He knew that time could slip away. He knew that intervals end. He prayed not for more time but for wisdom to see clearly the time he had.

"Teach us to number." We do not naturally number our days. We assume more will come. We defer, postpone, delay. The heart that does not number its days is the heart that wastes them.

But numbering is not morbid. It is clarifying. The person who knows their days are finite lives differently than the person who assumes infinity. The traveler who sees the destination approaching does not dawdle.

Throughout this book, we have been learning to see. To see the interval (Chapter 9). To see the two pillars (Chapter 3). To see the hidden currencies (Chapter 17). To see the crucible (Chapter 18). Now we see the container itself—the numbered days within which all seeing occurs.

The "heart of wisdom" is the heart that sees time rightly. Not as burden but as gift. Not as pressure but as opportunity. Not as scarcity but as sacred.

How many days remain in your interval? You do not know. Neither do I. But we know the number is finite. We know the window will close.

Teach us to count rightly. Give us hearts that see.

The Theft That Cannot Be Repaid

What is not done in time cannot be done at all.

Martha was busy with many things. Her house was full of activity, her hours full of tasks. She was not idle—she was occupied. But Mary sat at Jesus's feet, listening. When Martha complained, Jesus replied: "Mary has chosen the good portion, which will not be taken away from her" (Luke 10:42).

One filled her time. The other invested it. The difference was eternal.

The five virgins who lacked oil were not wicked. They were unprepared. They assumed more time. "While they were going to buy, the bridegroom came, and those who were ready went in with him to the marriage feast, and the door was shut" (Matthew 25:10).

The door was shut. Not as punishment but as reality. Time had passed. The opportunity was gone. What could have been prepared was not prepared. What could have been purchased was not purchased.

The servant who buried his talent thought he had time. He did not refuse the investment—he deferred it. The master returned when the servant did not expect. The interval ended, and the talent remained uncompounded.

Procrastination of eternal investment is not postponement. It is forfeiture.

You cannot make up for lost time. You can only redeem what remains. The formations that didn't happen, the treasure that wasn't deposited, the becoming that didn't occur—these are not delayed. They are lost.

"I'll get serious about formation later. I'll invest more later. I'll become the person I should be later."

Later may not come. And if it does, what was lost in "now" is still lost. The door closes once. The arrow does not return.

Both Pillars Require Duration

Return now to the two pillars—but see them through the lens of time.

The doing pillar. Every investment takes time. The giving that becomes treasure requires sustained generosity over years—not a single gift but accumulated faithfulness. The serving that becomes cities requires labor over decades. The witnessing that brings souls requires patient presence, repeated conversations, prayers spanning years. The compounding of Chapter 17 requires duration. Interest grows over time. There are no shortcuts, no instant returns.

The becoming pillar. Formation is incremental. There is no instant character. The virtuous spiral of Chapter 3 requires repetition—habit forms through repeated action over time. You cannot become patient instantly; patience requires time to develop patience. Endurance requires duration to become endurance. Love deepens through years of loving. The soul is shaped incrementally, day by day, choice by choice, moment by moment.

Both pillars are built within the container of time. Without time, neither exists. No time means no formation and no investment.

This is why the book is titled *The Interval*. The interval is not merely a span to be endured but the arena where becoming happens. We are not static beings but temporal becomings. God is eternal Being —"I AM." We are finite becoming—"I am being made." The interval is where that becoming occurs—where the soul that will exist forever is being formed through the choices made in time.

Everything converges here. The doing pillar requires time to deposit treasure. The becoming pillar requires time to form character. Both operate within the numbered days. Both depend on the unrepeatable resource.

What you are doing—right now, in these numbered days—is determining what treasure you will steward forever. Who you are becoming—through the choices of this interval—is the person who will carry that treasure into eternity.

Time is the medium of both.

Witnesses to Time's Weight

Blaise Pascal: The Diagnosis

Pascal (1623-1662) was a mathematician and physicist before he was a theologian. His *Pensées* contain the most penetrating analysis of how humans waste time.

He called it *divertissement*—diversion. We fill our hours with noise, entertainment, busyness—anything to avoid thinking about death and eternity. "All the unhappiness of men arises from one single fact," Pascal observed, "that they cannot stay quietly in their own chamber."

The restlessness is not accidental. It is evasion.

"The only thing which consoles us for our miseries is diversion, and yet this is the greatest of our miseries. For it is this which principally hinders us from reflecting upon ourselves... But diversion amuses us, and leads us unconsciously to death."

The busy person is not necessarily the investing person. Busyness can be escape. Entertainment can be anesthesia. Activity can be avoidance.

Pascal saw that time-wasting is often eternity-avoidance. We fill the hours because we dare not face what empty hours would reveal—our mortality, our accountability, our need.

The diagnosis: we divert ourselves from what matters most. The cure: face the eternal directly, then live accordingly.

Pascal died at thirty-nine, having faced the eternal and lived accordingly.

What are you using to avoid facing eternity?

Dietrich Bonhoeffer: The Response

If Pascal diagnosed the evasion, Bonhoeffer (1906-1945) demonstrated the alternative.

"Every moment and every situation challenges us to action and to obedience," he wrote in *The Cost of Discipleship*. "We have literally no time to sit down and ask ourselves whether so-and-so is our neighbor or not. We must get into action and obey."

No postponement. No deferral. The call is now; the response must be now.

"When Christ calls a man, he bids him come and die."

Bonhoeffer's letters from prison show a man who knew time might be short—yet continued to write, think, form others. He did not waste his remaining days in despair. He invested them to the last.

THE INTERVAL

On April 9, 1945—weeks before the war ended—Bonhoeffer was hanged at Flossenbürg concentration camp. He had used his time.

Pascal diagnosed how we waste time. Kierkegaard revealed what time holds. Bonhoeffer showed how to spend it. Together they testify: the interval is brief, the moments touch eternity, and the response is now.

Urgency Without Anxiety

A necessary word.

Godly urgency is not worldly panic. The difference: worldly panic is self-driven, fear-based, exhausting. Godly urgency is God-driven, love-based, energizing.

Jesus was never frantic, yet intensely purposeful. "I must work the works of him who sent me while it is day; night is coming, when no one can work" (John 9:4). Urgency and peace. Purpose and rest.

We are not earning salvation—that is settled, as Chapter 9's threefold framework established. We are investing toward reward and formation, enabled by grace. The same grace that saves equips the investing. The Spirit who empowers formation also gives peace.

This should produce focus, not fear. Every day matters—but every day is also held by grace. The pressure is real; the peace is also real. We work out our salvation with fear and trembling—and God is the one working in us (Philippians 2:12-13).

The person who understands the interval lives with heightened awareness, not heightened anxiety.

The Now That Contains Forever

You are in the interval now.

The hours behind you are gone—whatever was formed in them is formed, whatever was lost is lost. The hours ahead are not guaranteed. Only this moment is yours.

And this moment holds more than it appears to hold. It is an intersection where temporal touches eternal. What you do with it can carry weight into forever.

The soul reading these words is a soul in formation. The moment of reading is a moment within the interval. What you do next—literally, when you set down this book—is part of your eternal becoming.

The treasure you will steward forever is being deposited now.

The character you will carry into glory is being formed now.

The capacity for joy you will experience eternally is being enlarged now.

There is no later—not really. There is only this moment touching eternity, and then the next, and then the next, until the interval closes and what remains is what was formed.

This is not threat. It is invitation. It is reality.

The question is not whether your time will pass. It will. The question is whether your time will be invested—redeemed—converted from mere duration into eternal weight.

What will you do with the time you have left?

The market is still open. The moment still holds eternity. The arrow has not yet reached its mark.

Begin.

INTERLUDE
THE WEIGHT OF NOW

We have traveled far.

Through Scripture and history, through fathers and mystics and modern voices, through parables and paradoxes, we have traced a single reality: eternal life has already begun, and within the brief window called the *interval of grace*, you are becoming someone who will exist forever.

Before we turn to practice—before we ask what this means for Tuesday morning and decade-long faithfulness—we pause. Not because the journey is complete. It is not. But the foundation has been laid. And foundations bear weight.

Feel it now.

You have learned that you are not waiting to begin eternal life. You are in it. The border between this age and the next runs not at death but at conversion. Everything that follows—every ordinary hour, every hidden choice, every unremarkable Wednesday—occurs within the age to come, already inaugurated, not yet consummated. You have

INTERLUDE

learned that in this interval you are doing two things at once: laying up treasure in heaven and becoming the soul who will steward it forever. The doing and the becoming cannot be separated. They are not sequential but simultaneous, not alternatives but aspects of a single life hidden with Christ in God. You have learned the *continuity principle*: the self being formed here is the self that will exist there. Not a different person. Not a replacement. You—stretched, refined, perhaps transformed, but continuous. What is being written into your character is being written in permanent ink.

You have learned the *kiln of death*: the moment when formation ends and evaluation begins. The clay hardens. The wet cement sets. What has been shaped is what will be weighed. Death fixes what life forms. You have learned the mathematics of *heaven's economy*—the great inversion, where last becomes first and hidden becomes manifest and what earth dismisses heaven records. The ledger no one sees. The currencies no one counts. The compound interest of faithfulness sustained across years. You have learned the *crucible of character*: that suffering produces what ease cannot, that the crown of life can only be earned under conditions that will not exist in eternity, that what looks like interruption may be acceleration. You have learned the *unrepeatable resource*: time does not return. What passes is gone. The interval is not unlimited. The window will close—for you, specifically, at a moment you likely do not know.

This is what you have learned.

Now feel what it weighs.

The truths of this book are not ideas to be filed. They are realities to be inhabited. And to inhabit them is to feel the ground shift beneath your feet.

INTERLUDE

You are standing in the interval now. Not eventually. Not when circumstances change. Now. As you hold this book. As your eyes move across these words. As your lungs draw breath and your heart marks time.

The clock is running. Your numbered days are numbering down. The choices you will make today—the small ones, the ones that feel inconsequential—are pressing into the soft clay of your soul. Something is being formed. Someone is becoming.

This is not theory applied to life. This is life—your life, the only one you will ever live, the one whose shape will persist when the kiln fires and the evaluation begins.

The commute you endure. The conflict you are avoiding. The person you have been meaning to call. The habit you keep meaning to break. The practice you keep meaning to start. The conversation you have been postponing because there will always be time. There may not always be time. There is only now.

And yet. This weight is not meant to crush. It is meant to clarify.

The God who established the interval also established the grace. The same Father who sees in secret—who records the cup of cold water and the tear shed in private and the faithfulness no one applauds—is the Father who sustains what He demands. The One who will evaluate your work is the One who empowers your working.

You are not alone in the interval. You are not scrambling to impress a distant auditor. You are seen—intimately, attentively, lovingly—by the One who knows your frame and remembers that you are dust. The weight settles. But underneath the weight are everlasting arms.

INTERLUDE

What, then, is this pause for?

It is for presence. For letting the truths accumulate until they press upon the soul. For moving from *understanding* to *feeling*, from *knowing* to *knowing in your bones*.

The danger of a book like this is rushing to application. *What do I do now? Give me the steps. Show me the practices.* We will come to practice. The next section turns there directly. But application without weight becomes technique. Practice without presence becomes striving. And striving in your own strength is precisely what the interval is not about.

So we pause here. At the threshold between foundation and building. Between what is true and what we do about it. Feel the weight. Let it settle. The interval is real. The stakes are eternal. The grace is sufficient.

Here is what this pause is not.

It is not a moment to calculate your failures. You have not read these chapters to be condemned. Whatever has passed—the wasted years, the squandered opportunities, the formations that should have happened but did not—is held by the same grace that holds your future. The clay is still soft. The kiln has not fired. What remains can still be redeemed.

And here is what this pause is.

It is a moment to see clearly. To feel the texture of reality as it actually is. To stand in the interval with open eyes—knowing what is at stake, knowing what is being formed, knowing what is being recorded, knowing that the window will close. The ancient prayer rises: *Teach us to number our days, that we may get a heart of wisdom.* We are asking to see. And seeing changes everything.

INTERLUDE

The next section will turn to practice. How to live within the interval. How to conduct the audit of your own soul. How to discover your eternal vocation. How to begin—today, this week, this numbered life.

But first: receive what has been established. Let the weight find its place. The foundation does not move. The truths do not change. The interval remains. Everything you do is forming someone. Everything translates.

The Father who sees in secret is watching—not with suspicion but with attention, not with impatience but with the long patience of a craftsman who knows what the clay can become.

You are in the interval. You are becoming. The question is not whether formation will occur—it will. The question is what kind of soul is being formed, and for what eternal purpose.

The clock is running.
The grace is sufficient.
And you are still here.

Draw my gaze from the passing to the permanent,
From the urgent to the eternal,
From what fades to what remains.

Upward, then.
To where the treasure waits.
To where the becoming finds its home.
To You, who hold what I cannot yet see.

PART SIX
THE PRACTICE
CHAPTERS 20–21

CHAPTER 20
THE ETERNAL AUDIT

Standing Before the Gaze

Kierkegaard insisted that before God, every person stands alone—not in loneliness but in irreducible singularity. The crowd disperses. The comparisons fall away. It is just you and the One who sees.

He called this standing as "the single individual"—the posture of one who has stopped hiding in the mass, stopped measuring against neighbors, stopped performing for audiences. Before God, you are not a demographic or a role or a reputation. You are *you*—known, seen, evaluated as the particular soul you have become.

"The crowd is untruth," he wrote. But the single individual standing before God is where truth happens.

This chapter is an invitation to stand there now—voluntarily, while adjustment is still possible—and ask what God sees.

"No creature is hidden from his sight, but all are naked and exposed to the eyes of him to whom we must give account" (Hebrews 4:13).

The language is almost violent. *Naked. Exposed.* The word translated "exposed" refers to bending back the neck—the posture of an animal laid bare for sacrifice, throat vulnerable. Nothing hidden. Nothing protected.

This exposure is coming. The Bema is certain. The question is whether that Day will be your first experience of the light—or whether you've practiced standing in it.

The eternal audit is not morbid introspection. It is not anxious self-measurement against standards you can never meet. It is *invitation*—asking the Surgeon to show you what needs healing before the window closes.

Psalm 139 gives us the posture: "Search me, O God, and know my heart. Try me and know my thoughts. And see if there be any grievous way in me, and lead me in the way everlasting."

David does not claim to know his own heart. He asks God to search it. He does not trust his self-assessment. He trusts the assessment of the One who sees truly.

This is the audit: not self-examination but *consented examination*. You are not the searchlight. You are the one stepping into it.

The light does not reveal merely what you have done. It reveals what you *love*. And what you love is who you are becoming.

Where did your time go? There your heart was. Where did your treasure flow? There your heart was. Who did you become in the presence of those God gave you? That is the person being formed.

Augustine saw it: "Love, and do what you will"—because what you love determines what you will. The audit is not primarily behavioral. It is affectional. It exposes the loves that have been shaping you, choice by choice, hour by hour, into the soul you now are.

The purpose is not guilt. The purpose is *alignment*—bringing your life into congruence with what will be revealed when every hidden thing becomes manifest. The one who practices the audit now will not be surprised at the Bema. The light will feel like home.

You have read about the gaze. Now you are in it.

Not eventually. Not when you finish the book. Now. The Father who sees in secret is seeing. The One to whom all are naked and exposed is looking at your life—your actual life, the one you lived yesterday, the one you will live tomorrow.

What does He see?

Not what you intend. Not what you present. Not what others assume. What is *there*?

This is not condemnation. If you are in Christ, condemnation is behind you. This is something more intimate—the gaze of a Father who knows what you could become, who sees what you are becoming, who waits for you to stop hiding and simply stand.

The light is not punishment. The light is love.

But love sees. Love does not look away. Love holds you in the gaze until you stop performing, stop comparing, stop defending.

Before God, you are the single individual. Just you. Just Him. Just the truth of what your life has been and is becoming.

What does He see?
Stand here.
Not rushing to fix.
Not cataloging failures.
Not comparing.
Just standing. Seen.

Let the question find its depth:
What does God see when He looks at my life?
Not the life you project.
Not the life you intend.
The one you are actually living.
Carry this into silence. Let it press.
The searchlight is not yours to control.
But the consent is yours to give.

Search me, O God, and know my heart.
Try me and know my thoughts.
See if there be any grievous way in me,
and lead me in the way everlasting.

CHAPTER 21
YOUR ETERNAL VOCATION

What You Are Being Prepared For

In the wilderness, while Moses received the Law, God spoke a name: "See, I have called by name Bezalel the son of Uri, son of Hur, of the tribe of Judah, and I have filled him with the Spirit of God, with ability and intelligence, with knowledge and all craftsmanship" (Exodus 31:1-3).

Bezalel was a craftsman—a worker in gold, silver, bronze, stone, and wood. And God called him *by name* for a specific work: building the tabernacle, the place where heaven and earth would meet.

The Spirit filled him not for preaching or prophecy but for *craftsmanship*. His hands were his calling. His art was his vocation. The skills he carried—perhaps developed over years in Egypt, perhaps seeming pointless in the wilderness—were preparation for something God had planned before Bezalel knew it himself.

You too have been called by name. You too are being filled for specific work. Could it be that the shaping has been underway all along?

Chapter 4 established the continuity principle: the self being formed here is the self that persists there. You carry through death.

And you carry through for a reason. Your formation isn't random—it's preparation. For what?

The new creation is not unemployment. It is assignment. Vocation. Responsibility proportional to what was formed. Revelation speaks of the kings of the earth bringing their glory into the New Jerusalem (21:24). Human work, purified and incorporated. Your labor now is not filler until heaven—it is apprenticeship for eternal assignment.

What you build with your hands, what you create with your mind, what you cultivate with your care—these are not discarded at death. N.T. Wright, in *Surprised by Hope*, calls this the surprising news: that human work, purified by fire, will find its place in the new creation. The singer is not wasting her voice. The craftsman is not squandering his skill. The artist is not indulging vanity. They are preparing instruments for eternal use. The same Spirit who filled Bezalel for tabernacle work fills you for yours.

You are being prepared for something. The preparation is happening whether you notice or not. The invitation is to notice—and cooperate.

Vocation emerges at the convergence of four realities:

Gifting. What are you able to do that others find difficult? What comes so naturally you assume everyone can do it? Your gifts are not accident. They are given—placed in you by a God who equips for purpose.

Longing. What makes you ache? What vision of flourishing—for people, for creation, for justice, for beauty—keeps returning even when you suppress it? The desire that won't die may be the arrow pointing toward assignment.

Perceived Need. What gap do you see that others walk past? The Spirit opens your eyes to specific lacks—certain needs grip you while leaving others unmoved. The need that haunts you may be the need you were made to meet.

Formation. What has your suffering prepared you for? What do you know in your bones that comfort could never teach? The crucible was not pointless. The wound that healed has become the place of ministry.

THE INTERVAL

Where these four converge, you are standing near your eternal vocation.

But how do you know you're reading the convergence rightly?

There is something beneath the four—not another category but a confirmation. The prompting you cannot dismiss. The thought that keeps returning. The direction that, even when it makes you nervous, carries an undertone of peace.

Not ease—the path may be difficult. Not certainty—questions may remain. But peace. The quiet yes of the Spirit beneath the noise.

This is how seasons are discerned. Not by strategy but by prompting. Not by optimization but by peace. When gifting, longing, perceived need, and formation align—and the prompting confirms with that strange, steady peace—you are standing at the threshold of what you were made for.

You are being prepared for something.

Not generically. Not abstractly. *You*—the particular soul you are, with the particular gifts you carry, the particular longings that won't release you, the particular suffering that has marked you.

God does not waste formation. The wilderness years are not filler. The wounds are not accidents. The desires that keep you awake are not distractions.

Something is being assembled in you. Capacities are being built. A soul is being shaped for specific purpose—purpose that will extend into the new creation, purpose that will matter forever.

You were not made for generic existence. You were called by name —like Bezalel, like Jeremiah who was consecrated before birth, like every soul God forms with intention.

The preparation is underway. It has been underway longer than you know.

What is becoming clear?

Sit with the convergence.

What are you able to do that others find difficult?
What longing will not leave you alone?
What need has the Spirit opened your eyes to see?
What has your suffering uniquely prepared you for?

Do not rush to answer. Let the questions find their depth.

Vocation is not chosen. It is recognized—seen at last, after it has been forming in secret. The call was always coming. Moses simply had to turn aside and see.

Perhaps the answer is not yet clear. That is expected. Formation is still underway. But you can begin to notice. You can begin to cooperate with what is being prepared instead of resisting it.

The Father who sees in secret is forming you for something.

What is He making?

INTERLUDE
THE OFFERING

A crowd of thousands. A day without food. The disciples calculating —and failing. Then Andrew, almost apologizing: "There is a boy here who has five barley loaves and two fish, but what are they for so many?" (John 6:9).

What are they for so many? The answer was: nothing. The boy's lunch could not feed five thousand. The math didn't work. The offering was absurd. But the boy offered it anyway. He did not feed the multitude. Jesus did. The boy simply opened his hands. He gave what he had—not because it was sufficient, but because it was *his* to give.

You have stood in the light. You have asked what God sees. You have sat with the convergence. You have asked what He is making. Now comes the moment that is not a chapter, not a lesson, not a step. Just this: the opening of hands.

You cannot complete your own formation. You cannot engineer your eternal vocation. You cannot, by effort alone, become who you were meant to be.

But you can offer what you have.

The formation in process—
incomplete, imperfect, still being shaped.
Offer it.

The time that remains—
unmeasured, unguaranteed, unrepeatable.
Offer it.

The vocation emerging—
unclear, glimpsed, held loosely.
Offer it.

The wounds. The gifts. The longings that won't let go. The prompting beneath the noise. All of it. Whatever you have. However insufficient it seems.

The boy did not instruct Jesus on how to use the loaves. He did not strategize the distribution. He simply handed them over. The miracle was not his to engineer. It was his to participate in—through release.

This is not the end. It is the beginning that lets God do what only He can do. You are not the one who completes your formation. You are not the one who redeems your time. You are not the one who brings the vocation to fulfillment. You are the one who offers. He is the one who multiplies.

Here I am, Lord.
Here is what I am becoming—incomplete, still being shaped.
Here is the time I have left—unknown, uncounted.
Here is what I think you may be making me for—
held loosely, offered freely.
I do not know how you will multiply it.
But it is yours.
I open my hands.

PART SEVEN
THE VISION
CHAPTERS 22–24

CHAPTER 22
THE BEMA SEAT

The Day of Revealing

Paul stood before tribunals his entire apostolic life. Sanhedrin councils. Roman magistrates. Caesar's representatives. He was beaten, imprisoned, shipwrecked, stoned. Yet none of these verdicts troubled him.

"With me it is a very small thing that I should be judged by you or by any human court. In fact, I do not even judge myself... It is the Lord who judges me" (1 Corinthians 4:3-4).

Every human tribunal was shadow. The only verdict that mattered was coming.

"We must all appear before the judgment seat of Christ, so that each one may receive what is due for what he has done in the body, whether good or evil" (2 Corinthians 5:10).

Paul did not dread this Day. He pressed toward it. The One who would judge him was the One who had saved him. The evaluation was certain—but so was the Evaluator's love.

This is the Day toward which everything in this book has been pointing. Not to frighten, but to prepare. Not to burden, but to clarify what matters.

The Bema is coming. For every one of us.

The Bema is not the Great White Throne of Revelation 20—that judgment is for the lost, and the verdict is condemnation. The Bema is for believers. Those already in Christ. Those for whom there is "no condemnation" (Romans 8:1).

The question at the Bema is not "Will you enter?" That is settled by grace through faith. The question is: *What did you do with the life you were given? And who did you become in the living of it?*

The two pillars—doing and becoming—both stand under evaluation. Stewardship and formation. The treasure laid up and the soul being shaped. Everything this book has traced arrives here.

Paul tells the Romans: "Each of us will give an account of himself to God" (Romans 14:12). The Bema is personal. Individual. Unavoidable. No one gives account for another. No one hides behind the crowd. You stand alone before the One who knows you fully.

The stakes are not salvation—that gift remains secure. The stakes are reward. And reward, as this book has argued throughout, matters eternally. Capacity. Assignment. Joy. The difference between ruling over ten cities and five. The difference between arriving wealthy in what survives and arriving with nothing but your rescued soul.

At the Bema, what was hidden becomes visible.

Jesus warned of this: "Nothing is covered up that will not be revealed, or hidden that will not be known. Therefore whatever you have said in the dark shall be heard in the light, and what you have whispered in private rooms shall be proclaimed on the housetops" (Luke 12:2-3).

The secret faithfulness no one applauded—manifest. The hidden compromise no one caught—manifest. The motives beneath the actions—manifest. The prayers in the closet. The bitterness nursed in silence. The generosity no one recorded. The envy no one suspected.

Paul understood this total exposure: "Therefore do not pronounce judgment before the time, before the Lord comes, who will bring to light the things now hidden in darkness and will disclose the purposes of the heart" (1 Corinthians 4:5). Not just deeds but *purposes*. Not just actions but the hearts behind them.

This is terrifying or liberating depending on one thing: whether you have practiced standing in the light.

Chapter 20 invited you into the eternal audit—standing before God's gaze now, voluntarily, while the clay is soft, while adjustment is possible. That was rehearsal. The Bema is the Day itself.

For those who have practiced the audit, the disclosure holds no ambush. The light will feel familiar. The exposure will feel like relief—everything finally seen, nothing left to hide, no more pretending.

For those who avoided the light, who hid from examination, who never invited the searchlight—the Bema will be their first exposure. And the disclosure will be jarring.

Chapter 12 traced the fire that tests. Here it arrives.

"Each one's work will become manifest, for the Day will disclose it, because it will be revealed by fire, and the fire will test what sort of work each one has done. If the work that anyone has built on the foundation survives, he will receive a reward. If anyone's work is burned up, he will suffer loss, though he himself will be saved, but only as through fire" (1 Corinthians 3:13-15).

Gold, silver, precious stones survive. Wood, hay, stubble burn. The materials were chosen in the interval. The fire merely reveals what was already true.

Notice what endures: that which was built on the foundation of Christ, with motives purified by love, through power supplied by the Spirit. And notice what burns: that which was built for self—however impressive it appeared, however much applause it gathered, however successful by earthly metrics.

The fire is not punishment. It is revelation. It discloses what was real.

This brings us to the sobering reality of two outcomes.

Some will hear: "Well done, good and faithful servant. You have been faithful over a little; I will set you over much. Enter into the joy of your master" (Matthew 25:21).

Others will be saved "only as through fire"—escaping, but just barely. Smelling of smoke. Carrying nothing. Grateful to have survived, but grieved at what was lost.

Both outcomes involve salvation. The Bema does not determine destiny—it determines reward. Even the one who arrives with nothing but smoke-stained clothes is *saved*. The foundation of Christ holds.

Yet the difference between the two outcomes is not trivial. It is not temporary. It is eternal.

The one who built with gold hears "Well done" and receives expanded capacity, greater responsibility, brighter glory—forever. The one who built with stubble is saved but impoverished—forever carrying the weight of what could have been.

This is why the interval matters. This is why this book exists. Not to create anxiety but to clarify stakes. There is still time to build differently. There is still time to offer what you have to the One who multiplies.

But here the chapter turns. Because for those who have been practicing—the Bema is not threat.

It is vindication.

The Day when every cup of cold water given in Jesus' name is remembered: "Whoever gives one of these little ones even a cup of cold water because he is a disciple, truly, I say to you, he will by no means lose his reward" (Matthew 10:42).

The Day when the Father who sees in secret rewards openly: "Your Father who sees in secret will reward you" (Matthew 6:4).

The Day when the hidden ledger—Chapter 16's record of what no human eye observed—is read aloud for all creation to hear.

The widow's mite, honored. The prayer no one heard, answered and acclaimed. The years of faithfulness in obscurity, finally seen.

For those who stood in the crucible and let suffering form them—vindication.

For those who invested the hidden currencies of time and pain—vindication.

For those who offered their incomplete formation, their uncertain vocation, their insufficient loaves—vindication.

The Bema is the Day when what no one saw, everyone sees. When the last become first. When the overlooked are honored. When the quiet faithfulness that never made headlines is announced from the throne.

Paul finished his course anticipating this: "There is laid up for me the crown of righteousness, which the Lord, the righteous judge, will award to me on that Day, and not only to me but also to all who have loved his appearing" (2 Timothy 4:8).

All who have *loved* his appearing. Not dreaded. Loved. The Bema is anticipated by those who have lived in light of it.

If you have practiced standing in the light—you have been preparing for this Day.

If you have offered what you have—you have nothing to fear.

What remains is joy.

The evaluation is not the end. It is the threshold.

Beyond the Bema lies reunion—the communion of saints, the restoration of all that death stole, the company of the redeemed from every tribe and tongue and nation.

Beyond the Bema lies the morning—the new creation, the eternal vocation, the endless advance into God.

The Bema is the door. And the One who stands as Judge is the same One who died to open it.

The Lamb who was slain. The Savior who bled. The Lord who interceded for you across every failing, every stumble, every wood-hay-stubble compromise. He is not waiting to condemn. He is waiting to reward.

The question is not whether you will stand before Him. You will.

The question is what that Day will reveal—and there is still time to build what survives.

The Bema is coming.

But so is the "Well done."

CHAPTER 23
THE GREAT REUNION

Far Better

Paul was torn.

Not torn between good and evil, or between obedience and rebellion. He was torn between two goods—two glories, each pulling at him with legitimate force. "I am hard pressed between the two," he admitted. "My desire is to depart and be with Christ, for that is far better. But to remain in the flesh is more necessary on your account" (Philippians 1:23-24).

Notice his language. Not merely "better." *Far* better. The Greek is intensive—*pollō mallon kreisson*—much more better, exceedingly superior, better beyond comparison. Paul had seen the risen Christ on the Damascus road. He had been caught up to the third heaven and heard things that cannot be told (2 Corinthians 12:4). He knew what waited on the other side of death. And his settled judgment, writing from prison with execution looming, was that departing to be with Christ was *far better* than anything this life could offer.

But why? What makes it far better?

Paul's longing reveals a crucial insight: the superiority of being "with Christ" is not merely a change of scenery. It is the cessation of sin's power. For Paul—a man who battled daily with the reality of sin dwelling within him, who cried out, "I do not do what I want, but I do the very thing I hate" (Romans 7:15), who groaned under the weight of a body of death (Romans 7:24)—to be "at home with the Lord" is to be finally and permanently freed from the internal war that plagues every believer. Heaven is "far better" because it is the state of perfect holiness—uninterrupted communion with the Holy One, unmarred by the sin that has dogged every step of our earthly pilgrimage.

Every mature Christian knows this war. The desire to pray, undermined by wandering thoughts. The intention to love, corrupted by selfish motives. The resolve to obey, eroded by persistent weakness. We fight and fail and repent and fight again—and the fight never fully ends, not on this side of the grave. But heaven is where the fight ends. Not in defeat but in final victory. The flesh that warred against the Spirit is left behind. The soul that strained toward holiness finally arrives.

This is what awaits us.

When the last breath leaves and the eyes close and the heart stills, the believer does not drift into oblivion. There is no annihilation. No soul sleep. No gray shadowland between worlds. In that instant—that very moment—the soul enters the presence of Christ. "Away from the body and at home with the Lord," Paul wrote (2 Corinthians 5:8). The transition is immediate. The destination is glorious. And the war is over.

This is heaven. And it is far better than we have dared to imagine.

Paradise Today

Jesus made the promise explicit.

On the cross, with nails through his wrists and the weight of the world's sin pressing down, he turned to a criminal dying beside him. The man had moments to live. He had no time for baptism, no opportunity for good works, no chance to prove the sincerity of his repentance. He had only a prayer: "Jesus, remember me when you come into your kingdom" (Luke 23:42).

THE INTERVAL

And Jesus answered: "Truly, I say to you, today you will be with me in paradise" (Luke 23:43).

Today. Not eventually. Not after a period of purification. Not when the resurrection comes. *Today*—before the sun sets on this awful Friday, before your body grows cold, before the soldiers break your legs to hasten death—you will be with me. In paradise.

The word itself is borrowed from Persian—*paradeisos*—a walled garden, a royal park, a place of beauty and rest reserved for the king's delight. Jesus promised the thief immediate entry into the garden of God's presence. No delay. No waiting room. The moment death closes our eyes here, glory opens them there.

This is the consistent witness of Scripture. Stephen, as stones crushed his skull, saw "the heavens opened, and the Son of Man standing at the right hand of God" (Acts 7:56). His last words were not a cry of despair but a prayer of arrival: "Lord Jesus, receive my spirit" (Acts 7:59). He knew where he was going. He knew who would receive him.

The believer who dies tonight will wake in paradise tomorrow. The grandmother who slipped away last year is not floating in some intermediate void. She is with Christ. Present to him. Conscious in his presence. At rest in a way that makes even the best of this life seem dim by comparison.

The Communion of Saints

Imagine the moment of arrival.

Your grandmother who prayed for you through decades of wandering—she is there to greet you, her face radiant with the joy of answered prayer finally witnessed. The mentor whose words shaped your calling—waiting with the same steadiness that marked him on earth, now purified of every limitation. The friend who fought cancer with faith and lost the battle but won the war—standing at the threshold, whole, laughing, more alive than you ever saw her. The child who left too soon, whose absence carved a permanent hollow in your heart —running toward you, known and knowing.

Heaven is not a solitary experience. It is populated with everyone who has trusted Christ across every age—and those who loved you, who shaped you, who went before you, they are already there.

The writer of Hebrews lifts the veil on this reality: "You have come to Mount Zion and to the city of the living God, the heavenly Jerusalem, and to innumerable angels in festal gathering, and to the assembly of the firstborn who are enrolled in heaven, and to God, the judge of all, and to the spirits of the righteous made perfect, and to Jesus, the mediator of a new covenant" (Hebrews 12:22-24).

Consider the company. *Innumerable angels*—not a sparse gathering but a multitude beyond counting. The *assembly of the firstborn*—every heir of promise from every generation, enrolled in heaven's registry by the blood of Christ. The *spirits of the righteous made perfect*—every saint from every age, from Abel to the believer who died this morning.

This is not a hushed sanctuary. This is a *festal gathering*. The Greek word is *panegyris*—a festive assembly, a public celebration, a gathering for joy. Heaven is not muted or somber or quietly reverent in some austere way. It is celebratory. The saints are not pacing in holy boredom, waiting for something better. They are gathered in worship, fellowship, and joy—present to Christ and present to one another.

The communion of saints spans millennia. Abraham is there. David is there. Mary and Peter. Augustine and Aquinas. Edwards and Willard. The missionary who brought the gospel to your great-grandmother's village. The Sunday school teacher who planted the first seeds of faith in your parents. The network of grace that brought you to Christ—they are all there, and when you arrive, you join a fellowship that has been building since Abel's blood cried out from the ground.

The Welcome That Waits

And here is what deepens the joy: you are not merely arriving—you are being received.

We think of heaven as a destination we travel toward—and so it is. But Scripture reveals a startling reversal: heaven is also traveling toward us. The saints who have gone before are not passively present.

They are watching. Waiting. Anticipating the moment when those they loved join the company.

The Father who ran to meet the prodigal saw him "while he was still a long way off" (Luke 15:20). The father had been watching. Waiting. Hoping. When the son appeared on the horizon—still distant, still uncertain of his welcome—the father *ran*. Dignity forgotten. Propriety abandoned. The welcome was prepared before the son arrived: the ring, the robe, the fattened calf, the feast. Not obligation but desire. Not duty but delight.

C.S. Lewis captured this in a haunting scene from *The Great Divorce*. A woman arrives in heaven—not famous on earth, not a saint whose name history recorded. But she is radiant now, attended by angels and redeemed souls who pour out to celebrate her coming. Who is she? Lewis's guide explains: she had loved many into the kingdom. The people whose lives she touched, whose trajectories she bent toward God, who owe their presence in glory to her faithful investment—they have come out to meet her. The reunion is not merely her finding them. It is them welcoming her, crowning her arrival with their joy.

In Revelation, John sees the souls of martyrs under the altar, given white robes, told to rest "until the number of their fellow servants and their brothers should be complete" (Revelation 6:11). They are watching. They are waiting. They are anticipating the completion of the gathering—and that includes anticipating *you*.

The friend who reached the other shore first has been watching for your arrival. The father who died when you were young is hoping for the day when your name joins the registry. You are wanted. You are hoped for. You are awaited with the same fierce joy that met the prodigal on the road.

Rest and Worship

"Blessed are the dead who die in the Lord from now on." "Blessed indeed," says the Spirit, "that they may rest from their labors, for their deeds follow them" (Revelation 14:13).

The word is *rest—anapauō—*a cessation from toil, a release from the weariness that marked this life. The saints in heaven are not striving. They are not anxious. They are not carrying the burdens that bent their shoulders on earth. The labors are finished. The race is run. What remains is rest—not the rest of inactivity but the rest of completion, the satisfaction of a task fulfilled.

And yet this rest is not passive. The throne room scenes of Revelation pulsate with activity—worship, praise, adoration offered with full-throated abandon. "Holy, holy, holy, is the Lord God Almighty, who was and is and is to come!" (Revelation 4:8). Day and night, without pause, the inhabitants of heaven pour out praise. Not because they are compelled but because they finally see what deserves such praise. The dimness is removed. The glory is unveiled. And the only fitting response is worship.

Imagine what it will feel like: the first moment when you see clearly, when the veil lifts entirely, when you behold the face you have loved but never seen. Every distraction that pulled your mind during prayer—gone. Every doubt that whispered during worship—silenced. Every weight that made praise feel like effort—lifted. For the first time, you will worship with your whole being, undivided, unhindered, fully present to the One who has always been fully present to you. The friction that marked every act of devotion on earth will simply be absent. And praise will flow like water downhill—natural, inevitable, unforced.

Jonathan Edwards spent his life contemplating this reality. Heaven, he argued, is not a place where joy plateaus but where it perpetually increases—like a fountain that rises higher with each passing moment, or a river that grows broader as it approaches the sea. The saints in glory are not bored. They are increasingly ravished by the beauty of God, discovering depths they had not yet plumbed, ascending heights they had not yet scaled.

The souls of the righteous are "made perfect" (Hebrews 12:23)—*teleioō*—brought to completion, to the full measure of what they were created to be. The sin that clung is gone. The weakness that hindered is removed. The potential that was glimpsed on earth is realized in glory.

But heaven is not only rest and worship. The saints explore, learn, serve. The God who is infinite cannot be exhausted in a trillion years of knowing him. There are depths to plumb, heights to scale, mysteries to enter. The curiosity that flickered on earth—often distracted, often dulled—burns bright and clear in paradise. And the service that felt burdensome here flows freely there, for it is service without sin, without fatigue, without the friction of a fallen world.

The Crown Has Faces

In Chapter 15, we traced how souls are the only treasure that transfers from earth to eternity—the currency that crosses over when everything else stops at death's door. Now we see that currency present in heaven.

The people you loved into the kingdom—they are there. The neighbor who heard the gospel from your lips and believed. The child you raised in faith who now raises praise. The stranger you served with a cup of cold water in Jesus' name. They have faces, names, places in the assembly. And they remember what you did.

Paul understood this with pastoral ferocity. "What is our hope or joy or crown of boasting before our Lord Jesus at his coming? Is it not you? For you are our glory and joy" (1 Thessalonians 2:19-20). The Thessalonians themselves were Paul's crown. Not a separate reward for investing in them—*they themselves* were the reward. Living testimonies. Souls saved. People he would see in glory and know that his labor was not in vain.

When you enter heaven, the souls you invested in will be part of your welcome. The coworker whose spiritual interest you cultivated through a hundred small conversations—if he came to faith, he will be there, and he will know what you did. The young woman you mentored through her first years of marriage—she will greet you with gratitude that has only deepened through years of glory. The teenager you taught in youth group who went on to plant churches in Southeast Asia—he will be surrounded by faces you never met, but who owe their presence in part to your faithfulness.

This is what we meant when we said everything translates. The doing of the interval—the investment, the sacrifice, the faithful pouring out of time and energy and love—translates into heaven. The crown has faces. The treasures can talk. And you will see them there.

The Soul Who Enters

But here is the question this book has been pressing: *Who* enters?

Not merely *that* you enter—that is secured by grace through faith, sealed by the Spirit, guaranteed by the blood of Christ. But who is the person who walks through those gates? What soul arrives to join the communion of saints?

The soul you have been becoming.

This is the thesis we have traced from the beginning: eternal life has already begun. The interval of grace is not waiting for eternity to start. It is eternity's opening movement. What you do and who you become during this window shapes what you carry into the age to come. The doing and the becoming are not separate tracks that merge at death. They are the single life you are living, hidden with Christ in God, now being revealed, one day fully unveiled.

The generous soul arrives in heaven generous still—and finds a welcome commensurate with the generosity that preceded. The faithful soul arrives faithful still—and enters a fellowship that recognizes faithfulness as native tongue. The soul shaped by suffering arrives with a depth that only suffering carves—and brings something to heaven's worship that the comfortable never developed.

Heaven is not a great equalizer that flattens all distinctions. It is a great revealer that manifests what was forming in secret. The person who cultivated capacity for God during the interval possesses that capacity still. The person who developed rich interior life arrives with rich interior life. The person whose capacity remained modest arrives with that same capacity—full to the brim with joy.

The thimble and the ocean both enter heaven. Both are filled to the brim with joy. Both overflow with the presence of Christ. But the ocean holds more—more capacity to receive what God endlessly gives, more depth to explore the infinite, more room for the joy that perpetually increases. When the fountain of heaven's delight rises higher each moment, the ocean rises with it; the thimble, already full, can receive no more. Both are blessed. Both are grateful. But the ocean was shaped in the interval, and the shaping matters forever.

And There Is More

Heaven is glorious.

Heaven is real. Heaven is far better than anything this life offers. Heaven is presence with Christ, communion with saints, rest from labors, worship without hindrance, joy without shadow. Heaven is the hope that has sustained martyrs and comforted the grieving and drawn the dying peacefully through the valley. Heaven is true.

And yet—

The martyrs under the altar cry out: "O Sovereign Lord, holy and true, how long before you will judge and avenge our blood on those who dwell on the earth?" (Revelation 6:10). They are in heaven. They are blessed. They are clothed in white robes. And still they ask: *How long?*

Something remains incomplete.

Heaven is glorious beyond words. But God made us for bodies—for hands that touch, feet that walk, arms that embrace. The saints in glory await the resurrection of theirs. They enjoy the presence of Christ with an intimacy we can barely imagine, but they do not yet enjoy the fullness of embodied existence. And embodiment awaits.

The saints in glory await the new creation. They dwell in paradise, but paradise is not yet united with earth. Heaven and earth remain distinct. The prayer "on earth as it is in heaven" has not yet been finally answered. The dwelling place of God is *with* the saints, but not yet *on the earth* as John saw in his vision.

Heaven is not the final chapter. It is a glorious chapter—more glorious than we have words to capture. But the story continues. Christ will return. The trumpet will sound. The dead will be raised. The city will descend. And the marriage supper of the Lamb will inaugurate an eternity that exceeds even the present glory.

To that consummation we now turn.

CHAPTER 24
THE NEW CREATION UNVEILED

The Trumpet Sounds

Heaven is glorious. And there is more.

The saints in glory know this. They wait with holy impatience, crying "How long?" not from discontent with present blessedness but from anticipation of coming consummation. They possess the firstfruits—presence with Christ, communion with saints, rest and worship and joy—but they await the full harvest. They see through the veil what we can only glimpse: a Day is coming that will exceed even the exceeding glory of heaven as it now exists.

Paul traced that Day for the anxious Thessalonians:

"For the Lord himself will descend from heaven with a cry of command, with the voice of an archangel, and with the sound of the trumpet of God. And the dead in Christ will rise first. Then we who are alive, who are left, will be caught up together with them in the clouds to meet the Lord in the air, and so we will always be with the Lord" (1 Thessalonians 4:16-17).

The Lord himself descends. Not an angel sent in his stead. Not a representative bearing his authority. The Lord himself—the same Jesus who ascended from Olivet, who was taken up in a cloud while the disciples strained to see, who will return in the same way (Acts 1:11). The One who departed will return. The One who sits at the Father's right hand will rise from that throne and descend with a shout.

And at that shout, everything changes.

The dead in Christ—the saints who have been in heaven, present with the Lord though not yet reunited with their bodies—they rise first. Their bodies, long buried, scattered to dust, dissolved into the elements, are reconstituted and glorified. The soul that departed at death is reunited with the body that was laid in the grave. But this is not resuscitation to the same weak, corruptible flesh. This is resurrection—transformation into something imperishable, glorious, powerful.

"We shall all be changed, in a moment, in the twinkling of an eye, at the last trumpet. For the trumpet will sound, and the dead will be raised imperishable, and we shall be changed" (1 Corinthians 15:51-52).

In a moment. In the twinkling of an eye. The transformation is instantaneous. The bodies that were sown in dishonor are raised in glory. The bodies that were sown in weakness are raised in power. The natural body is transformed into a spiritual body—not "spiritual" as opposed to physical, but physical existence animated and empowered by the Spirit without limit.

But this transformation is more than physical. The Image of God, marred by the Fall, is not merely restored but perfected, enabling us to reflect and serve Christ without hindrance. Our glorified bodies will be the permanent instruments of worship and work, finally matching the intention of our redeemed souls. What we have been becoming in the interval—the character formed, the capacity developed, the soul shaped by grace—now receives its fitting vessel.

The resurrection body of Jesus is the prototype. He could eat fish on the beach with his disciples (John 21:12-13). He could be touched —"Put your finger here, and see my hands," he told Thomas (John 20:27). He retained the wounds of crucifixion, glorified but visible. And yet he could appear in locked rooms (John 20:19), vanish from sight (Luke 24:31), ascend through the clouds (Acts 1:9). The resurrection body is not less physical than our current bodies. It is more—physical existence raised to capacities we cannot now imagine.

This is what awaits us. This is why the saints in heaven wait with eager expectation. Blessed as their present state is, embodiment is what we were made for. And embodiment—glorious, powerful, imperishable embodiment—is coming.

Beyond the Bema

Beyond the Bema, the fire has finished its work.

The evaluation is complete. What was hidden has been revealed. The secret acts of faithfulness, known only to God, have been announced before the assembly. The souls who invested in hidden currencies—who served without recognition, who gave without publicity, who persevered without applause—they have been vindicated. Their Father who saw in secret has rewarded openly.

And the souls who built with stubble have been saved, yet as through fire. They enter the joy of their Lord, genuinely grateful, genuinely blessed—but beginning the eternal journey from a lower summit than they might have. The thimble enters alongside the ocean. Both will grow forever; both will advance into God without end. But the starting point differs, and what could have been formed in the interval remains unformed. Yet even here, grace abounds. The stubble builder is not condemned to static poverty but invited into endless expansion. The journey will be glorious.

The Bema is not the end. It is the final threshold, and beyond it lies the feast.

The Marriage Supper of the Lamb

"Then I heard what seemed to be the voice of a great multitude, like the roar of many waters and like the sound of mighty peals of thunder, crying out, 'Hallelujah! For the Lord our God the Almighty reigns. Let us rejoice and exult and give him the glory, for the marriage of the Lamb has come, and his Bride has made herself ready; it was granted her to clothe herself with fine linen, bright and pure'—for the fine linen is the righteous deeds of the saints. And the angel said to me, 'Write this: Blessed are those who are invited to the marriage supper of the Lamb'" (Revelation 19:6-9).

Here is the consummation toward which all history has been building.

The marriage of the Lamb. The Bridegroom who loved the church and gave himself up for her, who has been preparing a place for her, who endured the cross for the joy set before him—he now receives his Bride. She is ready. She is clothed in fine linen, bright and pure—not her own righteousness but the righteous deeds of the saints, granted to her by grace, woven into a wedding garment by the Spirit's work through the interval.

The imagery draws from ancient Jewish wedding custom. The betrothal had been sealed long ago—at Calvary, where the dowry was paid in blood. The bridegroom departed to prepare a place—"In my Father's house are many rooms... I go to prepare a place for you" (John 14:2). Now he returns for his bride, and the wedding feast begins.

"Blessed are those who are invited to the marriage supper of the Lamb."

This feast is not a brief reception. It is the threshold event that marks the transition from the present age to the age to come—the inaugural celebration of the eternal state. Jesus had anticipated it at the Last Supper: "I tell you I will not drink again of this fruit of the vine until that day when I drink it new with you in my Father's kingdom" (Matthew 26:29). The meal he shared with twelve in the upper room was a foretaste. The supper of the Lamb is the fulfillment.

And it is embodied. This is crucial for understanding why the feast follows resurrection rather than occurring in the intermediate heaven. A feast is a communal, physical event—eating, drinking, reclining at table, sharing food and fellowship. The saints in heaven, blessed as they are, await their resurrection bodies precisely so they can participate fully in this celebration. The marriage supper is not for disembodied spirits. It is for glorified bodies gathered in joyful assembly.

Imagine the moment. You are seated at a table that stretches beyond sight, surrounded by the redeemed of every age—faces you recognize and faces you have longed to meet. The cup is raised—the fruit of the vine that Jesus promised to drink new with us (Matthew 26:29)—tasted with a real tongue, swallowed by a real throat. And across the table, close enough to touch, sits the One for whom you have waited your whole life. His eyes meet yours. He raises his cup. "I told you I would drink it new with you," he says. And the first sip of that wine—the first taste of joy unmixed with sorrow, of celebration untainted by the knowledge that it must end—that first sip inaugurates forever.

The exact timing and location of this feast has been debated among theologians, and we should hold our conclusions with appropriate humility. (The same is true of the thousand-year reign described in Revelation 20. Faithful Christians differ on its nature and timing, but sequencing these events lies beyond the scope of this book.) The strongest biblical evidence suggests that the marriage supper occurs after the resurrection and marks the inauguration of the new creation—embodied celebration on the renewed earth, the threshold of eternity.

"Many will come from east and west and recline at table with Abraham, Isaac, and Jacob in the kingdom of heaven" (Matthew 8:11). Recline at table. Meal language. Fellowship language. The language of bodies gathered for feasting. The kingdom is not ethereal but earthy—not earthy in the sense of fallen and corrupt, but earthy in the sense of physical, tangible, real. And the feast is the doorway.

The City Descending

The ending is not what we expected.

We have imagined it wrong for centuries—souls drifting upward into clouds, leaving earth behind like a burning ship, escaping matter for pure spirit. The hymns taught us to "fly away" to a home "beyond the blue." The funeral sermons promised that our loved ones had "gone to a better place." And we pictured that place as elsewhere—above, beyond, away from the messy materiality of bodies and bread and blood.

But that is not how the story ends.

"Then I saw a new heaven and a new earth, for the first heaven and the first earth had passed away, and the sea was no more. And I saw the holy city, new Jerusalem, coming down out of heaven from God, prepared as a bride adorned for her husband. And I heard a loud voice from the throne saying, 'Behold, the dwelling place of God is with man. He will dwell with them, and they will be his people, and God himself will be with them as their God'" (Revelation 21:1-3).

Read it again. Slowly.

The city comes down. Heaven descends to earth. God's dwelling is with man—not humanity extracted to God's realm, but God taking up residence with humanity on a renewed creation. The movement is not evacuation but arrival. Not escape but consummation. The final scene is not spirits floating in ethereal bliss but the Creator making his home among his creatures on the ground he first called good.

N.T. Wright, in *Surprised by Hope*, has captured this with a memorable phrase: "life after life after death." When believers die, they go to be with Christ in heaven—that is life after death, and it is real and good. But it is not the final chapter. The final chapter is resurrection, renewed creation, heaven and earth united. That is life after life after death. That is the Christian hope fully realized. That is the new earth—our eternal home.

The implications are staggering. We are not being prepared for ethereal existence. We are being shaped for resurrection life in a physical world healed of every wound. The soul you are becoming will inhabit a glorified body on a glorified earth, doing glorified work that matters forever. The interval is not preparation for disembodiment. It is training for re-embodiment—richer, fuller, more capacious embodiment than we have ever known.

What Makes It New

But what is genuinely new about the new creation? If *kainos* means renewal rather than replacement, what distinguishes the new earth from Eden restored?

First, the presence of God reaches an intimacy never before known. In Eden, God walked in the garden in the cool of the day—

present, yes, but also separate, arriving and departing. In the new creation, he *dwells*. "Behold, the dwelling place of God is with man." The tabernacle and temple were shadows of this—God's presence localized, mediated, approachable only through sacrifice and priesthood. Now the shadow gives way to substance. No temple stands in the New Jerusalem because the Lord God Almighty and the Lamb *are* its temple (Revelation 21:22). The presence that Moses glimpsed from the cleft of the rock, that Isaiah saw in the year King Uzziah died, that the disciples witnessed on the Mount of Transfiguration—that presence fills everything, and we bear it without being consumed.

Second, the garden has become a city. The New Jerusalem is the ultimate fulfillment of the Cultural Mandate (Genesis 1:28)—the original divine commission to fill and subdue the earth. What began as untamed potential has been developed into civilization. Innocence has matured into wisdom. Potential has been realized. The tree of life remains, but now it stands in an urban garden, straddling the river that flows through the city's heart (Revelation 22:1-2). The story has gone somewhere—and it has gone where God always intended.

This is not Plan B. It is Plan A fulfilled—the original design brought to its intended completion through the long arc of redemption.

Not Escape but Renewal

The biblical story does not end with destruction. It ends with healing.

This is God's consistent pattern throughout Scripture. The flood did not annihilate creation; it cleansed and renewed it. The exile did not end Israel; it purified and restored her. The cross did not defeat Christ; it became the instrument of victory. God's way is not to abandon what he made but to redeem it.

So it will be with creation itself.

"For the creation waits with eager longing for the revealing of the sons of God. For the creation was subjected to futility, not willingly, but because of him who subjected it, in hope that the creation itself will be set free from its bondage to corruption and obtain the freedom of the glory of the children of God" (Romans 8:19-21).

Creation waits. Creation hopes. Creation groans in labor pains, Paul says, longing for the day when the children of God are revealed—because on that day, creation itself will be liberated. The trees and mountains, the rivers and fields, the physical stuff of the universe—all of it will be set free from the decay that sin introduced. Renewed. Healed. Glorified.

The Greek word in Revelation 21:5 is *kainos*—"Behold, I am making all things new." It does not mean replacement, as though God scraps the old and starts fresh with something else entirely. It means renewal, transformation, restoration. The same creation, healed. The same earth, glorified. The same bodies, raised imperishable. Continuity through transformation—not annihilation and recreation.

This is why the garden imagery of Genesis returns at the end of Revelation. The tree of life reappears, bearing twelve kinds of fruit, yielding its fruit each month, its leaves for the healing of the nations (Revelation 22:2). The river of life flows through the city, bright as crystal, proceeding from the throne of God and of the Lamb (Revelation 22:1). What was lost in Eden is recovered—but more than recovered. The garden has become a city. The innocence of the beginning has been transformed into the maturity of the end. Paradise is not merely restored; it is consummated.

What We Are Being Prepared For

Now we can see why formation matters with such permanent weight.

We are not being shaped for disembodied floating. We are being prepared for resurrection life on a renewed earth—life that involves work, creativity, relationship, and endless advance into God. The capacities developed in the interval are the capacities deployed forever.

Consider work. Every gardener knows the frustration: the weeds that return no matter how often they are pulled, the pests that devour what was carefully cultivated, the weather that ruins what was ready for harvest. The curse declared that the ground would produce thorns and thistles, that labor would be marked by sweat and frustration (Genesis 3:17-19). But on the new earth, the curse is lifted. "No

THE INTERVAL

longer will there be anything accursed" (Revelation 22:3). You plant, and it flourishes. You build, and it stands. You create, and nothing corrupts your creation. The resistance is gone. And the capacity for such work—the skills honed through years of faithful labor against the thorns—that capacity remains, now deployed without opposition.

Consider creativity. Every artist knows the gap between vision and execution—the painting that never quite matches the image in the mind, the song that falls short of the melody heard in the soul. In the new creation, that gap closes. The glorified mind conceives; the glorified hands execute. The soul who cultivated creativity in the interval —who practiced and failed and practiced again, who developed craft through decades of discipline—that soul brings more to the new earth than the one who let creative capacity atrophy. The trained hand creates what the untrained hand cannot.

Consider relationship. No more misunderstanding. No more betrayal. No more walls between souls. The communion of saints is not a one-time greeting but endless fellowship—and the capacity for such fellowship was forged in the interval, through the difficult work of loving imperfect people, through forgiveness extended and received, through community practiced despite its cost. The soul who learned to love amid difficulty brings that capacity to the city where difficulty is no more.

And consider presence. "They will see his face, and his name will be on their foreheads" (Revelation 22:4). The beatific vision—the direct, unmediated experience of God—is the constant state of the redeemed. We will see him face to face, not in momentary glimpses but in permanent, unbroken communion. The resurrection body does not merely house the soul; it becomes the instrument of encounter with God—hands that serve him, eyes that behold him, a voice that praises him. The embodied habits formed in the interval— the gestures of kindness, the postures of prayer, the physical practices of presence—persist in the body that is raised.

This is what you are being prepared for. The soul formed through decades of faithful becoming is the soul who will work and create and relate and worship on the new earth. The capacity developed now is the capacity deployed forever.

The Glory of the Nations

There is one more dimension to the new creation that Scripture reveals—a dimension that ties directly to everything we have traced about doing and becoming.

"By its light will the nations walk, and the kings of the earth will bring their glory into it, and its gates will never be shut by day—and there will be no night there. They will bring into it the glory and the honor of the nations" (Revelation 21:24-26).

The kings bring their glory. The nations bring their honor. Something from earth enters the New Jerusalem. This is the fulfillment of the Cultural Mandate—that original commission, now complete. The gates stand perpetually open, and through them streams the fruit of faithful stewardship.

What is this "glory of the nations"? Commentators have puzzled over it for centuries. But the logic of this book suggests an answer: it is the treasure that transfers. The cultural achievements of humanity, purified of sin, are incorporated into the new creation. The work that was done "in the Lord" is not lost. Paul's declaration rings with new significance: "Therefore, my beloved brothers, be steadfast, immovable, always abounding in the work of the Lord, knowing that in the Lord your labor is not in vain" (1 Corinthians 15:58). Not in vain—because it enters the city. It contributes to the glory.

And remember what we traced in Chapter 15: the currency of souls is the only treasure that transfers fully. The people you invested in—the neighbor whose faith you watered, the child you raised to know Christ, the stranger who saw something in your life that made the gospel plausible—they walk through those gates too. They are part of the glory you bring. They are the treasure that speaks, the crown with faces, the investment that multiplied across the interval and now enters the city in glorified bodies.

Imagine the procession. The kings of the earth approach—but not only the kings history remembers. Here comes the grandmother who reigned over a kitchen and a Sunday school class, who governed three generations with prayer and wisdom. Here comes the businessman who built with integrity when corruption would have been easier, whose company blessed thousands. Here comes the artist whose work opened hearts to beauty, the teacher whose words shaped minds, the pastor whose faithful presence held a church together through decades of obscurity. They bring their glory—the fruit of what they did and who they became.

We are the glory. We are what enters. The "glory of the nations" includes the glorified saints themselves—the people transformed by the Spirit, the character forged in the crucible of faithfulness, the souls shaped for capacity they will now deploy forever.

Revelation 21:24-26 is the eschatological fulfillment of everything this book has argued. What we do and who we become—both matter eternally. Both enter the city. Both contribute to the consummation.

Gregory of Nyssa and the Endless Advance

But here a question presses: If the new creation is "final," does that mean growth stops? Does perfection imply stasis? Will eternity be an endless plateau—beautiful, perhaps, but unchanging?

Gregory of Nyssa—whose vision of epektasis we explored in Chapter 6—answered this question with a truth that still startles: even in glory, even in perfection, the soul continues to advance into God.

He called it *epektasis*—from Paul's language in Philippians 3:13 of "straining forward" toward what lies ahead. Gregory argued that even in glory, even in perfection, the soul continues to advance into God. Why? Because God is infinite. No creature—however glorified—can exhaust the infinite. There is always more of God to know, always deeper into the divine nature to go, always further up and further in.

"This is the most marvelous thing of all," Gregory wrote, "that the perfection of human nature consists perhaps in its very growth in goodness." The journey does not end at the gates of the New Jerusalem. It begins there. Eternity is not arrival at a destination but embarkation on an endless voyage.

We traced this in Chapter 6. Now we see its consummation. The *epektasis* that began in the interval continues forever on the new earth. But—and here the stakes sharpen one final time—the starting point differs.

Two souls enter the new creation. Both saved. Both glorified. Both blessed beyond all earthly imagination. But one begins the eternal advance from a higher summit, having climbed further during the interval. The other begins lower—yet both begin, and both will climb forever.

We return to the image one last time: the thimble and the ocean. Both enter the city. Both are filled to the brim with joy. Both overflow with the presence of Christ. Both will grow forever as the fountain of heaven's delight rises higher each moment. The ocean began with greater capacity; the thimble began with less. But both are expanding into God without end—glory upon glory upon glory.

This is not speculation but the consistent witness of Scripture—"star differs from star in glory," Paul wrote, "so also is the resurrection of the dead" (1 Corinthians 15:41-42)—and the unanimous teaching of the church across twenty centuries.

This is why formation matters. The ocean was shaped in the interval.

Dallas Willard and the Divine Conspiracy

Dallas Willard spent his life trying to help Christians understand that the new creation is not a retirement home for souls who barely squeaked through. It is a working kingdom, a realm of responsibility, a cosmos under renovation that requires competent, formed, trustworthy agents.

He saw resurrection life as active participation in God's ongoing creative work. "We will not sit around looking at one another or at God for eternity," he wrote, "but will join the eternal Logos, 'reign with him,' in the endlessly ongoing creative work of God."

This is what Jesus promised. The servant who proved faithful with little is given authority over cities (Luke 19:17). Not a gold watch and a rocking chair. Cities. Governance. Stewardship over realms of the renewed creation. The new earth is not passive enjoyment but active vocation—and the capacity for that vocation was developed in the interval, through decades of faithfulness in small things that trained the soul for cosmic responsibilities.

THE INTERVAL

The soul formed for that work is the soul being formed now.

Toward the Everlasting Morning

The night is nearly over. The dawn approaches.

This is the vision that has sustained the church across two millennia—through persecution and plague, through empire and collapse, through every darkness that threatened to swallow the light. The martyrs died with it on their lips. The saints lived with it in their hearts. The faithful ordinary believers—the ones whose names no history records—they held to this hope when nothing else remained.

The new earth is coming. Christ will return. The trumpet will sound. The dead will be raised. The Bride will be united to her Bridegroom at the marriage supper. Heaven will descend to earth. God will wipe away every tear. Death will be swallowed up in victory. And those who have trusted him, followed him, allowed him to form them—they will inherit the earth.

Not float above it. Inherit it.

The meek receive what was promised. The pure in heart see God —finally, fully, face to face. Those who hungered and thirsted for righteousness are satisfied—satisfied and still hungry for more, because the infinite cannot be exhausted, because *epektasis* continues forever, because the journey into God has no end.

C.S. Lewis saw it with blazing clarity in *The Weight of Glory*: "There are no ordinary people. You have never talked to a mere mortal." The person standing in front of you is becoming an eternal creature of staggering glory—and your interaction with them, your words, your service, your investment, tilts the scale. The currency of souls is always being exchanged. The treasure that transfers is always being accumulated or neglected.

This is not burden. It is privilege. It is the weight of glory—the weight that would bow our shoulders if we could see it now, the splendor being prepared, the magnificence that will be unveiled.

You are part of that unveiling. You are being unveiled. The hidden life you have been living—hidden with Christ in God (Colossians 3:3) —will be revealed. "When Christ who is your life appears, then you also will appear with him in glory" (Colossians 3:4). The character developed in obscurity will shine before the assembly. The soul formed in secret will be manifested in public.

And so we return, one final time, to the question this book has pressed from its opening pages: *Who are you becoming?*

The Bema has been traced. The reunion has been promised. Heaven has been celebrated. The new creation has been unveiled. What remains is response.

The clay is still soft. The wheel is still turning. The interval of grace is still open.

Not the accomplishments that impressed the world—they will not matter. Not the wealth that could not cross the threshold. Not the reputation that died with the body. What will matter is this: Did you become someone who can flourish in the presence of God? Did you develop capacity for him—capacity to see him, know him, serve him, enjoy him? Did you invest in the treasure that transfers? Did you steward the currencies that cross over? Did you cooperate with the Spirit's shaping work, even when the wheel turned painfully, even when the fire burned hot?

The new earth is home for the transformed. And transformation happens here, now, in the interval that remains open while you read these words.

The everlasting morning is coming.

Who will you be when it dawns?

KEY PHRASES

Continuity principle — The self that dies is the self that rises; identity persists through death and resurrection, transformed but recognizable.

Currency of souls — People are the only treasure that transfers into eternity; those brought to faith become the believer's "crown of boasting."

Eternal audit — The practice of standing before God's evaluating gaze now, voluntarily, rather than waiting for the Bema.

Forming room — What the interval actually is, contrasted with the waiting room fallacy; the place where eternal souls are shaped.

Grace of now — The present opportunity while the clay remains soft; the invitation implicit in every moment before the kiln fires.

Great inversion — Heaven's opposite economy, where the last become first, the hidden is revealed, and earthly values are reversed.

KEY PHRASES

Heaven's economy — The eternal value calculation system where what matters to God differs radically from what matters to the world.

Hidden ledger — God's record of unseen faithfulness; the secret acts of obedience that will be revealed and rewarded.

Interval of grace — The unrepeatable span between conversion and death when eternal formation remains possible.

Kiln of death — The moment when formation ends and fixity begins; death fires what has been shaping into permanence.

Threefold framework — The distinction between salvation (by grace through faith), formation (by Spirit-enabled cooperation), and reward (by grace-enabled faithfulness).

Two pillars — Doing and becoming; the inseparable dimensions of faithful response that shape eternal capacity.

Unrepeatable resource — Time that cannot be recovered once spent; the finite currency of the interval.

Vicious spiral — The descending dynamic where unfaithful choices diminish capacity, leading to further unfaithfulness.

Virtuous spiral — The ascending dynamic where faithful action builds character, which enables greater faithfulness.

Waiting room fallacy — The assumption that earthly life is mere endurance until heaven, rather than the forming room for eternity.

VOICES FROM THE CLOUD OF WITNESSES

Thomas Aquinas (*Summa Theologica*) — Fixity of the will at death; the soul's orientation becomes permanent.

Augustine of Hippo (*City of God*) — Saints shine with different degrees of radiance; personal history persists into resurrection.

Jacob Böhme (*The Way to Christ*) — The will shapes itself, choice by choice, into what it will remain forever.

Dietrich Bonhoeffer (*The Cost of Discipleship*) — Every moment challenges us to action and obedience; when Christ calls, the response must be now.

Meister Eckhart (*Sermons*) — The God-seed planted in the soul, growing toward eternal fruition.

Jonathan Edwards (*Charity and Its Fruits*) — Vessels of different sizes cast into an ocean of happiness; every vessel full, though some far larger.

VOICES FROM THE CLOUD OF WITNESSES

Gregory of Nyssa (*Life of Moses*) — Epektasis: eternal progress into the infinite God, never reaching a final limit.

John of the Cross (*Dark Night of the Soul*) — The dark night is God's purifying work; what feels like absence is actually surgery.

Søren Kierkegaard (*The Concept of Anxiety*) — Øjeblikket: the moment where time and eternity touch; every instant is a decision point where the temporal can receive the eternal.

C.S. Lewis (*Mere Christianity; The Great Divorce*) — We are, choice by choice, becoming creatures of heaven or hell.

Maximus the Confessor (*Ambigua*) — Christ formed in us through the virtues we cultivate.

Blaise Pascal (*Pensées*) — Divertissement: we fill our hours with noise and busyness to avoid facing death and eternity; time-wasting is eternity-avoidance.

Thérèse of Lisieux (*Story of a Soul*) — Thimble and tumbler: both full, each holding all it can contain.

A.W. Tozer (*The Pursuit of God*) — Christ conquered death by letting death conquer him; surrender is victory.

Simone Weil (*Gravity and Grace*) — Decreation: the soul empties itself that God might fill it.

Dallas Willard (*The Divine Conspiracy*) — Grace is not opposed to effort but to earning; the person we become is what we take from this life.

N.T. Wright (*Surprised by Hope*) — Life after life after death: the intermediate state followed by bodily resurrection.

APPENDIX
A NOTE ON DIFFERENTIAL GLORY

Introduction

Throughout this book, we have employed the image of the thimble and the ocean to illustrate a crucial claim: all believers are equally saved and filled to capacity with joy, but capacity itself differs based on formation during the interval of grace. The ocean holds more than the thimble—not because God withholds from the thimble, but because the thimble cannot contain what the ocean receives. Both overflow. Neither lacks. Yet one possesses greater capacity for God than the other.

This concept—known historically as "Graded Glory," "Differential Reward," or *Capacitas Dei*—has strong biblical warrant and represents the consistent teaching of the church across twenty centuries. This appendix provides the scriptural, theological, and historical foundation for readers who desire a more rigorous defense.

I. THE BIBLICAL CASE

The New Testament explicitly teaches that believers will receive differentiated rewards based on faithfulness during earthly life, and that resurrection glory itself admits of degrees.

A. Differentiated Rewards

The Parable of the Minas (Luke 19:11-27) provides the clearest dominical teaching on this subject. Each servant receives the same amount—one mina—but their faithfulness differs. The outcomes are strikingly unequal: the servant who gained ten minas receives authority over ten cities; the servant who gained five receives authority over five cities (vv. 17, 19). Jesus does not say "both receive equal standing in the kingdom." He assigns proportional responsibility based on demonstrated faithfulness.

The Parable of the Talents (Matthew 25:14-30) reinforces this principle. Though the amounts entrusted differ based on ability, the reward structure remains proportional: "Well done, good and faithful servant. You have been faithful over a little; I will set you over much" (v. 21). The "much" varies according to the "little" faithfully stewarded.

Paul's teaching on the Bema Seat (1 Corinthians 3:10-15) establishes that believers' works will be evaluated by fire. What survives—gold, silver, precious stones—is rewarded. What burns—wood, hay, stubble—is lost. Crucially, Paul states that the one whose work burns "will suffer loss, though he himself will be saved, but only as through fire" (v. 15). The loss is real. It is not the loss of salvation but the loss of reward—what might have been carried into eternity but was forfeited through unfaithfulness.

The sowing principle of 2 Corinthians 9:6 generalizes this pattern: "Whoever sows sparingly will also reap sparingly, and whoever sows bountifully will also reap bountifully." While Paul applies this to financial generosity, the principle extends to all grace-enabled investment. The eternal harvest corresponds to the earthly sowing.

APPENDIX

B. Differentiated Glory

Paul addresses resurrection glory directly in 1 Corinthians 15:41-42: "There is one glory of the sun, and another glory of the moon, and another glory of the stars; for star differs from star in glory. So also is the resurrection of the dead."

The analogy is explicit. Just as celestial bodies differ in brightness —all glorious, yet not equally glorious—so resurrection bodies will differ in splendor. Paul does not say all stars shine identically. He says they differ. And he applies this directly to the resurrection: "So also is the resurrection of the dead." The thimble shines. The ocean shines brighter. Both shine—but not equally.

Daniel 12:3 reinforces this: "Those who are wise shall shine like the brightness of the sky above, and those who turn many to righteousness, like the stars forever and ever." The shining is permanent ("forever and ever") and connected to earthly faithfulness ("those who turn many to righteousness"). This is not temporary recognition but eternal differentiation.

Jesus himself teaches differentiation within the kingdom in Matthew 5:19: "Whoever relaxes one of the least of these commandments and teaches others to do the same will be called least in the kingdom of heaven, but whoever does them and teaches them will be called great in the kingdom of heaven." Both are in the kingdom. Both are saved. But one is "least" and the other "great." The distinction is real and permanent.

C. Capacity as Developed

Scripture presents the capacity to receive God as something that grows through faithful cultivation. Paul prays that the Ephesians would "have strength to comprehend with all the saints what is the breadth and length and height and depth, and to know the love of Christ that surpasses knowledge, that you may be filled with all the fullness of God" (Ephesians 3:17-19). The capacity to comprehend and to be filled is not static. It requires "strength" that must be developed.

Similarly, Paul prays for the Colossians to be "filled with the knowledge of his will," "increasing in the knowledge of God," and "being strengthened with all power" (Colossians 1:9-11). Peter commands believers to "grow in the grace and knowledge of our Lord and Savior Jesus Christ" (2 Peter 3:18). If growth is commanded, it can be neglected. If it can be neglected, outcomes differ. The soul that grew possesses what the soul that stagnated does not.

II. THE THEOLOGICAL CASE

The biblical data finds systematic expression in three theological concepts that illuminate the thimble/ocean distinction.

A. Capacitas Dei

The doctrine of *Capacitas Dei* (Capacity for God) holds that while God gives himself fully to every redeemed soul, the subjective reception of that gift varies according to the creature's developed capacity. God is infinite; creatures are finite. No finite being—however glorified—can exhaustively contain the infinite. Therefore, the joy experienced is limited only by the soul's ability to receive it.

The thimble receives all of God that a thimble can hold. The ocean receives all of God that an ocean can hold. Both receive God fully in the sense that neither is denied access to him. But the ocean's greater capacity means it contains more of the inexhaustible divine life. The difference lies not in God's giving but in the creature's receiving.

B. The Beatific Vision

The ultimate blessing of the eternal state is the direct vision of God: "They will see his face" (Revelation 22:4). Jesus promised, "Blessed are the pure in heart, for they shall see God" (Matthew 5:8). But purity of heart is not uniform among believers. It is cultivated across a lifetime of sanctification—or neglected.

If the vision of God is granted to the pure in heart, and purity of heart admits of degrees during the interval, then the capacity for that vision is shaped by earthly formation. All see God. But the soul that cultivated profound capacity for intimacy with God perceives more of that unveiled glory than the soul that remained shallow. The thimble sees; the ocean sees more.

C. Essential vs. Accidental Reward

Medieval theology distinguished between essential reward (*praemium essentiale*) and accidental reward (*praemium accidentale*). Essential reward is salvation itself—union with God, freedom from sin, eternal life. This is possessed equally by all the redeemed, secured entirely by grace through faith in Christ.

Accidental reward encompasses the additional blessings that vary according to faithfulness: increased capacity for joy, expanded responsibility in the new creation, greater glory in the resurrection body. These are genuine rewards, truly possessed, yet they do not constitute salvation itself. The thimble possesses full essential reward—it is completely saved, completely united to Christ, completely free from sin. But its accidental reward differs from the ocean's. Both categories are gifts of grace; neither is earned apart from Christ's merit applied to the believer.

III. THE HISTORICAL WITNESS

This understanding represents not innovation but retrieval. The church has consistently affirmed differentiated capacity within universal blessedness.

Augustine (354-430) addressed the question in *City of God* (XXII.30), arguing that the blessed will possess differing degrees of glory proportioned to their merit, yet all will be perfectly satisfied. His analogy of vessels of varying sizes—each filled to capacity—establishes the principle that fullness is relative to the vessel. "No one will envy another's greater glory," Augustine wrote, "because the bond of love will reign in all."

Thomas Aquinas (1225-1274) developed this systematically in the *Summa Theologica* (I, q. 12, a. 6). The beatific vision, he argued, is received according to the soul's capacity, which is shaped by the "light of glory" possessed. "The more perfectly the soul possesses the light of glory, the more perfectly it sees God... Hence some see God more perfectly than others." The difference lies in the recipient, not in God's self-communication.

Gregory of Nyssa (335-395) contributed the concept of *epektasis*—the soul's endless advance into the infinite God even in glory. Since God cannot be exhausted, perfection consists not in stasis but in perpetual growth. If growth is eternal, starting points matter permanently. The soul that climbed higher during the interval begins the endless advance from a higher summit.

Jonathan Edwards (1703-1758) envisioned heaven as involving perpetual increase in joy—a fountain rising ever higher, a river growing ever broader. "The saints in glory will be progressive in knowledge and happiness to all eternity." If joy perpetually increases, the one who begins with greater capacity for joy possesses that advantage forever.

Thérèse of Lisieux (1873-1897) provided perhaps the most beloved expression of this doctrine's principle. Struggling with why God seemed to love some saints more than others, she received an insight she recorded in *Story of a Soul*... She considered vessels of different sizes—if both are filled to the brim, neither can hold more, and neither is empty. Both are completely full. The smaller vessel's size is not deficiency but distinct glory.

C.S. Lewis (1898-1963) employed similar reasoning in *The Great Divorce*, noting that a "pint pot" cannot envy a "quart pot" because the pint is full. It physically cannot contain the quart's volume. The feeling of lack is impossible in a state of complete fullness.

Randy Alcorn has defended this doctrine for contemporary evangelical readers in *Heaven*. He argues that if no differences existed in eternity, our earthly choices would have no eternal impact—contradicting the explicit teaching of Scripture. "If you have a small cup, full of joy, and I have a big bucket, full of joy, we are both full... but I have more capacity for joy because of how I lived my life."

The **Reformed tradition** likewise affirmed this teaching. The

Westminster Larger Catechism speaks of believers receiving "glory" at death, and Reformed theologians consistently maintained that glory admits of degrees. Charles Hodge wrote: "As there are to be degrees in the glory and blessedness of heaven, as our Lord teaches us in the parable of the ten talents, so there will be differences as to degree in the sufferings of the lost."

IV. ADDRESSING OBJECTIONS

A. "Doesn't this create envy or diminished joy?"

This objection assumes that awareness of another's greater capacity produces discontent. But this is impossible in a perfected soul for three reasons.

First, both vessels are completely full. The thimble does not experience 80% fullness while the ocean experiences 100%. Both are 100% full relative to their capacity. There is no unfulfilled desire, no sense of lack.

Second, envy requires willing against God's will. Dante addressed this brilliantly in *Paradiso* (Canto 3). When Dante asks Piccarda Donati—residing in the "lowest" sphere of heaven—whether she envies those in higher spheres, she answers: "Brother, the power of love quiets our will... In His will is our peace" (*E 'n la sua volontade è nostra pace*). To desire a higher place would be to disagree with God's placement, which a perfected will cannot do. The thimble loves being a thimble because being a thimble is what God willed for it.

Third, perfected love rejoices in another's good. The thimble celebrates the ocean's greater capacity to glorify God. Far from resenting the ocean, the thimble delights that God receives more glory through the ocean's greater capacity. This is love perfected—rejoicing in another's good as one's own.

B. "Isn't this works-righteousness?"

No. Salvation is by grace alone through faith alone in Christ alone. The thimble and the ocean are equally saved—justified by the same blood, clothed in the same righteousness, adopted into the same family. Essential reward does not differ.

What differs is accidental reward, and even this is grace. We do not earn capacity; we receive it through faithfulness to grace already given. The Spirit enables the growth; we cooperate with his enabling. The reward recognizes not autonomous achievement but grace-enabled faithfulness. As Paul wrote, "By the grace of God I am what I am, and his grace toward me was not in vain. On the contrary, I worked harder than any of them, though it was not I, but the grace of God that is with me" (1 Corinthians 15:10). The work was real. The grace was prior and enabling. Both are true.

C. "Doesn't grace level all distinctions?"

Grace saves equally; it does not sanctify identically. Scripture explicitly teaches that believers differ in their growth, their faithfulness, and their rewards. To deny differentiation is not to magnify grace but to contradict clear biblical teaching.

The parables of the Minas and Talents would be incoherent if grace eliminated distinction. Ten cities versus five cities is not symbolic language requiring flattening; it is Jesus's own description of differentiated reward. Grace is magnified, not diminished, by the diversity of its fruit.

D. "How can heaven be heaven if some have less?"

This objection imports a zero-sum economy into an infinite one. In earthly economies, if you have more, I have less. In heaven's economy, God's infinite self-communication means no one's abundance diminishes another's supply.

Moreover, "less" implies deficiency, which does not exist. The thimble possesses everything a thimble can possess. Its joy is not partial joy awaiting completion. It is complete joy—the fullness of what that particular soul can experience. The question assumes that the thimble should want to be an ocean. But the thimble, perfected in love and wisdom, wants to be exactly what God made it to be: a thimble, overflowing with as much of God as a thimble can contain.

E. "If formation is 'fixed' at death, how can the saints grow forever?"

The tension is apparent, not real. What is fixed at death is not growth itself but the foundation from which eternal growth proceeds.

Three things are established when the kiln fires: orientation (the direction of the will toward God), formed character (the specific capacities developed), and starting point (the level from which eternal advance begins). None of these impose a ceiling. All of them establish a floor.

Gregory of Nyssa's epektasis teaches that the saints advance into God forever because God is infinite and inexhaustible. But Gregory did not teach that all saints advance from the same starting point. The soul that climbed higher during the interval begins the endless journey from a higher summit. Both the thimble and the ocean grow forever —but the ocean's greater capacity means its growth encompasses more.

The kiln establishes the foundation; it does not impose a ceiling. The fixed starting point is precisely what makes eternal differentiation permanent—not because growth stops, but because growth continues from wherever the interval left each soul.

Conclusion

The "thimble and ocean" metaphor is not pastoral speculation but a visual expression of consistent biblical teaching and historic Christian doctrine. Scripture teaches differentiated rewards (Luke 19; Matthew 25; 1 Corinthians 3), differentiated glory (1 Corinthians 15; Daniel 12), and developed capacity (Ephesians 3; 2 Peter 3). The theological tradition—from Augustine through Aquinas, Gregory of Nyssa, Edwards, Thérèse, Lewis, and contemporary voices like Alcorn—has consistently affirmed that all the blessed are perfectly satisfied while possessing differing capacities for that satisfaction.

APPENDIX

This doctrine does not create anxiety but motivates faithfulness. The interval matters—not for salvation, which is secured by grace, but for the capacity we carry into eternity. We are not competing with one another; we are becoming ourselves. The goal is not to be the largest vessel but to be faithful with what we have been given, trusting that the God who evaluates the widow's mite knows exactly what each soul was capable of becoming.

The ocean was shaped in the interval. So was the thimble. Both are held in the same nail-scarred hands. Both overflow with the same infinite love. And both will spend eternity discovering that even the ocean has only begun to fathom the depths of God.

ABOUT THE AUTHOR

Jarred Fenlason, D.Min., is a teacher and writer whose work focuses on spiritual formation and the eternal weight of the Christian life. He holds a Doctor of Ministry from United Theological Seminary, where his research focused on discipleship and equipping believers to encounter the power, presence, and love of God.

He is also the author of *Encounter Discipleship: An Interactive Biblical Discipleship Program*.

His passion is to awaken believers to the eternal significance of ordinary days—and to the One who is shaping them for eternity.

Jarred lives in Charlotte, North Carolina, with his wife, Rochelle. They have three adult children.

Free Companion Resource

Visit www.intervalbook.com to download the free companion workbook. It includes deep-dive discussion questions and a structured 8-week guide explicitly designed for small groups and church studies.

www.ingramcontent.com/pod-product-compliance
Lightning Source LLC
Chambersburg PA
CBHW020923090426
42736CB00010B/1020